T0261186

# CYBERSECURITY PROGRAM DEVELOPMENT FOR BUSINESS

# CYBERSECURITY PROGRAM DEVELOPMENT FOR BUSINESS

## THE ESSENTIAL PLANNING GUIDE

Chris Moschovitis

WILEY

Published by John Wiley & Sons, Inc., Hoboken, New Jersey.
Published simultaneously in Canada.

For general information on our other products and services or for technical support, please contact our Customer Care Department within the United States at (800) 762-2974, outside the United States at (317) 572-3993, or fax (317) 572-4002.

Wiley publishes in a variety of print and electronic formats and by print-on-demand. Some material included with standard print versions of this book may not be included in e-books or in print-on-demand. If this book refers to media such as a CD or DVD that is not included in the version you purchased, you may download this material at http://booksupport.wiley.com. For more information about Wiley products, visit www.wiley.com.

*Library of Congress Cataloging-in-Publication Data is Available:*

ISBN 9781119429517 (Hardcover)
ISBN 9781119430056 (ePDF)
ISBN 9781119430001 (ePub)

Cover Design: Wiley
Cover Image: © phive2015/iStockphoto

Printed in the United States of America.

10 9 8 7 6 5 4 3 2 1

# CONTENTS

# FOREWORD

*If you know the enemy and know yourself, you need not fear the result of a hundred battles. If you know yourself but not the enemy, for every victory gained, you will also suffer a defeat. If you know neither the enemy nor yourself, you will succumb in every battle.*

— Sun Tzu, *The Art of War*

Who better to write a foreword for a cybersecurity book than a hacker? An "infamous hacktivist," as John Leyden called me five years back. After all, I'm the kind of person who, with help from this book, you will be prepared to defend yourself against!

I started out as a kid in the ghetto where I went into gang life and drug dealing. At some point I asked myself, "Do I follow in my father's footsteps, or do I find my own path in life?" I realized that living the fast life and being in the streets was only going to keep me there.

I wanted more.

I discovered the Internet at age 12. We're talking about a time when Google wasn't what it is today, and finding information online entailed going to forums, searching bulletin board system (BBS) archives, and relying on the likes of CompuServ, America Online (AOL), and Internet Relay Chat (IRC).

As I explored this world, I began to hear about certain mysterious figures who, like ancient sages, had a wealth of knowledge and experience that many Internet users lacked, but respected. I became attracted to the hacker ethic and lifestyle. Reading "The Hackers' Manifesto" cemented exactly what it was about being a hacker that I liked: that hacking was my decision, my choice, and no one could say otherwise.

I tried to reach out to hackers and join them. I was disappointed to learn these hackers belonged to invitation-only and private communities. It was impossible to speak to them. So, I made my own way. I chose a nom de guerre, "Sabu." As soon as I adopted this persona, I began to think differently, without boundaries.

To fully make the transition from Hector to Sabu required a lot of knowledge I didn't have. In short, I needed education. To compromise a server, I had to understand and be able to communicate with the underlying system, so I became a systems administrator of various UNIXes and POSIX systems. To write a proof-of concept exploit for a vulnerability, I had to learn several programming languages, and so on.

As I slowly grew out of my awkward teenage years, I became more interested in the world from a geopolitical perspective, which attracted me to "hacktivism," where you combine hacker skills with activist causes. In the year 2000, I began hacktivist operations against governments around the world. I went from a curious hacker to a persistent threat to governments I did not agree with. That decision ultimately led to my downfall as a hacker and a hacktivist.

Just before my arrest, I had decided to leave the hacking world. All my experience as a hacker, security researcher, and systems administrator provided me a wealth of experience that I could now apply to any business—and I did. I became senior systems administrator for one of the biggest nonprofit technology-oriented organizations in New York City. Life was good, and every decision I made, including becoming a foster parent, was positive.

That's when I made my mistake and got back in the game. I unretired Sabu and reconnected with the hacktivist scene. It was 2010, the height of Anonymous and online hacktivism. I involved myself in the Arab Spring, shutting down government communications at the apex of the Tunisian revolution, as well as targeting federal contractors and media platforms. This was a time when cybersecurity was forever changed—from the tools and the scope of attacks to how hackers were organized, were funded, and acted. I knew our world would not be the same again.

I am not proud of that time. But when I realized how far I'd overstepped the line, it was too late.

I was arrested, and "Sabu" became infamous.

I had to accept the consequences of my actions and change my life for good. This meant leaving behind most of my friends, expanding my perspective, and realizing what really meant the most to me in life: my family.

My life offers you a glimpse into the hacker world. It's important for you to understand that we come from all walks of life, from privileged suburbs to the ghetto. We may be working in so-called legitimate jobs one day and hacking the next. Some do it for the thrill, whereas others still do it to support their causes—as in my case.

But hackers also hack for revenge and out of greed. The varied nature of hacker threats and motives means that cybersecurity is not easy. It requires dedication to preparedness, education, and constant vigilance.

Those three things, preparedness, education, and vigilance, are what Chris Moschovitis's book is all about. I first met Chris at ISACA CSX, and we quickly discovered that our thinking on cyberthreats and possible solutions was in alignment. Most important, I share with him the critical importance of being prepared, staying informed, thinking ahead, and remaining vigilant. Chris and I agree: This is the only path to cyber-resilience.

Like the choices I made in my life, the choices you make in your organization have the potential to change its path. The things you will learn in these pages will help you get ahead of the curve, become cyber-resilient, and be prepared for the next time you "meet" a hacker, who, unlike me, is not in retirement.

Hector "Sabu" Monsegur
Director of Assessment Services
Rhino Security Labs

# PREFACE

"Enough already!"

This was the (only *half*-joking) reaction of a well-respected editor of a major publishing house when I suggested he produce yet another cybersecurity book. "Enough! You cybersecurity people have demoralized everyone so much that no one wants to hear, read, or talk about this any more. We're not publishing any more cybersecurity books! Done! Finished!"

I couldn't argue with him. He's right. Cybersecurity experts have done a wonderful job of terrorizing everyone about the threats while doing nothing by way of offering some hope, some light at the end of the tunnel. Every security discussion seems to boil down to the same, dire predictions of cyber-doom:

> *"It's not if, it's when!"*
> *"There are only two kinds of companies:*
> *Those that have been hacked and those that don't know it!"*

Got it! We're all done for, thank you very much. Now what?

## Something Completely Different

What if there was a book that put the whole cybersecurity thing into perspective, using simple, direct language? What if there were sections and chapters explaining what is going on, what the risks are, and what all the technobabble really means? And what if the book had a step-by-step, actionable approach on what you can do about all this? A book that aggregated the current best practices, put them in perspective, injected my experience and my own point of view, and how I applied all this across all our clients? All the while poking a little fun at ourselves, too?

I thought that this would be a great idea! And since I couldn't find any, I decided to write one.

Throughout my career, I've felt an attraction to science, technology, management, and governance, as well as a deep empathy for my clients' businesses. No matter what their industry, I understood their struggles, their anxieties, and what it means to make payroll no matter if it is for 10 employees or 5,000. I understood that I was their Rosetta stone—someone who could translate tech-speak to business-speak—and I felt the weight of that responsibility. My clients count on me and my recommendations. They are placing their trust and their businesses in my hands. My recommendations and my opinions matter in ways far more impactful than just tech. They affect people, their jobs, and their privacy.

This is exactly why I wrote this book.

This book is for them and for you: a businessperson, either running your own business or responsible enough to need to know how to protect the one you're employed at—no matter the size. You don't want to be at the mercy of experts talking above your head and around you. You want to participate in the conversation; you want to know what you're getting into. You are also an individual concerned about your privacy. You are alarmed about all the stuff about cyberattacks, hackers, and the like bombarding you in the news, and you want to stop feeling helpless about it. You are also a pragmatist who knows you can't spend your day being terrorized into hiding, paralyzed with inaction, or crippled by the costs of compliance and cyber-protection.

This book will prepare you for all this, step by step. We'll develop your cybersecurity program together, using the information presented here as well as by reviewing case studies from different industries and businesses.

Speaking of case studies, we need a case study disclaimer. The case studies presented throughout this book are aggregated from our work and from the work of colleagues who were gracious enough to share their experiences, some as named contributors. As you would expect, all names, industries, and geographies have been changed to protect the anonymity of the clients. The goal has been to distill the essential lesson from each case while protecting the identity and respecting the privacy and confidentiality of every client. You will find these case studies sprinkled throughout the book, especially as we dive into the specifics of cybersecurity program development.

My original title for the book paraphrased the great Stanley Kubrick and his film, *Dr. Strangelove*. I was going to call it *How to Stop Worrying about Cybersecurity and Learn to Love the Hackers!* The wise people at Wiley talked some sense into me and changed it for the better, but my goal remains the same.

It is my hope that when you're done, you will stop worrying about cybersecurity and will have learned to love the hackers!

# ABOUT THE AUTHOR

I was born in Athens, Greece. After high school I chose to come to the United States to study physics and computer science. I did that at The College at Brockport, in upstate New York. My years at Brockport were formative to me as a person, a scientist, and as a professional. Words for the gratitude and respect I have for the dedicated faculty that shaped my life can easily fill a couple of books, but that is for another time.

After graduating with my bachelor's degree in science, I became an instructor of computer science and a computer systems manager at the Stratford School in Rochester, New York. Following brief graduate work stints at the Rochester Institute of Technology and the University of Rochester, I moved to New York City to serve as the director of academic computing at the Pratt Institute. There, under the direction of the vice president of information technology (there were no "chief information officers" back then), I was responsible for the building and management of four computing centers of excellence, each focusing on a specific discipline (art, architecture, engineering, and information science). From there, I was recruited to be the vice president of information technology at the O'Connor Group, a real estate manager and developer in New York City. Then, in the middle of the Reagan Recession, I decided that there was no better time than the present to start my own company, which I did in 1989.

I have been running my own firm ever since, surrounded by partners and colleagues who teach me more and more every single day, and together we deliver a broad spectrum of IT consulting services. I have been privileged to partner with great clients, to engage in fantastic projects of business and technology transformation, and to collaborate with teams that push boundaries and develop incredible business solutions. I lived through the amazing advances in computer science that are now the stuff of lore: I was there during BitNet, sending email messages and watching the message hop from node to node. I was amazed at formatting the first 10MB hard disks of IBM's new personal computer. I've fed endless floppies in and out of the first Macs. I've built muscles carrying the Compaq "Portable," which was nicknamed "luggable" for good reason. I've carried pagers and cellphones the size of suitcases. I subscribed to CompuServe and AOL, and still have a working Hayes 14.4 modem.

Throughout it all, I have always been fascinated by security, privacy, and the protection of data. Even before "cybersecurity" was a word, I insisted that the sites we designed and managed implemented business-appropriate computer security and disaster recovery. Maybe it was because George, a partner of mine at the time, was a computer virus collector (he still has them). Maybe, because I remain culturally Greek, naturally cautious and private. Whatever the reason, I always asked, "What happens if 'this' gets out?" or "How fast can we be back up and running?" Any of my consultants will tell you that even now, the first thing they are taught when they start working for me is that "not checking the backup is a career-ending mistake."

Following decades as a practitioner of both IT governance and cyber-security management, I decided to make it official and joined Information Systems Audit and Control Association (ISACA), an independent, nonprofit, global association that was founded in 1969, engaging in "The development, adoption and use of globally accepted, industry-leading knowledge and prac-tices for information systems." Joining ISACA was one of the smartest things I ever did. Through ISACA, I got certified in two areas: one in IT governance, becoming Certified in Governance of Enterprise IT (CGEIT), and another in cybersecurity, becoming a Certified Information Security Manager (CISM). As of this writing, I am proud to have the highest scores in the New York chapter in both, as well as membership in the top 5 percent of those tested worldwide for CISM, and the top 10 percent for CGEIT.

# ACKNOWLEDGMENTS

This book reflects a long, personal, and professional journey. Over the course of some 30 years in the industry, I have had the privilege to meet hundreds of professionals, experts, partners, clients, and vendors who have shaped my thinking, formed my experiences, and honed my expertise. From my original partner in the business, George Whelan, who religiously collected and kept live computer viruses on floppy disks, to instructors like Jay Ranade, who has forgotten more than I'll ever know, to clients who partnered with me, and staff who tirelessly worked to solve problems, I owe each one a debt of gratitude that no acknowledgment can do justice. I start, therefore, with an apology for my omissions. They are entirely my own.

First and foremost, I want to thank our clients, our true partners to success. Every day, we are honored and privileged to be your allies and to contribute to your success. We are humbled by all the things that you teach us every day. I would be remiss if I didn't single out the Hoffman family, Andrew, Mark, and Steve, who have been loyal supporters and mentors since I started the firm; the executive leadership at the 4As for defining and living into a true partnership of success; the founding partners at Allegaert Berger and Vogel, Chris, David, and Michael, for their trust in us, loyalty, and wise counsel through thick and thin; the president of the LaSalle Academy, Dr. Cathy Guerriero, and her team, for infusing us with creativity and vigor, and for taking the time to listen even when they are running at 1,000 mph; and finally, the leadership team at the Packer Collegiate Institute, Bruce Dennis, Elizabeth Winter, and Jim Anderson, for their trust, engagement, and reminding us how to be brave in the face of change.

In the same breath, I want to thank my own partners and associates, whose incredible expertise, loyalty, dedication, skills, empathy, and personal engagement make our clients' success possible. They are, alphabetically: Anna Murray, Atsushi Tatsuoka, Frank Murray, Greg Andrews, Haleigh Westwood, Jonathan Ongvano, Justin Schroeder, Leon Tchekmedyian, Pedro Garrett, Protus Miyogo, Sotos Antoniades, Steve Vance, Thomas Hussey, Yeimy Morel, and Zachary Tereska. Thank you for all you do, day and night, and thank you for allowing me to shut my door and write, write, write! Without your help, this book would still be on the drawing board.

Whenever there is a book, there is an editor and a publisher. I have been the luckiest of authors to have the best in both. First, my eternal gratitude to the amazing Hilary Poole, my editor, coauthor, and friend of countless years and as many books. You are simply amazing. I refuse to go next to a keyboard unless I am reassured you'll edit the outcome. Thank you!

To everyone at John Wiley & Sons, one of the most professional and exceptional publishers in the world, and especially to my executive editor, Sheck Cho, captain and commander extraordinaire; Judy Howarth, manager of content enablement and operations; and my developmental editor, Christina Verigan. This book is as much yours as it is mine, and I am grateful for all your help, guidance, and support.

To all the cybersecurity and governance professionals around the world, working tirelessly in the field, in academia, in research institutions, in government agencies, and militaries, this book pales in comparison to your achievements every day. Without your endless efforts in breaking new ground, expanding and enhancing our scientific understanding, and guiding us through the turbulent and terrifying waters that cybersecurity is, we would be lost. Your work represents the lighthouse that helps us navigate, and if I aspire to anything, it is for this book to aid in reflecting your light, interpreting your guidance, and adding wind to the sails.

To the many international organizations that help all practitioners learn, hone, and apply their craft, as well as develop the frameworks we depend on, my gratitude for your ongoing contributions, tireless curation, and unending support. I must particularly single out (ISC)$^2$, CERT, ENISA, ISACA, ISECOM, ISO, ISSA, OECD, OWASP, and SANS, with my apologies for omitting the many other deserving organizations worldwide. My specific thanks to Dr. Christos K. Dimitriadis, chairman of the ISACA board of directors, and Matt Loeb, ISACA CEO, for their continuous support, and the ISACA New York chapter for making the chapter a home away from home for me and countless professionals in the New York metro area.

To the book's direct contributors and supporters, Anna Murray, F. Charlene Watson, Frank Downs, and Mark Thomas, thank you for allowing me to include your expertise and to share it with my audience. This book is richer and more useful because of your contributions. And to Mike Barlow, an early supporter and advocate for the book, as well as an accomplished writer in his own right, thank you for everything. Your guidance, advice, and support mean the world to me.

Finally, to Anna Murray, a name that keeps on repeating in these acknowledgments, but from where I sit, not enough! You are the most brilliant, expert, capable, tenacious, fierce, loving, accepting, and giving professional and writer I know! Every day I thank my lucky stars that brought you to my life as my partner in the business and my partner in life. You are, and always will be, the brightest star in the dark of night, guiding me home. Thank you.

# CHAPTER 1

# Understanding Risk

I f you're reading this book, I'd hazard a guess that you've read some of the doom-and-gloom cybersecurity books out there as well. There are many, and many are great (see the bibliography for suggestions). What's more, I am sure you have had your fill of statistics. Dreadful statistics showing how cybercrime is increasing by the day. I'll include some of those, too, just to satisfy any morbid curiosity left in you, but they are essentially useless. By the time the ink is dry on these pages, the numbers have changed. For the worse.

## A BRIEF SAMPLING OF DREAD

- Hacker Attack Rate: 39 Seconds
    Assistant Professor of Mechanical Engineering Michel Cukier at the A. James Clark School of Engineering conducted the study that profiled the actions of hackers using brute-force methods to gain access to a set of exposed computers. The results showed that the computers were attacked about 2,244 times per day.
- More than 33 percent of United States consumers have experienced a cyberattack.
    This was reported in a survey by Zogby Analytics commission for the Hartford Steam Boiler Inspection and Insurance Company (HSB), with the most likely victims being between 18 and 24 years old. Moreover, the associated incident costs ranged from $500 for 56 percent of the cases to between $1,000 and $5,000 for 23 percent of the cases.
- According to the "Internet Security Threat Report—Symantec 2017" (Volume 22, April 2017):

- It takes on average two minutes for an Internet of Things (IoT) device to get attacked.
- The average ransom amount for a ransomware attack went from $373 in 2014 to $1,077 in 2016.
- Over the last eight years, more than 7.1 billion identities have been stolen as a result of data breaches.
- In 2016, the United States was number one both in number of data breaches (1,023) and in identities stolen (791,820,040).

■ According to the "2017 Data Breach Investigations Report" (Verizon):

- 75 percent of the breaches are perpetrated by outsiders, versus 25 percent involving insiders.
- 62 percent of breaches featured hacking, of which 81 percent leveraged stolen or weak passwords.
- 66 percent of malware was installed through malicious email attachments.
- 73 percent of the breaches were financially motivated; 21 percent were espionage-driven.

■ According to the "Small Business Trends" website (https://smallbiztrends.com):

- 43 percent of cyberattacks target small business.
- Only 14 percent of small businesses rate their ability to mitigate cyberrisks vulnerabilities and attacks as highly effective.
- 60 percent of small companies go out of business within six months of a cyberattack.
- 48 percent of data security breaches are caused by acts of malicious intent. Human error or system failure account for the rest.

■ According to Juniper Research's study titled "The Future of Cybercrime & Security: Financial and Corporate Threats & Mitigation" (Juniper Research, Ltd.):

- Cybercrime is expected to cost businesses over $2 trillion by 2019.

- Although North America has seen the lion's share of these breaches (60 percent in 2015), the proportion will level off as global digitization levels the playing field.
- According to "Cybersecurity Ventures' Predictions for 2017 through 2021":
  - The cost of cybercrime damages worldwide is estimated to be $6 trillion annually by 2021.
  - In 2016, the cybersecurity unemployment rate dropped to zero percent, and it is expected to remain at that level through 2021, with a projected job-to-skills shortfall of 1.5 million positions by 2019.
- ISACA's *2016 Cybersecurity Global Data Snapshot* lists social engineering, insider threats, and advanced persistent threats as the top-three threats facing organizations.
- According to Barkly Protects, Inc.:
  - One-third of the IT professionals surveyed by Barkly reported their security had been bypassed by a cyberattack in 2016.
  - 71 percent of organizations targeted with ransomware attacks were successfully infected.
  - Over half the organizations that suffered successful cyberattacks in 2016 are not making any changes to their cybersecurity posture in 2017, with budgetary constraints cited as the main block to improved cybersecurity.

## How Much Is It Worth to You?

In the misty past, a person's most valuable possessions were things he could see: his castle, gold, tapestries, even his heirs! Their value was tied to their physical existence.

Today, the concept of *value* has expanded beyond tangibles to include intangibles such as data, intellectual property, and reputation. As a matter of fact, many intangibles hold more value than tangibles. Consider, which is more important: an artisanal pizza or the *recipe* for the artisanal pizza? It's no accident that the phase following the Industrial Revolution has been nicknamed the Information Revolution.

The rise of intangible valuables affects every individual as well as businesses of all sizes. These things of value that individuals and businesses create are—like all things of value—coveted by others and therefore warrant your protection. So, just like you would protect your valuable jewelry, you must protect your valuable data. It's a simple concept.

What is interesting in this analogy is the assumption that we all share a common understanding of what is *of value*. You certainly have no problem intuiting that a set of diamond earrings is valuable and should therefore be stored in a secure place. Which place and how secure? That, too, is straightforward to understand. We have an innate sense of value to guide us in these decisions—something that tells us that a $300 pair of earrings is safe in the jewelry box in the apartment while a $30,000 pair of earrings is best protected in a bank's safe deposit box. Easy to understand and easy to make a value judgment on.

We make these types of judgments every day, and we're very good at it. We understand what's of value, and we understand the risks to this value:

Earrings? Theft!
Property? Fire!

It ends up that we are very good at making complex risk management decisions on a daily basis. Who knew?

## Risk! Not Just a Board Game

Consider this situation: It is 11:00 at night, and you just finished dinner with friends at your favorite restaurant. Walking to your car, you reach an intersection and see that the walk signal is red. You look left. You look right. You see a car down the block, shrug it off, and cross the street. No problem.

Now, let's change this scenario a little. Same story, only this time you are pushing a stroller with your baby in it. What's the decision now? Do you cross the street or wait for the signal to change? My bet is you wait.

We just stumbled on the concept of *risk acceptance*, which will prove to be of real importance in the pages that follow. The bottom line is that we all live with risk every single day of our lives. We constantly make decisions about risk and, when we're done evaluating, we take action signifying our acceptance of this risk.

In the example just suggested, in one case you accepted the risk that you can cross the street against the light, and in the other case, when you had your baby along, you did not. How does this translate to the cyberworld? In some cases, we accept the risk of having our information available out there (e.g., when using Facebook, Instagram, Swarm, and the like), and in others we do not (e.g., when we are using our credit card or revealing our medical records).

Studying risk is taking a trip down a fascinating, complex, and intricate labyrinth. It is hard-core science—involving complex mathematics, ethics, and philosophy—with potential life-and-death implications (e.g., the risk of reprisals when we attack a terrorist group, the risks that first responders take every day, etc.). This is certainly not a book to start you on this type of journey, although I have included a selected bibliography for you to consider at the back of this book. The purpose of this book is to expose you to some risk management and tech concepts so that we can develop a common language when discussing how to protect your things of value from cyber-based threats. With that in mind, let's start with a simple definition. What is risk?

*Risk is the combination of the likelihood of an event and its impact.*

What's the risk of a hurricane in Miami?

Well ... how likely is it, and what will its impact be when it hits?

Why do you need know this? Because, for starters, the answer determines whether you want to move there, if you want to start a business there, if you want to send your kids to school there, and how much your insurance will cost you to protect you from this risk, and so on.

How can you determine the likelihood that a hurricane will strike Miami? You have tons and tons of statistical data that give you a good sense of the frequency of hurricanes hitting the area over the past couple of hundred years.

What's the impact? There is the cost of rebuilding, the cost of business losses, environmental damage, and the potential of loss of life, among many others. You get the picture. Who is good at keeping these types of statistics? Insurance companies. But this alone is not the complete picture. Let's fill in the blanks.

First, let's assume you have decided that you want to live in Miami. That's key. That decision (like the road-crossing example discussed earlier) implies some degree of risk acceptance out of the gate. You know that hurricanes strike Miami, yet you choose to live there. Fine. (Who am I to judge? I live in New York!)

But you're not simply living in Miami. Knowing that hurricanes may hit Miami, you have chosen to live in a "hardened" house, meaning a house that is as hurricane-proof as you *choose* to make it. Before buying the house, you did your research, compared options, and decided to buy a house that can withstand a Category 3 hurricane. That was your choice. It was a very important one: You didn't just choose any house. You chose to get a hardened one. This hardened option? That's a *control*. Controls act against risks. Your control was to buy a house that can withstand a Category 3 hurricane. That *mitigates* your risk: If a Category 3 storm hits, you are protected.

But what happens if a Category 4 storm hits? Well … you have to deal with that risk.

So, how do you deal with the Category 4 risk? You call your insurance company and tell them that you need hurricane insurance. They quote you an outrageous amount, to which you respond with "Wait! I have a Category 3 hurricane-proof home!" They go recheck their numbers and come back with a much more reasonable amount, but they tell you they will cover only Category 4 storm damage and higher. Nothing below. You sign on the dotted line.

You have now *transferred the risk* of a Category 4 storm and higher to the insurance company. Now, you're breathing more easily. What did you accomplish?

First of all, you *assessed the risk* of your desire to live in Miami and decided that *this was worth it to you*. You *applied a control* to *mitigate this risk* by buying the hardened house. You then *transferred the rest of the risk* to the insurance company.

Did you eliminate the risk? Nope! You can still get hurt if a tree falls on you during a Category 3 storm and the insurance will not pay for your medical bills. In other words, no matter what you do, there is always some risk that is left over. Always. *Risk is never zero.* This leftover risk is called *residual risk* and that's the risk that you choose to accept.

Or not.

If you don't accept the risk, you can do more to make it more to your liking. You can apply more controls. For example, you can invest in a Category 4 hurricane-proof home and renegotiate with the insurance company to cover more or different kinds of risk. You can buy your own weather station to predict hurricanes before anyone else does and evacuate the area. You can build a bunker. You can do all sorts of things insofar as the things you do to mitigate your risk don't exceed the value of what you're trying to protect. In risk management terms: The cost of controls cannot exceed the value of the asset you're trying to protect. That would be silly, and clearly, you're very smart, so you wouldn't be doing this anyway.

One last thing: There are all sorts of controls. Broadly speaking, they fall into one of the following categories: *preventative, detective, corrective*, and *compensatory*. Your weather station is a detective control, the hardening of your home is a preventative control, and your bunker is a compensatory control. What's the corrective control? The insurance inspector who comes once a year to confirm that the house remains hardened. (Notice that your insurance policy is not a control. It doesn't *do* anything to reduce risk; it only accepts some of the risk you transfer to it. You're still the one incurring the risk; it's just that you're not on the hook for the damages that may result.)

What happens if you employ all these controls at once? Well—you risk strategist, you!—you just developed a *defense-in-depth* strategy to mitigate your risk. You rolled out your controls in a way that they complement one another; if the first fails, the next kicks in, and so on.

Okay, now we're talking the same risk management language. Enough for our purposes (secretly, we haven't even scratched the surface of the risk management field, but let's accept this and move on). But wait, you say: How does the hurricane example apply to my data in New York? Believe me, it does, and I'll show you how. For now, just note those definitions and examples. We'll apply them to your data universe shortly.

But I need to come clean about something before we go further down the cyberpath: Remember all these statistics about likelihood that the insurance company had? How useful they were in determining risk and so forth? Well … we don't really have any of those for cyberattacks. Not enough to build a very robust statistical model about likelihood. At least not yet.

We certainly have a good sense of the *impact*: Your life (or your business) will be in shambles if someone steals your identity (or your business data), so we're all pretty clear on impact. The rest, *you* are going to estimate. Notice the change from "we" to "you"? Excellent! I am betting that you, of all people, know best when it's okay to cross the street. I trust you.

This all makes sense when the risk is personal, right? You get to make the call on what risk you're willing to accept. But what if the risk is to a business? The same concept applies. The people who decide whether or not to accept business risk can only be the owner(s) of the business. No one else. If it is a small business, the owner (usually the president or CEO) is responsible for accepting or rejecting risk. For larger firms, the board of directors is ultimately responsible for risk management decisions. In the absence of a board, then it is the CEO or the executive appointed by the shareholder(s) to run the company. If you are not "them," then you need to trust them that they are making the right decision. That's why they are there. The responsibility is theirs, and theirs alone, to decide whether it is safe to "cross the street." It is your responsibility to advise them one way or another.

To summarize our risk definitions:

- *Asset*: Anything of value
- *Risk*: Likelihood of an event, multiplied by its impact
- *Mitigated risk*: Existing risk after controls have been applied
- *Residual risk*: What's left over after risks have been mitigated or transferred as much as possible
- *Accepted risk*: Residual risk that has been accepted, aka *the risk of doing business*
- *Controls*: Active countermeasures, be it processes, systems, or applications, that prevent, detect, correct, or compensate against risk

# CHAPTER 2

## Everything You Always Wanted to Know About Tech (But Were Afraid to Ask Your Kids)

How much do you need to know for us to have an intelligent conversation about your business data, your personal information, potential threats, and your options to address those threats? The answer is surprisingly fluid, as it is with any fast-changing field. How much do you need to know about medicine to have a meaningful conversation with your doctor about your health? How much do you need to know about law to understand and engage with your attorney? How much do you need to know about cars to talk to your mechanic?

It's a tricky question with no easy answers, and to some degree, it involves lots of individual choice. Some people dive deep into research before consulting with a medical expert; doctors jokingly refer to these folks as "Google Medical School graduates." Others shy away from research entirely, depending on the expert advice of professionals. But no matter where on the spectrum you find yourself, everyone around the table should at least speak a common language. For example, you may not know precisely how your engine *works*, but you know what an engine *is*.

Not so much with technology. The minute we start talking tech, eyes glaze over, mouths yawn, and palms sweat. For some reason, we forget we share a common language ... and we need to fix that!

Of course that is more easily said than done, especially when it comes to tech. Still, the success of this book's message rests in its ability to reach you, be understandable, and actionable. We definitely need to be able to communicate at some level. To do this, I have chosen to abuse metaphors, go back to basics as needed, keep everything as simple as possible, use short case studies to illustrate examples, and live by Mark Twain's adage: *Humor is the good-natured side of a truth*.

Our goal is a simple one: When done with this section, I'd like you to have the same tech facility you have when talking about your car. I am not expecting you to be a mechanic but I am hoping that you'll get to know a bit about its history, the location of the engine, what the steering wheel does, and how to start it.

It will also be good if you get to learn to drive the thing without killing anyone!

## In the Beginning...[1]

There was darkness. And void. It was probably pretty cold, too. Then, the lights came on, rocks started spinning in the heavens, and before you know it, fish were walking on land, and all creatures big and small were living in glorious, albeit analog, bliss. Shortly thereafter, an English mathematician by the name of Charles Babbage came up with something he called the Difference Engine, now credited as the first computer. Three years later, it was hacked by Ada Lovelace when in 1843 she published "Sketch of the Analytical Engine," officially firing the starting gun and setting the world racing down the information highway. Moving right along, past the invention of the telegraph, the telephone, and the radio, almost a hundred years after Ms. Lovelace, Alan Turing, another Brit, published a paper titled "On Computable Numbers," detailing the design of a digital computer.

It didn't take long for the rest of the world to get into the game. In 1938, Konrad Zuse built the first electromechanical binary computers, the Z1 and—of course—the Z2. A year later, John Atanasoff completed the first entirely electronic binary computer. World War II drove the development of electronic deciphering devices of which the German Enigma and the British Colossus are the best known. The public didn't get to see a computer until 1944, when IBM constructed a room-sized machine, the sexily named Automatic Sequence Controlled Calculator, at Harvard University (it was

---

[1]An extraordinarily brief history of computers, networks, the Internet and everything, creatively pilfered from *History of the Internet: A Historical Encyclopedia: A Chronology, 1843 to the Present*, Christos J.P. Moschovitis, Hilary Poole, Erica Pearson, Tami Schuyler, Theresa Senft. ABC-CLIO 2005.

nicknamed Mark I by Harvard engineers). Not to be left behind, in 1946 the University of Pennsylvania inaugurated ENIAC, which weighed over 30 tons with its 17,000-plus vacuum tubes.

Things were going splendidly in 1947, when a dead moth was found short-circuiting the vacuum tubes of a Mark II computer, giving rise to the term *bug*, usually preceded by several expletives. The same year, John Bardeen, Walter Brattain, and William Shockley, working at Bell Labs, invented the first transistor. The rest, as they say, is history: In the blink of an eye, we went from massive mainframe computers to personal computers, tablets, smartphones, wearables, and even quantum computers. As of this writing, there is even experimental work of storing terabytes worth of data in *biocomputers* that use the DNA helix for memory. So much for *digital* devices!

Paralleling the development of all these computers is the development of the networks that connected them. It started when the United States, quite annoyed by the incessant *blip-blip-blip* of Sputnik, formed the Advance Research Projects Agency (ARPA) in 1958. ARPA's head of its command-and-control division, J.C.R. Licklider, sent a memo to his colleagues boldly asserting that the time was right for a network of interconnected computers. He was right. Several geniuses later (Leonard Kleinrock, Robert Taylor, Paul Baran, Ted Nelson, and more) and ARPANET was born!

From then on, everything is a blur. Between 1969 and 1990, we had NET-mania: ARPANET, ALOHANET, TELENET, USENET, and—yes—FIDONET, to name a few. At some point, all these NETs were talking to one another and everyone agreed to call the collection of all these connected networks, computers, and devices INTERNET and get it over with.

In between all that, Ray Tomlinson invented email, and soon he received one from a Nigerian prince asking for money. Skipping past some incredible advances in computer science with even more funky acronyms (UNIX, ETHERNET, TCP/IP, RSA, DNS, PING, and so much more), we finally arrive at the glorious year of 1990, when Tim Berners-Lee and Robert Cailliau first use the phrase "World Wide Web" as the name of a hypertext system that they had just developed, filling the world with links, most of which you should avoid clicking on.

And here we are!

## Key Definitions

We have a big advantage in our vocabulary-building exercise in that, unless you've been living under a rock (in which case I am flattered that this is the first book you chose!), you already know most of the terms you need.

This, therefore, should help clarify the terms as opposed to introduce them:

- *Hardware*: Any physical device that can store, process, or transmit data in digital form. Examples include everything from supercomputers to personal computers, laptops, tablets, cellphones, wearables, switches, routers, and digital appliances of every imaginable (and some unimaginable!) kind. Going forward, and as a matter of convenience, I will be using the term *digital device* as synonymous with *hardware*.
- *Software*: In its broadest definition, software is a set of instructions that guide hardware in performing a task. Nothing happens without software. Think car and driver. You may be familiar with the distinction between the operating system (OS) of a computer or phone and its applications (or apps), but while they are indeed different, both are software; they just do different things. The OS is the software that controls the use of the actual hardware while the applications make requests of the operating system to have the hardware perform specific tasks.
- *Network*: In this context, a network is a collection of connected (again, most often digital) devices. You can have a network of computers—such as the one in your office that enables you to send a document to your office printer—and you can also have a network of networks—such as your point-of-sale terminal network that connects to a credit-card authorization network. Whatever its size, the point of a network is to enable communications. Networked devices can share data and software, leveraging their connection to increase processing power. The Internet is a network of networks. In fact, it is *the* network of networks—you might think of the Internet as one giant ocean but in fact it's more like a huge number of interconnected streams, rivers, and lakes. And like Tolkien's "one ring," the Internet is there connecting them all!
- *Digital Services*: Simply put, a *service* delivers value to a customer through action (a human doing a task for the customer) as opposed to manufacturing (producing a product). Similarly, for digital services: A collection of hardware and software, networked or not, combines to deliver value. For example, a digital service can be something as simple as digital storage. Other digital services include access to processing power or to a particular application.
- *Hosting*: Be it a business (such as hosting a website) or a service (hosting storage), the term *hosting* means the capacity to deliver digital services located off-premises (remote) to the consumer. There are many nuances to the term (for example, *near hosting, far hosting, distributed*

*hosting*), but the easiest way to think of it is that the computers are located in someone else's office—that office hosts the computers on your and others' behalf. That other firm runs and maintains them, pays the electric bills, and so on—while you get to use the computers by accessing them remotely.

- *Cloud*: Or, cloud computing, is the delivery of hosted digital services, on demand, over a network, and commonly over the Internet. If these services are being delivered through private and proprietary means, then the term used is *private cloud*. If the network is the Internet, then it's called *public cloud*. If we combine them, we refer to it as a *hybrid cloud*. Terms like Software as a Service (SaaS) and Infrastructure as a Service (IaaS) are now used to differentiate between cloud-delivered application services and hardware services.

The "as a service" tag is getting appended to more and more digital services these days, for example, Architecture as a Service (AaaS), Platform as a Service (PaaS), and Everything as a Service (XaaS). The main advantage of cloud computing is its scalability, redundancy, reliability, pricing, and on-demand availability. The main disadvantages are that all of these "as a services" are nothing more than "hosted subscriptions," rather than items you own. "As a service" is kind of like renting an apartment in a location you can't always control, with co-tenancy issues (you moved from your apartment to one with roommates), conflicts of interest (the renter has different priorities from the landlord), and potential problems with accessibility (no Internet access means no cloud access).

- *Digital Ecosystem, Digital Realm, Digital World, Cyberworld, and the like*: The collection of all of these definitions (hardware, software, networks, services, etc.) also sounds really smart and cool when you use it in a bar.

One more definition—my favorite!—and we're done with this chapter:

- *Cybersecurity*: Cybersecurity is the ongoing application of best practices intended to ensure and preserve confidentiality, integrity, and availability of digital information and the safety of people and environments.

# CHAPTER 3

## A Cybersecurity Primer

This chapter is your core resource for cybersecurity. You can refer to it again and again to refresh your understanding, look up a term, and review essential principles.

## Cybersecurity Defined

This is my definition of cybersecurity:

*Cybersecurity is the ongoing application of best practices intended to ensure and preserve confidentiality, integrity, and availability of digital information as well as the safety of people and environments.*

There are other definitions out there, most with more complexity. But I—and I'd hazard most businesspeople—needed something different: a simple, meaningful definition we can pin to our monitors, consult frequently, and easily understand.

This definition includes the dynamic nature of the field (it's *ongoing*) and the four best-practice pillars: *confidentiality, integrity, availability,* and *safety.*

The pillars of cybersecurity used to be a triad: *confidentiality, integrity,* and *availability. Safety* is the newest member of the roster, making it a lovely quartet, and introduced to address everyday-life threats posed by the Internet of Things (IoT).

## The Meaning of Security

The word *security* is at the heart of cybersecurity. So, let's take a moment to break it down. Security is a practice dealing with all aspects of prevention, protection, and remediation from any type of harm to an asset. The bullet-proof glass in front of the Mona Lisa is security.

Information security is also a practice, one that aims to protect any type of information assets. The fireproof safe where you keep your will is a form of information security.

Now: Cybersecurity is a subset of information security, focusing specifically on protecting digital information assets in their ecosystem.

## Confidentiality

*Confidentiality* is the term of the four that prompts the most debate. Because it's the most controversial, we'll deal with it first.

Most people think of *confidential* as being synonymous with *private* or even *secret*. We're all on board with the definition, except for one thing: Who, exactly, gets to decide what's private or secret? That depends on whose stuff it is and who may want access to it.

What makes the concept of confidentiality so tricky is that the definition truly lies in the eye of the beholder. What's more, even if we agree on what's confidential today, we may disagree tomorrow. For example, a husband and wife may agree that their emails are confidential right up until the moment divorce proceedings begin. Two corporations may agree that their transaction records are confidential until they sue one another for breach of contract. Two allied countries share intelligence today until they are allies no more.

Of course, one could simply decide to trust no one, but we have a job to do here. We must develop a framework on which to build our defenses, and to do that, we need definitions.

Therefore, as in the case of risk, I will look at you as the expert. I assert, and firmly believe, that you and you alone can determine what *confidential* means to you, just as you and you alone ultimately determine your acceptable level of risk. This works if you're an individual, and it works if you're a CEO of a business, or a board member of a multinational corporation. You get to decide what's confidential and what's not, and—more importantly—to what *degree* it's confidential.

Degrees of confidentiality? Of course! This is not a black-and-white world, is it? Not only are there degrees of confidentiality, but confidentiality itself has a life cycle during which its degree can change.

In general, there are three accepted degrees of confidentiality: top secret, secret, and confidential. Conveniently, the European Union in its 2013 council decision, pretty much agreed, and made it sound even sexier in French by publishing the following definitions (*emphases* are mine):

(a) TRÈS SECRET UE (EU TOP SECRET): information and material the unauthorized disclosure of which could cause *exceptionally grave prejudice to the essential interests* of the European Union or of one or more of the Member States;

(b) SECRET UE (EU SECRET): information and material the unauthorized disclosure of which *could seriously harm the essential interests* of the European Union or of one or more of the Member States;

(c) CONFIDENTIEL UE (EU CONFIDENTIAL): information and material the unauthorized disclosure of which *could harm the essential interests* of the European Union or of one or more of the Member States;

(d) RESTREINT UE (EU RESTRICTED): information and material the unauthorized disclosure of which *could be disadvantageous to the interests* of the European Union or of one or more of the Member States.

You might wonder why we are talking about nation-state security when you are running a business. The reason is simple: States have spent centuries thinking about these definitions, so it's helpful to leverage their expertise. You'll notice these classifications go by degrees of harm. Disclosure of information could cause:

- Exceptionally grave prejudice
- Serious harm
- Harm
- Disadvantage

Most businesses have information assets that, if disclosed, would cause various degrees of harm. As a business, you will likely want to add more classification levels. You probably already have certain clearances to see particular types of sensitive information; for example, your accounting department likely has access to financial data other employees don't. Furthermore, there is information open at a corporate level, such as the details of your benefit program, but not available to the public. And, finally, there is information open to the public, such as the annual report.

Determining your levels of confidentiality will be important as we move to the topic of asset valuation. For each asset, you'll need to classify its confidentiality status (among others), and—to the degree applicable—its life expectancy. For example, your tax returns may be kept and labeled CONFIDENTIAL for seven years, and BURN, BABY, BURN thereafter.

## Integrity

*Integrity*, our next term, is an easier topic to get your head around than confidentiality.

If you ask an accountant to define *integrity*, she may refer you to the American Institute of Certified Public Accountants 2013 publication titled "Information Integrity," which sports the following definition:

> *Information integrity is defined as the representational faithfulness of the information to the underlying subject of that information and the fitness of the information for its intended use.*

This is painstakingly accurate and also why I don't ask my favorite accountants to define things for me. I have synthesized instead the following definition of integrity in the cybersecurity context:

> *Integrity is the set of practices and tools (controls) designed to protect, maintain, and ensure both the accuracy and completeness of data over its entire life cycle.*

In short, you want to have a way to make sure that the numbers in your Excel spreadsheet don't change *on their own*. If you are wiring $5,000, you don't want it to morph into $50,000 without your approval. You want to be assured that the payroll is correct, and that your love letter addressed to Anna doesn't suddenly start with "Dear Monica ...." That would be a serious integrity problem.

How do you achieve integrity? You do it by implementing digital signatures, write-once-read-many logging mechanisms, and hashing. These conversations tend to be a bit too technical, so suffice to say that you need to know about them enough to understand your cybersecurity expert's explanation and recommendation for your specific requirements.

## Availability

*Availability*, pillar number 3, is *the set of practices and tools designed to ensure timely access to data*. If your computer is down, availability is compromised. If your Internet connection is moving at a snail's pace, availability is compromised. How do you ensure availability? In one word? *Backup*. In two words? *Redundancy* and *backup*.

## Safety

Finally, term number 4: *safety*. It is the newest pillar in cybersecurity, but one whose impact is potentially the most critical. This is where cybersecurity incidents could result in injuries, environmental disasters, and even loss of life.

You may be a user of a connected medical device, potentially putting you at mortal risk if that device is hacked. Or, you may be in a connected car, plane, or train. Or, you may be in charge of a business that is responsible for water purification for thousands of people, or of a utility that millions of people rely on for life-sustaining services like electricity.

The concept of safety steers the cybersecurity conversation away from the purely technical to more of a people-centric approach. Therefore, as you approach your own cybersecurity program development, keep this last pillar at the forefront of your thinking. Ask yourself how your cybersecurity decisions go beyond information security and potentially involve the prevention of physical harm to human beings or the environment.

# Measuring Cybersecurity's Success

Here's a key question: How do you measure cybersecurity's success?

Ask yourself: How do you measure any security effort's success? By the absence of impact. If you have a house that keeps getting broken into and you install an alarm system and the break-ins stop: *Ta-da!* Success. No more impact of break-ins. If you're riding in your bulletproof limo and you're peppered by bullets? No problem; you keep on trekking. No impact! (I might advise that you reconsider your life choices, but that's a different matter.)

Success in cybersecurity, therefore, will be the absence of impact on confidentiality, integrity, and availability of digital information no matter where it is (stationary/stored, traveling/transmitted, or processed). What about safety, you ask? Same metric. We want to look at the absence of impact on the safety of any assets governed or affected by digital information. This is, by the way, one of the arguments used against including safety as a fourth cybersecurity pillar: ensuring zero impact on confidentiality. Integrity and availability implies—some argue—that you already have safety. I do see their point. Personally? I feel safer in the redundancy of including it!

It's important to note that *absence of impact* does not mean that the effect of your cybersecurity efforts can't be quantified. There are tools that will quantify the number of attacks your business systems are currently enduring, likely many without your knowledge. That's right, you may already be experiencing digital break-ins even if you are not aware of them. Establishing these baselines will be a key step, and we will discuss cybersecurity success metrics in more detail in Chapter 4.

## Ensuring and Preserving

Remember our definition? *Cybersecurity is the ongoing application of best practices intended to ensure and preserve confidentiality, integrity, and availability of digital information as well as the safety of people and environments.*

Let's focus on *ensure* and *preserve* for a moment. How does one go about it, exactly? This question has engaged scholars, scientists, legislators, and citizens the world over for many years. The results of their hard work are expressed in the form of standards.

In the most abstract sense, a standard is a set of properties that something must meet to be considered appropriate to its function. This something can be a product or a service, or even a material. For example, people know that 24-karat gold is 100 percent pure because they have accepted that standard of purity. Similarly, people may be familiar with the International Standards Organization (ISO) 9001 quality management standard, the Institute of Electrical and Electronics Engineers (IEEE) 802.3 Ethernet standard, or, the ever-so-popular American National Standards Institute (ANSI) Z315.1-2012 Tricycle Safety Requirements standard.

Now, get ready for a dizzying assault of acronyms that you must memorize fully. There will be a quiz!

When it comes to cybersecurity the main standards that apply are (alphabetically):

1. The European Telecommunications Standards Institute (ETSI) TR 103 family of standards
2. The IASME standards for small and medium-sized enterprises (IASME stands for Information Assurance for Small and Medium-sized Enterprises)
3. The Information Security Forum (ISF) Standard of Good Practice (SoGP)
4. The International Society for Automation (ISA) ISA62443 standards for industrial automation and control systems
5. The Internet Engineering Task Force (IETF) via their Request For Comments (RFC) 2196 memorandum
6. The Information Systems Audit and Control Association, now known only as ISACA, through their COBIT framework and Cybersecurity Nexus (CSX) resources
7. The Institute for Security and Open Methodologies (ISECOM) with their Open Source Security Testing Methodology Manual (OSSTMM) and the Open Source Cybersecurity Playbook
8. The ISO 27000 family of standards (ISO 27000–ISO27999)
9. The National Institute of Standards and Technology (NIST) Cybersecurity Framework (CSF)

10. The North American Electric Reliability Corporation (NERC), which via its Critical Infrastructure Protection (CIP) family of standards addresses electric systems and network security

Believe it or not, even this list is far from complete, and I will bet you several copies of this book that there are at least half a dozen more international standards organizations that are going to send me nasty letters for my obvious and glaring omission herein for which I sincerely apologize.

Now, please, don't get me wrong. This whole book lives and dies on the work of the thousands of dedicated experts who've toiled in endless committee meetings and real-life environments to produce this extensive body of knowledge. I cannot be clearer on this: Without their continuing and never-ending dedication, skills, expertise, and hard work, we would all be in the dark, not even knowing where to start addressing cybersecurity. I am eternally grateful to their work and will acknowledge them in every opportunity I get. They are the true visionaries in cybersecurity, the ones we all learn from and are guided by, including the advice in this book.

Why is all this important? Because meaningful advice must be grounded on solid research and hard science. Because no one person can possibly master a subject as deep and complex as cybersecurity, let alone information security. And because we must check our own interpretation of what's right and filter our own opinions and experiences through the lens of proven, peer-reviewed, work.

This book draws from all these standards. It is my interpretation and translation of their advice into what I consider appropriate for the current business climate and threat landscape. My personal favorite, and most prominently influencing this book, is number 9 in my alphabetical list here: the NIST CSF. I feel that NIST, despite being U.S.-based, has truly managed to incorporate a universal approach to their framework. They make this available to everyone for free on their website https://www.nist.gov/cyberframework. Moreover, I believe that the NIST CSF is truly extensible, adaptable, and easily mapped with many governance frameworks, an excellent example of which is the ISACA COBIT to NIST mapping (a must-read for all you framework buffs!).

Acronyms aside, what do all these standards tell us about *ensuring and preserving confidentiality, integrity, and availability of digital information as well as the safety of people and environments?*

Each standard has its own spin on this. My favorite, NIST CSF, does so by recommending five key functions: *identify, protect, detect, respond,* and *recover.* I trust you'll immediately notice something missing? Think about it while we review the five functions:

1. The *identify* function is where you develop an understanding of what your risks are, what your assets are, and what your capabilities are.

2. *Protect* is your set of plans and actions that put in place the right controls (remember: controls do stuff) to protect the assets.
3. *Detect* is the set of plans and actions that you will use to identify, classify, etc., an attack against your assets.
4. *Respond* is the set of activities that you engage in response to an attack.
5. Finally, *recover* refers to whatever plans or protocols you have in place to bring things back to normal after an attack.

Each one of these core functions needs to be looked at, and each one will be different from individual to individual and business to business. Believe it or not, experts agree a good cybersecurity program should have tremendous freedom and latitude in approach. You have to do what is right in your world without imposing some monolithic, one-size-fits-all solution.

## A QUICK NOTE ABOUT YOUR IT DEPARTMENT

Businesspeople often overly rely on their IT team to "do cybersecurity." Keep in mind that your IT and development teams may be security savvy, but they are not necessarily security professionals. If you sense them being dismissive or defensive on this matter, you must take a step back and engage with a security professional to give you an honest opinion on your possible exposure and development of a cybersecurity program.

Now, did you come up with what might be missing from the five functions: *identify, protect, detect, respond,* and *recover?*

*Retaliate* or *revenge* might come to mind. It's a thought. It's also a highly illegal thought, so we'll just leave it at that and move on!

What about *prevent?* Isn't that something you would hope is a function of a good cybersecurity program?

It depends. First of all, there are those who would argue that prevention is a fool's errand. How do you prevent a nation-state from launching a cyberattack? How do you prevent a cybercriminal from targeting a financial institution, or you personally?

In essence, how do you prevent crime? Okay, if *prevent* is unattainable, how about *deter?*

These are questions that criminologists have studied for more than a hundred years. The answers are complex, vary by region and culture, and even by circumstance. How do we even begin to incorporate prevention or deterrence in the new cyber-front? Perhaps it is best to focus on what we can do rather than waste time on prevention?

I disagree with this view. I believe that there are meaningful steps that we can take to both prevent and deter cybercrime.

In early 2017, I wrote an editorial titled "Clear and Present Danger." It presented my thinking on prevention at the nation-state level. You will find the complete editorial in the Appendix, but my recommendation essentially was:

> *We need a concentrated effort in this new front for the survival of humanity. We need our leaders to be educated and alert to the danger this poses. We need our people to be sensitized to the danger of cyberattacks—think "duck and cover" for the cyber-age. We need our allies to reinvigorate their frameworks for resolving conflicts peacefully to include cyberwarfare. A cyberattack to one country should be considered an attack to us all, with the commensurate and immediate response. And, we need our international organizations to recognize the danger of cyber-actor proliferation and take immediate and decisive action.*

My point with this editorial should be obvious: Just as alliances and treaties help prevent war, there should be new alliances and new treaties to prevent a cyberwar. And there absolutely are preventative steps we can take. Certainly, there are at the nation-state level. But what about closer to home? Can we prevent or deter cyberattacks against businesses or individuals? I believe we can.

## Deter, Identify, Protect, Detect, Respond

Certainly, the right legal and technical frameworks can deter cybercriminals from attempting an attack. They attack us because that's where our money is. Make it hard enough to get at the money and some attacks can be deterred before they even occur.

How do you do this? You start by deploying the best preventative control ever devised: education! Endless studies prove that cybersecurity awareness training is the most effective preventive control deployed in any organization. Certain industries that follow a rigorous, engaging, and interactive cybersecurity awareness training program have reported attack reductions in excess of 40 percent. If that's not deterrence, I don't know what is!

Thus, we should add *deter* in front of *identify, protect, detect, respond,* and *recover.* Deterrence is a critical function of any cybersecurity program, and an integral part of our responsibility to any organization we're charged to protect.

It also serves as a constant reminder that cybersecurity is people-centric, not technology-centric. It is people who make a cybersecurity program a success, and it is the same people who, left in the dark, can be the weakest security link.

Deterrence is not a question of education alone. It is also built on reducing what's called your *attack surface*. As part of the *deter* function you need to take a close look at your business. What do you do, who are your partners, what are the threats, and how have they changed over time? There may be things that you can do to further deter cybercriminals from targeting your organization by changing certain things about the business itself. A slight change in workflow may make it not worth the trouble for someone trying to breach your data.

For example, a client of mine who is an immigration attorney used to accept scans of sensitive documents by email and, worse, upload the documents to his website unencrypted. A simple change—moving this workflow to a secure, encrypted provider—reduced his attack threat significantly. Now, instead of having to hack some simple hosted marketing website, the potential attacker would have to breach a Fort Knox–like level of security made affordable through cloud services. The same type of simple solution may work for your company. Just shifting from an unsecured handshake with a partner to a secure one is not only prudent, but may prove to be a significant deterrent to an attacker.

Establishing a cybersecurity culture across the company has multiple deterrence benefits. Not only does the ongoing awareness make for better and safer employees, but the same employees can contribute their thoughts and ideas on how to reduce your attack surface and, most importantly, they are sensitized to both external and internal threats. Now, they know that if an employee is snooping around the network and copying files onto USB drives, they may constitute a real cybersecurity threat to the business and they can raise the alarm accordingly. This, in itself, is a deterrent to a potential insider threat from manifesting itself. In short, a cyber-aware employee can be your best cybersecurity control yet!

Speaking of which, it is time that we take a deeper dive into what these controls are all about.

## Cybersecurity Controls and Defense in Depth

Now that we have our six functions—deter, identify, protect, detect, respond, and recover—the next obvious question is, *where do we go from here?*

First you develop a strategy that's right for you. What does this look like? It depends on your business. As you would expect, cybersecurity strategy will vary greatly from business to business, just as marketing strategies or daily operations vary from firm to firm. No two companies are exactly alike, even within the same industry. What is right for one law firm may be too much for another. One may be dealing with intellectual property (IP), trademarks, and patent law, versus another that may focus on criminal law, and a third on tax and estate law. All want to be secure, of course, but the priorities and data life cycles can be very different.

You'll recall that controls are actions that mitigate risk. They, generally speaking, will prevent, detect, correct, or compensate against risk. More specifically:

- *Preventive controls* are designed to prevent the attack from reaching the asset in the first place. A nondigital preventive control might be a pair of big burly guys, armed to the teeth, who physically guard your assets. Digital preventive controls include, as we already discussed, cybersecurity awareness training as well as more technical controls like firewalls, intrusion prevention systems (IPS; designed to both detect and thwart an attack).

- *Detective controls* are designed to identify that an attack is occurring, including what kind of an attack, where it came from, what it used, and, if you're lucky, who may be behind it. For example, motion detectors that set off sirens waking up the aforementioned big burly guys and send them to go chase the intruder are detective controls. These days, these motion detectors can take the form of sophisticated cameras, detecting motion, plus capturing images and sounds. Digital detective controls include antivirus and antimalware systems, as well as intrusion detection systems (IDS; designed to detect abnormal patterns in networks or systems and raise the alarm).

- *Corrective controls* are designed to minimize the damage from an attack. Examples include restoring from backup, patching the systems with the latest security fixes, upgrading to the latest version of applications and operating systems, and the like.

- *Compensating controls* are designed to compensate for the failure or absence of other controls and mitigate the damage from an attack. Examples include having a hot failover site (a geographically separate site that mirrors your environment, available the instant you need it), isolating critical systems from the Internet (aka air-gapping), and, in general, backup and disaster recovery plans that can keep the lights on while everyone else is in the dark.

Now, we can talk strategy!

## Defense in Depth

The best way to use all these controls is by layering them across systems in a way that achieves what is called defense in depth. This has the effect of putting multiple and diverse barriers (controls) between the attacker and the asset.

This strategy looks different from case to case, but has proven to be the best way to protect yourself and your assets. Think moats, slippery walls, hot boiling oil, tar, arrows, secret tunnels, and all the fun, creative ways people used to protect their castles and their lives. Now translate those to the electronic realm, and you've got the defense-in-depth concept down pat.

We'll spend more time with defense in depth in subsequent chapters. For now, you understand the key concept behind it, as well as its main goal:

*Protect the organization from cyberrisk.*

## The Threats

> *Just because you're paranoid doesn't mean they aren't after you.*
> —Joseph Heller, *Catch-22*

We have just done a high-level walkthrough of the building blocks of a cybersecurity program. All of this, of course, exists in a broader context, usually referred to as the threat context or threat landscape.

Who is out there? What harm are they attempting to cause you and why? As you would expect, threats vary business to business: The threat context for a restaurant is going to be quite different from that of a brokerage firm or a utility company.

It's important to distinguish between a threat (the impending prospect of something bad happening) and an attack (the realization of a threat). Keep in mind that cyberattacks are not accidental—they don't just happen; they are planned. Cyberattacks involve organized efforts by someone(s) to accomplish something particularly wicked with regard to your digital assets. Attackers will be stealthy, they will be persistent, and they will not stop unless they are either successful, or busted.

The people behind such cyberattacks are called a lot of things, but this is a family book, so we'll stick to threat agents.

## Threat Agents

The European Union Agency for Network and Information Security (ENISA) produces an annual report titled "ENISA Threat Landscape

Report." The 2016 report (published in January 2017 as *ENISA Threat Landscape Report 2016—15 Top Cyber-Threats and Trends*) lists the following threat agents. For good measure, I have added a motive summary (i.e., likely reasons for why are they doing what they're doing). You will want to take a look at this list to see which threat agents are most likely to apply to your business context.

1. **Cybercriminals**
   *Motives:* "Show me the money," plain and simple.
2. **Insiders (e.g., employees)**
   *Motives:* money and revenge, not necessarily in that order.
3. **Nation-States**
   *Motives:* cyberwarfare or intellectual property theft, competitive intelligence gathering, etc.
4. **Corporations**
   *Motives:* cyber-corporate-warfare or intellectual property theft, competitive intelligence gathering, etc.
5. **Hacktivists**
   *Motives:* activism of one sort or another, often but not always altruistically motivated (freedom of speech, fight against injustice, etc.).
6. **Cyber-Fighters**
   *Motives:* nationally motivated "patriots" like the Yemen and Iranian Cyber Army.
7. **Cyberterrorists**
   *Motives:* to create fear, chaos. Terrorist by any other name.
8. **Script Kiddies**
   *Motives:* young people "hacking for the fun of it" and causing havoc, be it intentional or not.

## Key Trends Influencing Threat Agents

The preceding threat agents are flourishing in today's technology environment thanks to a variety of accelerating trends. ENISA has noted these four key trends that influence the activities of threat agents, still holding true today:

1. *Consumerization of cybercrime.* Just as Lowe's and Home Depot made home renovations more available to the masses, new tools are making cybercrime broadly accessible. There are many do-it-yourself hacking kits available for purchase or even free download. It is also fairly easy to hire a hacker to attack a target. Worse: There are both franchising

opportunities and affiliate programs for cybercriminals as well as exciting new commercial avenues like ransomware-as-a-service whereby you can get your own custom ransomware kit for little money up front for a percentage of the extorted profits. A financial win-win for everyone involved, unless, of course, you're one of the victims. All this leads to:

2. *Low barriers to entry for technical novices.* If you're motivated, you can start your career as a cybercriminal easily. There are hacker universities in which you can get training, and when you purchase some of the ready-made hacking kits you can even get expert tech support!

3. *Dark net mystique:* The dark net is now like how the Internet was in the 1990s. It is perceived as being used only by dangerous geeks, and normal users are discouraged from peeking in. For that matter, one has to jump through a whole set of technical hoops to gain access, further making the dark net an excellent hideout for cybercriminals.

4. *Low rates of attributions:* It remains practically impossible to arrest cybercriminals. Even after major cyberevents, commercial or espionage related, no meaningful attributions were made, and practically no arrests. This makes being a cybercriminal a low-risk/high-reward line of work.

Threats, threat agents, and trends. How do we go from that to hackers? Are hackers the threat agents? And, are hackers cybercriminals? Nothing could be further from the truth!

## The Nature of Hackers

Back when the Internet was a cyber–Wild West, the term *hacker* was no insult—quite the opposite, it was a term of respect. The Internet as we know it was created by people who proudly called themselves hackers because a *hacker* was anyone skilled at building, exploring, and expanding the capabilities of all sorts of systems.

Nefarious, bad-guy hackers should really be referred to as thieves, vandals, criminals, really-really-really-bad people, etc. Unfortunately, the distinction between good hackers and bad hackers never caught on, and these days the term *hacker* is usually not meant as a compliment. But not all hackers are alike: The differences between them can be night and day, black and white, Jedi-versus-Sith, or your choice of fundamental opposing forces.

Historically speaking, all hackers *do* have one thing in common: high levels of technical skill. Hackers explore the details of programmable systems and figure out how to stretch their capabilities. This is very important because the skills involved are far from inconsequential. It requires a combination of inborn talent and endless study, competition, and practice. All great hackers, irrespective of which side they are on—night or day, good or evil, black hat or white—share these hard-won attributes. You might not be surprised to learn then that many old-school hackers have been recruited (or volunteered) to solve some of the world's most intractable problems such as curing diseases, distributing vaccines, or developing next-generation safe nuclear reactors.

Hackers also, it should be said, tend to have very healthy egos and are usually not above showing off their skills. Knowing a bit about the hacker personality helps set the context for your cybersecurity program and—importantly—how you communicate about it.

For example, it is one thing to consider yourself fit because you go to the gym every day, and quite another to consider yourself an Olympic-level athlete. Similarly, it is one thing to work toward protecting your assets from cyberattacks, and quite another to try to bait a hacker by boasting of your unbreakable defenses. If you do, you do so at your own peril. Given the character of hackers, it is foolish to underestimate them and even more foolish to challenge them.

## Attack Process

Having been introduced to the hacker mentality, we are now ready to discuss the actual process of a cyberattack. How does it unfold, what does it entail, and what can you do about it?

Remember, at its core, a cyberattack represents actions taken by threat agents against your assets. All cyberattacks have certain attributes and will typically follow a general process, a cyberbattle plan of their own.

A cyberattack unfolds through an *attack vector*. That is the path that the attacker takes to compromise your asset. Although most attack vectors are pointing inward (ingress) toward systems and assets, there are attacks that point outward (egress). Those outward attacks focus on ways to extract data and assets as opposed to gaining access and potentially damaging data.

On the attack vector rides the *attack payload*. Think of this as a container (e.g., the outside of a bomb) that delivers the exploit (the explosives) that take advantage of one or more vulnerabilities exposing the target to the attacker. There are many types of payloads, all of which are essentially sections of malicious programming code most often wrapped in a layer of innocuous programming code designed to fool your defenses. There is a whole scientific discipline dedicated to analyzing and studying payloads, something far beyond the scope of this book for our purposes, but suffice it to say that payloads can be very complex, and very elegant at the same time.

## Types of Attacks

There are myriad classifications for cyberattacks. Here are some major vocabulary terms, the ones most commonly used and the ones you'll be hearing in cybersecurity discussions.

*Advanced persistent threat (APT):* An APT says what it does and does what it says—it's a coordinated, persistent, resilient, adaptive attack against a target. APTs are primarily used to steal data. They can take a long time to research, plan, coordinate, and execute, but when they succeed, they are frequently devastating. You definitely do not want to be on the receiving end of one, and if you are, you had best have a very strong incident response plan in place.

*Brute force attack:* If there is any elegance in hacking a system, then this method lacks it. A brute force attack, much like a brute, doesn't use any brains, only force—in this case, computing force. So, if I wanted to guess your password with a brute force attack, I would use a very fast computer to try every single combination possible of the number—a task that can take a large amount of time or a startlingly brief amount, depending on the complexity of the password. For example, a 4-digit numerical PIN takes only a few hours to crack by brute force. (If you would like to test your own password or PIN to determine how long it would take for a brute force attack to crack it go to http://passfault.com, an open web application security project (OWASP) site, and give it a try.)

*Denial of Service (DoS) attack:* DoS attacks come in two flavors: single-source and distributed. A single-source DoS attack occurs when one computer is used to drown another computer with so many requests that the targeted one can't function while a distributed DoS (DDoS) attack achieves the same result through many (meaning thousands or millions of) computers. In DDoS attacks, the computers are usually under the coordinated control of a botnet (see "A Brief Cyberglossary of Terms" in the next section), working together to overwhelm a target with requests, rendering the target computer inoperable. Of late, this type of attack has gotten more and more press because instead of using compromised computers as part of the botnet, the hackers have been using any digital device (such as nanny cameras, thermostats, etc.) that is connected to the Internet. Most of these devices lack even the most rudimentary security, and too many users don't bother changing the default password, further contributing to the ease of compromising these devices and using them as bots.

*Man-in-the-Middle attack:* In this type of an attack, the hacker intercepts the communication between two systems, replacing it with his own, eventually leading to his gaining control of both systems. For example, a man-in-the-middle attack can be used to gain access to credentials and to then fake normal operations while the attacker compromises the target.

*Phishing attack:* Phishing and spear phishing are attacks that use social engineering methods. *Social engineering* in this context is just a fancy word for lying. Hackers convince a victim that the attacker is a trusted entity (such as a friend, established business, institution, or government agency) and trick the victim into giving up their data willingly. The goal of these attacks is to gain your trust so that you divulge sensitive information to the attacker. The degree of sophistication of such attacks varies, from the infamous appeals for bank information from Nigerian princes, to emails that appear to be from a bank or the Internal Revenue Service, to extremely sophisticated cons that can trick even the best-prepared and skeptical victim.

## A Brief Cyberglossary of Terms

This brief cyberglossary includes most major terms in the cybersecurity parlance. This jargon gets hurled about in both the media and inside businesses. Some of the terms overlap. Therefore, it's handy to have a glossary to refer back to. Some terms you've heard about, some you've seen hanging in the post office, and some are likely new and exciting, like *rootkit*.

We'll go alphabetically, and keep in mind that this is only a partial list·

*Adware:* Those can be innocuous and very, very, annoying at the same time. They are nasty little programs that once on your computer they … show you ads! That is if you're lucky. Because these days adware has been replaced with much nastier wares.

*Botnet:* A composite name made up from roBOT and NETwork. It is used to describe both the tool (software) and the collection of connected compromised computers that can be used to launch a large-scale cyberattack, typically in the form of denial-of-service attacks, which we'll explore more further on.

*Industrial control systems (ICSs):* These are the small computers that run inside of large machines. Think of a fan in a factory that will turn on and off based on something such as temperature. ICSs are often a key vulnerability because they are often based on older technology and may not be easily updated with patches that protect them against attacks. Other terms in this category include SCADA systems (supervisory control and data acquisition distributed control systems) and PLCs (programmable logic controllers). ICSs are typically found in industries such as electric, water and wastewater, oil and natural gas, transportation, chemical, pharmaceutical, pulp and paper, food and beverage, and discrete manufacturing (e.g., automotive, aerospace, and durable goods). SCADA systems are generally used to control far-flung assets using centralized data acquisition and supervisory control. PLCs provide regulatory control.

*Internet of Things (IoT):* IoT refers to yet another network, this one made up of physical devices that aren't usually thought of as computers—for example, thermostats, appliances, cars, even wearables (devices that you wear as part of your clothing or accessories). These devices' main function is to sense and communicate to a controller that then takes action based on the sensor readings. IoT devices are often vulnerable to attacks because they use simple circuits that are not well defended or secured.

*Key loggers:* These are a subset of a larger class called spyware that can record everything as you type it and send it off. As you might imagine, they can be quite devastating since you type your passwords, secret documents, and even that secret recipe for grandma's meatloaf. Key loggers continue to evolve, and modern key loggers can trap keystrokes, mouse movement, and screen content. Nasty little bugs.

*Malware:* This is the general category for software designed to do bad things. A key logger is malware. So is adware. Although these types of software are all bad, it doesn't sound good to call them badware—so, malware it is. And yes, sometimes it seems there is more malware than goodware.

*Operational Technology (OT):* OT is synonymous with industrial control systems (ICSs), discussed earlier, but is used more narrowly for businesses as opposed to massive infrastructure.

*Ransomware:* A ransomware attack happens when a hacker locks your computer (typically by encrypting data), and extorts you for money to unlock it. The dark beauty of ransomware is that you can go big (as when hackers took over the computer system of a hospital in California and demanded thousands of dollars in ransom), or you can go small and hit thousands of computers asking for a few hundred bucks from each user. With so many options and so many vulnerable systems, ransomware has become a big and profitable business. So much so that on the dark web you can buy a "build your own ransomware kit" and deploy it to the target of your choice.

*Rootkit:* A rootkit is a collection of software that, once installed, modifies the operating system to hide itself and other nasty little bugs that are within it or will soon be forthcoming. A rootkit is the endgame, the goal of any sophisticated attack. Once a rootkit is installed, the intruders are set. They can stay as long as they want undetected, compromise additional systems, exfiltrate or corrupt data, and in general have their wicked way with your assets.

*SCADA:* Stands for "supervisory control and data acquisition." Do you remember an incident in 2010 when the Iranian centrifuges at their super-secret plant went all crazy and spun themselves to oblivion? That's because a SCADA controller was hacked. So, the best way to understand a SCADA device is by thinking about any of those fancy industrial controllers that monitor and direct industrial devices, like centrifuges, refrigeration systems, or power generators, etc. They monitor them, they process data from them, and directly interact with these devices to effect a result (such as the opening or closing of a valve, spinning up or down a centrifuge, cooling or heating a reactor, and so on). SCADA systems are often vulnerable because they generally run on older technologies that are difficult to patch and upgrade.

*Spyware:* This is the general name of a class of software designed to—you guessed it!—spy on you. Key loggers, already discussed, are part of this ever-growing family tree. There are "legal" spywares that an employer or a parent can deploy on a computer to monitor usage. I put "legal" in quotes because although you can purchase, install, and deploy these tools, their use is frequently challenged. For example, if a company has a bring-your-own-device (BYOD) policy to work, are they within legal bounds to install spyware on it?

*Trojan:* This term refers to the infamous Trojan horse that the Greeks used to take Troy. In case you're not up to speed with your Homer, after a futile 10-year siege against the city of Troy, the Greek army pretended to leave, built a huge statue of a wooden horse, hid a team of commandos in its belly, and when the Trojans (thinking the war was over) wheeled the horse in, the Greeks got out of the horse, opened the gates for the waiting army, and burned the place to the ground. Similarly, this class of malware disguises itself as a legitimate application, gains entry, and the rest is history.

*Viruses:* Viruses are a type of malware that your run-of-the-mill antivirus programs are supposed to catch before they do damage. They mimic biological viruses (hence the name), requiring a host and a trigger (don't click that link!). The problem with computer viruses is much the same as in the biological world: To inoculate against a virus, you must first kill it, rendering it harmless, and then inoculate the host to build antibodies against it. That's why the flu inoculations don't always work: You're being inoculated with last year's virus signature. If this season's virus is similar, you're in luck, but if not, you're in bed wheezing and sneezing. The same goes with your computer. If there is a signature for the incoming virus, then your antivirus application should catch it and stop it. If not, or if you haven't gotten the update, then get yourself a good backup!

*Vulnerability:* Vulnerabilities are a weakness in an information system, system security procedures, internal controls, or implementation that could be exploited or triggered by a threat source. There are millions of them in hardware, operating systems, and software ready to be exploited by adversaries. What's sad is that a vast number of technical vulnerabilities are known, and technical fixes (patches) exist for them. Unfortunately, in many cases these patches have not been applied, rendering systems open to attack.

*Worm:* This is a type of computer virus (defined earlier) that is designed to spread over computer networks by making copies of itself without any intervention by its maker.

*Zero Day:* Zero-day exploits are vulnerabilities in existing systems that are known only to the hacker. For example, let's say there is an undiscovered vulnerability in the new release of your favorite word processor; it's utterly unknown to the product developers and to the users, but it's lurking there nonetheless. This would be called a zero-day vulnerability because it is completely unknown to the world at large; therefore it has been exposed for zero days. Once the vulnerability is discovered, the race begins to fix (or patch) it before a hacker can use the vulnerability to damage the system in some way.

And how are zero-day exploits found? Hackers on the prowl for such vulnerabilities discover them and put them up for sale on the dark web. Depending on how serious the vulnerability is, this information can fetch significant amounts. Countries, other hackers, and of course the manufacturers are willing to pay top dollar to be the ones to have the secret. It is a "use once" vulnerability, though. Once revealed, it will be patched by the manufacturer or mitigated with some control or another, and the advantage will be lost.

That's it for our brief glossary of terms. For our purposes in this book, the preceding list should provide you with enough terminology to engage in and understand critical conversations around cybersecurity. There are, of course, many more terms, some quite technical in nature (e.g., *buffer overflow, spoofing, cross-site scripting, SQL injection,* etc.) that require security, IT, and development professionals to evaluate and address.

How much do you need to know about these extensive lists of threats and actors? Remember, I trust you to be able to make the right judgment call on what your risk is. Only you know the specifics of your environment. For example, you are aware if your business is likely to trigger the interest of hacktivists, those actors who might want to harm your system because of their allegiance to a certain cause or ideology. You are best in a position to know if your business relies on machinery using automated controllers (such as ICSs, PLCs, and SCADA systems). You will be the one to evaluate whether your intellectual property is valuable enough to your competitors, such as foreign companies looking for a shortcut, to become the target of a hack.

## PROJECT MANAGEMENT FOR CYBERSECURITY PROGRAM DEVELOPMENT

### Anna Murray, president emedia LLC, author of *The Complete Software Project Manager*, John Wiley & Sons, 2016.

Q: How do you eat an elephant?
A: One bite at a time.

This old joke captures why project management exists as a discipline. The main purposes of project management is to take endeavors that seem overwhelming—borderline impossible—and make them possible through plans, organization, and tracking.

In this article, I'm going to give you some essential points of project management specifically applied to Cybersecurity program development.

### Project Governance—The Steering Committee

At the outset of any project, you need to establish a governing body to oversee the project and make all of the major calls.

Think of the project as the "doing-the-do" part; before the "doing" is done, the project needs a governing structure of its own. This steering committee is this governing structure, the "boss" of the project. The project team is accountable to the steering committee for the project's successful completion.

The project steering committee will meet no less than monthly, and, depending on the project, weekly, to check in on project health. The project team reports to the steering committee on timeline and budget. The steering committee also helps the project team. They act as an escalation point, for example, when business stakeholders give conflicting directives. The steering committee decides direction to go in when problems arise and can remove barriers that crop up.

### Steering Committee Participants

The following roles are usually present on a project steering committee:

*Project Sponsor*

This is the person in the business with responsibility for the project's success or failure. Don't know who the project sponsor is? It's the person whom the CEO or board turns to and says, "Get it done!"

In the case of cybersecurity program development, this person is likely to be a chief information security officer (CISO) or, in the absence of one, you! (The CEO can, and frequently has turned to her IT resources like the CIO or CTO, but that has its own problems. That is bad cybersecurity governance! As we learn later in this book, IT creates value. Cybersecurity protects value. You can't have one do the job of the other. That's a conflict of interest.)

*Business Stakeholders*

Projects usually have many stakeholders. Take a website launch. Almost everybody in the business will have some skin in the game for this project. Sometimes a project has one main stakeholder. If you are putting new accounting software in place, the CFO will be your main stakeholder. In cybersecurity program development, there are many stakeholders because cybersecurity touches all areas of the business.

In cases in which there are many stakeholders, it's most common to get a key set of people who will then interact with their colleagues to communicate major decisions and get feedback.

These key "voices of the business" sit on the steering committee to act as representatives for those affected by the project.

*Project Management Staff*

All projects have one or more project managers. This person's role is to keep the project plans and timelines, track tasks, and report on project progress.

### Steering Committee Agenda

The steering committee agenda is very straightforward. Each meeting the project manager reports on the following:

- timeline,
- budget,

- key accomplishments,
- plans for the upcoming week(s), and
- problems or "gotchas" requiring steering committee decisions or input.

### The Project Team

Project team participants vary from project to project. For cybersecurity program development, your project team is likely to include:

- a project manager, who keeps track of to-dos, project time line, and budget;
- a business analyst whose specialty is capturing requirements and creating documentation;
- technical team members, such as networking and systems engineers;
- one or more cybersecurity experts, plus the in-house cybersecurity team (CISO, etc.).

In assembling a team, it's important to identify the roles necessary to the task at hand. That way you can decide if the roles can be filled internally—the "wearing many hats" scenario. Or, if you will need to bring in extra resources.

### The Project Plan

You may (or may not) be surprised to learn that many companies begin a project without a plan. This is especially true in projects like cybersecurity program development, in which there are clear to-do lists of things like asset classification and categorization. The thinking is, "We know what we have to do. Let's just get started and do it."

Put another way, it's tempting to just dive in when you have a good sense of what your end deliverables are.

In fact, this book specifies many deliverables, such as:

- asset classification,
- asset metadata,

▪ asset valuation, and
▪ business-impact analysis.

The problem with the just-get-started approach is that it's almost impossible to track progress. Another common difficulty is that projects veer off track and go down rabbit holes because there is no overall structure and a complete lack of milestones or reporting.

Every project needs a plan. A list of deliverables, while great, is not actually a plan.

### The Plan and the Murk

Even when you have a book as detailed as this one is, you are still mostly looking from the 30,000-foot view. You are understanding the major concepts of what you need to do to generate a cybersecurity program. Next, you are going to need to generate the detailed plan for *your* specific cybersecurity program.

I have found that human beings are pretty good at the high-level, the 30,000-foot view. And they are also really comfortable when they have a detailed list of to-dos, milestones, and timelines, even if that list is daunting. It is at least solid and knowable!

What human beings are *not at all good at* is deriving the detailed list from the high level. I call that "being in the murk." Overcoming the murk is the first and most difficult step in project management. Someone has to generate a project plan.

What usually happens in organizations is that nobody knows the project plan, everybody wants the project plan, and everyone thinks it's "the other guy's job" to generate a detailed project plan.

So how do you get out of the murk?

### Human Nature and the Problem with Murk: Tennis Players versus Novel Writers

In business, most of us spend our days in a kind of "tennis match." We go to meetings, respond to emails, and answer questions from our colleagues and bosses. It's a kind of where's-the-ball-get-the-ball rhythm, like in a tennis match. You must address something coming right at you.

There's a different type of work that's most easily compared to novel-writing. In this kind of work, you're called upon to generate something that does not exist, like a novel, or a project plan for your cybersecurity program! As with a writer who sits down to write a novel, you have an idea, maybe even an outline such as this book has given you. Then you face the proverbial blank page.

Step One is to write that first draft. Even if it's awful and has errors, at least you have something to work with.

## The Plan for the Plan

The best way to get out of the murk is what I call "planning for the plan." You don't have the plan yet, but you are figuring out a way to get there.

This stage is all about brainstorming, asking questions, and creating a rough draft. Maybe you need a colleague in the room to help you. Here are some questions you might pose to help you generate a project plan for your cybersecurity program development.

- What assets do I know exist the organization?
- Whom can I approach to fill in the gaps in my asset knowledge?
- Who knows where these things are, such as on the premises or in the "cloud"?
- What meetings will I need to schedule to fully flesh out the list?
- How long will that take? Don't know? Make an educated guess.
- Do vacations, conferences, maternity leaves, or holidays interrupt that schedule?
- Who in the organization will be needed to decide on things like confidentiality classification, criticality, and maximum tolerable downtime?
- Do I know who they are right now? Or do I need a meeting with someone to identify who they are?
- How long will it take to identify those people and meet with them to retrieve this information? Make an educated guess, please.

- Will I need any additional resources such as a contract business analyst, technical analyst, or cybersecurity specialist?
- How much will this cost?

By getting a list of questions out on the table and making some educated guesses, you can start to see a few things emerge in this "plan for the plan." First, your project is naturally shifting itself into phases (for example, asset identification—three weeks; asset classification—six weeks). Consequently, you are getting a general picture of the timeline and also some budgetary impacts.

You're also identifying the next level of meetings, which I call "breakout sessions." This is the time when you approach someone with greater knowledge of a specific area than you have (for example, with someone who has detailed knowledge of the assets), to start to fill in the gaps, identify further steps in the investigation, and firm up the timeline.

A good set of "plan for the plan" questions is usually followed by a few of the most important breakout sessions for your full plan timeline and budget to really take shape.

At the end of this process you should arrive at a project scope document.

### The Project Scope Document
This is the project team's charter. It enumerates what they plan to do, in what timeline, and on what budget.

A project scope document contains the following:

- a project summary and definition,
- project deliverables,
- a list of things that are out of scope,
- constraints,
- assumptions,
- risks,
- timeline,
- budget, and
- success metrics.

Let's look at these scope elements as they pertain to cybersecurity program development.

The *summary and definition* section of the scope document states what we are doing and why. An example in cybersecurity program development might go something like this: "ACME Co. has decided to implement a cybersecurity program to protect its assets, its employees, and to satisfy key clients who are requiring it of their vendors."

Other rationales might include competitive advantage, regulatory requirements, or board directives. In the future, someone such as a new executive might ask, "Why did we do that project?" Believe it or not, people *do* forget why an initiative was undertaken. Your project summary section should answer that question for now and for the future.

Project *deliverables* are the concrete things that you can point to when the project is done. In the case of cybersecurity program development, this is likely to be a set of documents and spreadsheets that constitute the program. Here is the place to state what exactly those will be. How many documents? How long? Be specific.

Deliverables might also include the identification of "child projects" that will be kicked off as a consequence of your cybersecurity program. For example, your cybersecurity program development will likely suggest controls (often subscription software products and services) that will need to be put in place. Your initial project plan would not go into those other subproject plans. It would simply state that such child projects will be identified.

Stating what's *out of scope* for your project is a critical part of the plan. This is because it's so common for business leaders and business stakeholders to get confused. If you are not clear about what is in scope and out of scope, you can easily end up in a situation in which a CEO says, "I really thought you were also going to identify and retain an incident-response expert."

If you don't plan to do it, say so up front.

*Constraints* are the limitations you face. For example, you may know that you have a custom-developed piece of software and that the person who programmed it is no longer available. Your discovery around this system is going to be limited. It's a constraint that should be stated up front.

Let's say that to be successful, you are going to need a certain time commitment from various business units. For example, you are going to need time with the IT department to walk you through all the IT assets and where they live (e.g., in the cloud or on the premises). You are also going to need time with business stakeholders to classify the criticality of assets. The understanding that these people will be available and give you the time—that's an *assumption*.

Of course, the *budget* and *timeline* will be included, how much this will cost and how long the parts will take, separately and in aggregate. You will use budget and timeline tracking tools to report out to the steering committee on how you're doing (e.g., asset classification was scheduled to take three weeks with 10 hours of an outside consultant's time budgeted, and we are right on track!).

Success *metrics* can be difficult to determine for many projects. For example, how do you know if a piece of software is successful?

In the case of cybersecurity program development, you will want to ask yourself these questions:

- How will I know if the company has adopted the cybersecurity program, or if it ends up as a document on the shelf? A pre-and-post-survey can help measure awareness and adoption.
- Are there pre-and-post metrics I can look at, such as the number of breaches, to determine the success of the program?

It's important in a project plan to state how you intend to measure success.

## Meetings and Communication

It's become *de rigueur* in the business world to be "anti-meeting." According to this line of thinking, meetings are not productive. They gather people together in a room (virtual or otherwise) to accomplish things that could better be handled in email.

But I disagree: I am a big proponent of meetings. Well-run meetings, that is!

Good, regular meetings are essential to keeping any project on track. I recommend a weekly check-in meeting following a disciplined meeting protocol.

1. *Circulate an agenda* ahead of time saying what you are going to discuss. The agenda for the meeting should usually be to report out on the major project tracks. This should be easy, because you have a project plan and scope document identifying the main project tracks.
2. *Discuss each track.* Identify progress, to-dos that have been "to done" for the week and what to-dos are expected to be complete in the following week. Address questions that arise.
3. *Avoid weeds. Schedule sidebar meetings.* If a particular thread takes the whole team very deep in the weeds, stop it and schedule a sidebar meeting. Agree to the time and date of the sidebar in the call.
4. *Avoid debate. Kick it upstairs.* A close sibling to "getting into the weeds," which takes a meeting off-track, is to get into a long policy or strategy debate. This usually means team members are inappropriately discussing strategic issues that they themselves cannot decide. So they talk about "what we should do" endlessly. Quickly identify strategic issues and business decisions that need to be kicked upstairs to a business stakeholder or the project steering committee. Get the facts you need and move on.
5. *Insist on attention.* State right up front that the meeting participants are expected to give the meeting their full attention and not multitask. Leaders should set the example by avoiding multitasking themselves!
6. *Timeliness.* Begin and end the meeting on time. People will show up to a meeting on time if they know it starts on time. Keep meetings to an hour, no more. A meeting that runs past an hour is not a meeting. It's a hostage situation.

7. *Notes.* All meetings should have follow-up notes capturing what was said with the action items. As I like to say, "If there are no notes, then everyone just wasted an hour of their time." And guess what! Your follow-up items comprise the agenda for your next meeting. It's a twofer.

## Prepare for the Trough of FUD

When you start a project, there is usually a set of heightened expectations about what the project will accomplish. In the case of cybersecurity program development, these expectations might go something like this: We will easily identify and classify all our assets. Within a few weeks, or perhaps a month, our systems will have detective, preventive, and compensatory controls in place as well as a robust incident-response program!

*Phew!* That's a lot. It's quite common for people to start a project with unrealistic expectations.

The Gartner Group has a now-famous tool called the Hype Cycle, which graphs the elevated expectations that happen with regard to technology in general. I have developed a similar tool when it comes to projects. It looks like Figure 3.1.

Take a look at the dashed line. This represents *reality.* Think of it as the cold, hard facts of the project scope document. Nothing more, nothing less. No emotions applied.

Now take a look at the solid line. It shows the *emotions* of the project. Business stakeholders start the project with high expectations and, dare I say it? Excitement! Then, as things take longer than they might have expected, problems arise, and the project does not meet the "white knight on a horse" standard they expected, emotions bottom out.

Emotions even dip way below the reality line. This is called the "Trough of FUD." FUD stands for Fear, Uncertainty, and Doubt. At this stage, business leaders and stakeholders may conclude that the project is a disaster, demand reviews, or cancel it entirely.

If the project is allowed to proceed, emotions level out as the business comes to a more realistic understanding of what the project was destined to be all along.

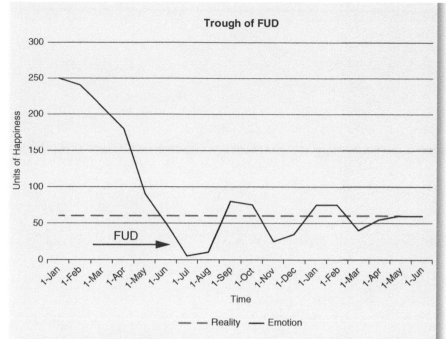

Figure 3.1   Trough of FUD

What can you do? I often show this graph to project teams and business leaders at the kickoff meeting. It has the effect of inoculating folks. They gain a sense of self-awareness of overblown expectations at the start; this awareness helps folks avoid deep depression in the middle of projects.

You should treat cybersecurity program development as a project, because it *is* one. As a matter of fact, it is several! And, it is likely a recurring one. Cybersecurity program management is a "living" project, and it also needs to be managed. You need to make sure you apply the appropriate methods, resources, and tools to make sure it gets done right. It is the only way to ensure its success.

Note: We're talking only about *project* governance here! This should not be confused with the governance of cybersecurity in the organization as a whole, which is covered in Chapter 4.

# Management, Governance, and Alignment

I f you have ever driven a car with wheels that are out of alignment, you probably experienced the joy of fighting the steering wheel to keep the car straight and on the road. If you're driving a company whose business goals, information technology, and cybersecurity are out of alignment, you'll experience the same issues: Depending on where the misalignment is, company goals may become increasingly difficult to achieve, technology may be out of sync with your needs, and cybersecurity may be protecting all the wrong assets. In short, your company is misaligned.

In our specific context, *misalignment* means that your technology and your cybersecurity are not working together in support of your business goals. The operative word here is *together*. They are pulling you in other directions as opposed to helping you achieve what you set out to do. Unfortunately, this is far more common that you'd think, and it plagues everyone from the lone wolf professional to vast multinationals. The reasons are surprisingly complex and often hidden under layers of confusion, indifference, and office politics. But misalignment ultimately boils down to two key problems: poor governance and poor management.

## Why Governance Matters

First, what is governance?

My definition is: *Governance is the collective set of principle-guided actions that when applied guide a company to the fulfillment of its goals.* I use principle-guided actions to distinguish governance from reactive management. I use "applied" to further drive home the idea that governance is something you need to think about, agree on, and consistently apply to get the results you want.

47

These principle-guided actions include a company's strategy, ways to measure success, ways to manage risk, and ways to exercise due care of company assets.

The difference between management and governance is in the "apply" part. The application of governance is what I call management. It is very important to separate the two: Governance is the collective set of principle-guided actions while management is the application of these principle-guided actions into the company's operations.

Although governance is frequently thought as overarching (i.e., across the whole firm), governance filters down and applies to each and every department as well. You need good governance in your IT department, in your cybersecurity department, in your marketing, product development, finance, facilities, etc. Management feedback, of course, is critical in both validating and influencing future governance, and it is this feedback loop that is absolutely essential in ensuring alignment.

Now, please remember: Bad governance will not invariably result in bad management. You can have a poor set of principle-guided actions that are very well applied. Similarly, good governance does not automatically result in good management. They are different things, both equally important. Why? Because if either of them is not up to task, then alignment suffers.

I keep referring to this alignment. What exactly is alignment, and why is it so important? I view alignment as the quintessential metric of value creation. A misaligned company is, at best, inefficient at value creation, and at worst... out of business!

Consider, for example, a company with a clear vision and mission statements, well funded, good, hard-working people, and with an excellent IT manager. She has gone out and procured state-of-the-art systems from top-tier vendors with the corresponding support agreements. She has bought the best her budget could get. Yet, all departments are complaining that nothing can get done in time. They find the systems onerous, and incapable of doing what they—the users—need. Where did the IT manager go wrong?

She didn't! She's managing the department just fine. Unfortunately, in the absence of proper governance, which would have ensured an alignment between IT and business goals, she was left to guess as to which system would be the best fit for what she thought the business needed, and with what she knew technology could provide.

Both governance and management are shared responsibilities. Governance must clearly spell out the set of principle-guided actions that need to take place for value to be created. Only then can management effectively integrate these into business operations. Similarly, if management fails to understand or properly implement what is being spelled out by governance, and give prompt and accurate feedback, then we'll have operational failure. Both cases damage the ability of the company to create value. Both cause misalignment.

Of course, governance and management practices differ from company to company, culture to culture, municipality to municipality, and state to state. Do they have anything in common? Is there a set of critical attributes that are essential to both?

Absolutely! The commonalities are: engagement, involvement, connection, and interest. These are critical ingredients to both governance and management, and they are some of the most difficult to find and cultivate, even among the most well-meaning executives. At their heart lies communication, and as we've discussed, failure to communicate is one of the core issues we are facing, something we are changing here by laying a common language foundation.

Which brings us to the bottom line: What do you need to know to facilitate alignment between your cybersecurity program and the rest of the organization? What is the practical nitty-gritty that you must own to make sure your program succeeds?

The first thing to consider is your strategy. Your strategy is there to realize your vision and mission for your company. Your vision and mission may not change, but your strategy might need to, in response both to your own innovations and to outside conditions.

Let's say your vision is to be the best, fastest, safest trucking company in Nevada. If that's the goal, what's the strategy? How are you going to make this a reality? Perhaps you'll decide on hiring only the best drivers, using only certain kinds of trucks, and so on. Then, you wake up one morning and right there on the front page is the leading story on the successful test of the first driverless truck fleet crisscrossing the country. How might this news change your strategy?

That brings us to the next question: How is your strategy being executed? For everything and everyone there is a structure that works. The self-employed businessperson is the chief cook and bottle washer. A business with staff, on the other hand, may have several layers, each with a role to play in executing the strategy, each in their own way steering the company toward the achievement of the goals. In one case, you have a steering committee of one, in the other, many. The responsibility is the same: Hands on the wheel, attention on the street, focus on getting to the destination.

There is one more question, and it is critical: How do you know you're making progress? For that matter, how do you know you've achieved your goal? In short, how do you define and measure success?

*There is surely nothing quite so useless as doing with great efficiency what should not be done at all.*
—Peter Drucker ("Managing for Business Effectiveness," *Harvard Business Review*, May 1963)

The more complex the strategy, the more ambitious the goal, the trickier it is to steer toward success. Things can get off the rails as different parts of the strategy get out of sync or misaligned. You have to have in place a way to monitor, a way to get back on track. The quote from Peter Drucker, possibly the greatest management consultant ever, speaks directly to the need for alignment. Let's not get ahead of ourselves, though. For now, let's get back in the car steering our strategy toward our goal.

How, exactly, are we steering? Yes, I know—hands on the wheel, eyes on the road. But *how* are we steering? Which side of the road? Are we steering in England or in the United States? Are we steering a bike, or the space shuttle? What are the rules of the road, and more importantly, how are we responding to them? Are we speeding recklessly? Are we tailgating? Is the blinker not shutting off? One way or another, we must balance the rules of the road, the kind of car we're driving, with the *where* and the *how*. We need a framework to follow that will give us our best chance of reaching our goal.

## Strategy, Steering, and Standards

Meet the three S's: *strategy, steering*, and *standards*—the governance triad most often applied when we talk about aligning technology and business. In my view, the three S's apply everywhere there is a need for alignment. We need to think of strategy, steering, and standards applied between cybersecurity and risk appetite. Between technology and business goals. Between risk and reward.

The good news here is that there is an enormous body of work in management science developed by brilliant people dedicated to advancing excellence in the field and success in business. I mentioned Peter Drucker already, but the list is long and the contributions many and ongoing. You will find a selected bibliography in the back of this book, but for our purposes, we'll stick to some key concepts and definitions, along with a business-centric overview of the tried-and-true frameworks that will apply to our work: aligning cybersecurity with our goals.

## Critical Success Factors

What does it take to support the three S's? Why, it's the four C's, of course! *competencies, conditions, conduct*, and *capabilities*. Jay Ranade, one of the most prolific authors in the IT governance and cybersecurity fields and an incredibly gifted instructor and mentor, drilled the notion that these four C's represent the critical success factors. He is, of course, right. Moreover, as he repeatedly pointed out, the four *C*'s may not be entirely under your control.

Jay is not alone in emphasizing the four *C*'s. In 2014, the U.S. Army produced a document called "Win in a Complex World 2020–2040." That document makes repeated references to the concept of the four *C*'s. Parenthetically (and all military jokes aside), one of the best centers of excellence in management studies is the U.S. armed forces. Some of the very best innovative and critical management thinking has come from our military.

But enough about them! What do the four *C*'s represent for us?

*Competencies* are the skill sets that we bring to the table. If you're a litigation law firm, a core competency would be engaging as many experienced litigators as you can afford. That's a core competency. Engaging real estate attorneys, as excellent as they may be, will not help you much in litigation.

*Conditions* are the environments in which competencies exist. Markets can be conditions. Geography can be a condition. Technology can also be a condition, and so can cybersecurity. Jay's point about "not always under your control" is abundantly clear when you think of market conditions.

*Conduct* refers to the set of actions that we take both within our company and within the conditions we operate in to accomplish our goals. Conduct can be ethical or unethical, legal or illegal, but it can also speak to company culture and work behavior. Conduct can have profound implications on the way you achieve your goal. The term "cost of doing business" hides a lot of conduct decisions within it, as does "risk acceptance."

Finally, *capabilities*. I like to look at capabilities as the set of competencies and the measure of competency throughput. Did I lose you here? Okay. Let's simplify! Think of capabilities as your capacity to generate value. Better? Okay, good! Now, how do you generate value with your capacity? Well, you are competent enough, and have enough bandwidth to apply your competency to value creation. In short, you're capable!

Perhaps the most complex of the four *C*'s, capabilities integrates concepts like capacity, resiliency, agility, and the like. For example, one may ask what are the capabilities of your law firm? The answer can be litigation only, or litigation plus real state plus corporate law. You can further ask, how many litigation cases can you handle at any one time? Or, can your corporate attorneys be leveraged by your litigation department? All of these are capability questions.

How do all of these factor into what we need to know to roll out a successful cybersecurity program?

## One Word: Alignment

What does alignment look like in practice? At the top level, your business strategy will inevitably determine the functions necessary to achieve it. These business functions, which are a direct consequence of your business strategy, determine the operations of the business. This applies whether you're a business of one or one thousand: business operations must be aligned with business functions, which are themselves the product of business strategy. Therefore, business operations must be aligned with business strategy.

You can write it out like this:

- Business strategy (determines): business functions
- Business functions (determine): business operations

Therefore:

- Business operations (must align with): business strategy

Right? A no-brainer!

Not so fast! If it were only that simple, we wouldn't be spending hours of uninterrupted fun trying to understand all this.

All too often, various business operations take on lives of their own and get out of alignment with the business strategy they were meant to serve. The closer to the core business strategy the function is, the easier it is to keep it in check. The further away it is, the harder it is to maintain alignment. Add the "foreign language" element of technology and cybersecurity, and you may soon be careening all over the road.

The way it is supposed to work is straightforward: The board defines business strategy and accepts risk. Their primary duty to the shareholders (read: owners and shareholders and partners) is to ensure value creation (goal setting and business strategy) and protect the business (monitor and manage risk). All those lovely principle-guided actions.

The executives take the board strategy and create the necessary business operations to achieve it.

Operations execute and provide input to a feedback loop that enables the executives and board to judge progress in value creation and adjust accordingly. See Figure 4.1.

How do you measure all this? You start by clearly setting the goals. You measure your progress toward achieving them by establishing key goal indicators (KGIs). You should also identify and establish what the critical success factors (CSFs) are, and communicate them across the company. Finally, you should be checking if you're on course or not through the establishment of key performance indicators (KPIs).

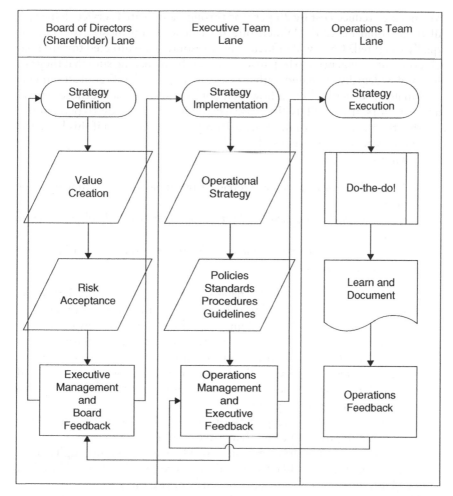

Figure 4.1   The Governance Swimming Pool

Some examples may help clarify these three acronyms.

The easiest example of a goal is sales. It's a number. You either hit it or not. If not, you can measure how far away you are from making that number. So, if your goal as a business is $10,000,000 revenue, and your key goal indicator is currently at $5,000,000, you're 50 percent there! (Hopefully, you also have six more months to go before having some explaining to do.)

Now, what are your CSFs for this goal? There can be several. One may be, "We need two new clients per month." Another may be, "We need to increase existing client spend by 10 percent per month." And, another may be,

"We need to reduce cost by 20 percent through automated service delivery." All three could be CSFs. Which one do you focus on most? Are they all equally weighted? CSFs will influence how resources are directed toward goal achievement, so you need to be particularly careful in making sure that they are clear and widely disseminated. Otherwise … you guessed it! Out of alignment.

Finally, your KPI tells you how well you're tracking against those critical success factors. If the CSF is "Increase existing client spend by 10 percent per month," then you can run a monthly KPI report that tells you if this has been met. Same with any (well-selected) CSF.

In summary:

- *KGI* = *key goal indicator* = Metric of progress toward achieving your goal.
- *CSF* = *critical success factor* = Metric of impact toward achieving your goal.
- *KPI* = *key performance indicator* = Metric of course deviation from achieving your goal.

Now, you may ask, do I really have to do all this? Do I need all these measurements and acronyms and tracking, and this, that, and the other? Yes! You do. But, don't worry. You're doing this already. This is simply putting it in more formal language. Even if you are a small, informal business, you have goals, KGIs, CSFs, and KPIs. You may not call them that, but you do. Your financial statements prove it! So does your success, your challenges, and even your failures. You use these tools—no matter what the terminology—to navigate your own world every day.

Why be all formal and keep track of all this? Because, at the end of the day, you cannot improve anything that you cannot measure.

Says who? Says Peter Drucker, and we need say no more. Although people have tried, with arguments like "You can't measure 'trust' or 'love.'" No. You cannot. (Unless you're a divorce attorney. Then, you can.)

I have argued from the beginning that everything we say here applies from the lone wolf to the multinational. Of course, a single practitioner doesn't have a board and an executive team, but that is because she is the board, executive team, and operations. A small business doesn't, either, but that is because these functions are divided up between the owner(s) and her team(s). And so on. The basic principles continue to apply.

## The Case for Frameworks

What is a framework? According to our friends at Merriam-Webster, it is a basic conceptual structure (of ideas). I like to think of frameworks as playbooks. Take football, for example. You have the rules of the game, and each team has a playbook. I consider that playbook the specific team's framework for winning. Not all playbooks work well for all teams, yet all teams must obey the same rules of the game. This is an important distinction, and it applies equally well in business.

In management science as a whole—and in technology and risk management in particular—there are several excellent, at times competing, at times complementing, frameworks. Note that a framework is different from a standard, which is itself different from a methodology (e.g., Six Sigma, Plan-Do-Check-Act, Kaizen, etc.). A standard, as per ISO, "is a document that provides requirements, specifications, guidelines, or characteristics that can be used consistently to ensure that materials, products, processes, and services are fit for their purpose." You either meet or do not meet a standard. For example, you are either PCI DSS–compliant or you are not.

Frameworks are different, and a bit looser. You can claim, and you would be right in doing so, that your technology follows the COBIT framework even though you are using only parts of it—the parts that apply to your organization.

This is exactly why you should consider adopting a framework as a guide in managing your technology and cybersecurity. A good framework should be comprehensive, flexible, adaptable, and straightforward to implement. Although not a complete list by any means, some of the better-known frameworks are: COSO (Committee of Sponsoring Organizations of the Treadway Commission), ITIL (Information Technology Infrastructure Library), BiSL (Business Information Service Management Library), CMMI (Capability Maturity Model Integration), COBIT (Control Objectives for Information and Related Technology), TOGAF (The Open Group Architecture Framework), and PMBOK (Project Management Body of Knowledge), which is more focused to the project management discipline but still overlaps with IT management and good management practices in general.

I have two personal favorites: CMMI, which was developed by Carnegie Mellon (recently acquired by ISACA) and used as a process improvement and appraisal framework, and COBIT, also by ISACA. If you'd indulge me, I'd like to briefly introduce you to both.

CMMI is all about process and process maturity. What is a process? Good question! It can be anything from software development to service delivery and everything in between. CMMI breaks down the maturity of a process into five levels: In Level 1, processes are unpredictable, ad hoc, and frequently changing in reaction to events. Level 2 processes are repeatable, and if you're lucky, with repeatable results. Level 3 processes are defined, they are documented, and are subject to review and improvement. Level 4 processes are managed using a variety of reliable metrics. Level 5 processes are optimized with a focus on continual improvement.

I am willing to bet you that you instinctively placed your organization in one of these levels. You know what CMMI level you are at. If you think you are at CMMI Level 3, you would be in good company, and in a decent rank! It ends up that CMMI Level 3 is the threshold you need to be at to implement a variety of other frameworks such as the Balanced Scorecard method (another personal favorite) for aligning performance, goals, strategy, and management. When it was introduced in 1992 by Norton and Kaplan, it revolutionized management thinking and introduced us all to the virtuous cycle of perspectives: learning, internal, customer, and financial. One affects the other, with learning being the key starting point. Absolutely delicious and highly recommended.

COBIT is the 800-pound gorilla of frameworks for the management and governance of IT. The one ring to rule them all. The unified theory of everything. The answer to the ultimate question about life, the universe, and everything. That's COBIT.

COBIT is based on five principles: Principle 1: meeting stakeholder needs. An excellent principle, really, leading to the goals cascade: Stakeholder drivers influence their needs. Then, stakeholder needs translate to enterprise goals. Those cascade to IT goals, and IT goals cascade to enabler goals. Principle 2 of COBIT: Cover the enterprise end to end. Nothing left out, everybody in the pool. Principle 3: Apply a single integrated framework. Principle 4: Enable a holistic approach. Principle 5: Separate governance from management.

Okay, so it's a bit heavier than CMMI, but it's all muscle. Not a gram of fat. I suspect, you got a bit overwhelmed by the principles. It makes sense that you would: Framework talk can appear overwhelming and intimidating.

The point is that these frameworks exist, and they evolve with the times. Brilliant people all over the world have dedicated their lives to building and refining these notions—not because everyone *must* implement them, but because everyone should know that there is a source of guidance, a place to get help, a resource with trusted, verified, scientific answers to problems.

That is the point. It's not whether you implement COBIT or not. It is that by its existence it is available for you to do a reality check on all the technobabble out there. You might never implement COBIT or CMMI, or the balanced scorecard or any of the other frameworks. But at least you know that they are there, and they can help you make the right decision objectively, each and every time.

Personally, I have staked my career—and this book—on them! I constantly interpret, derive, explain, get inspired by, and apply their advice on countless assignments, with consistently successful results!

## IT and Cybersecurity: Separation of Church and State

Having defined your business strategy, you then have a reasonable expectation that your technology operations need to be aligned with your business goals and that your cybersecurity program is aligned with your risk appetite.

What is the best way to make sure that this is a successful? Implement your KGIs, CSFs, and KPIs to be sure, but even more important:

*Keep technology and cybersecurity separate!*

Why? Because while the two may sound roughly the same, they actually have very different functions.

IT creates value. When properly aligned with your business strategy, your technology is an enabler, an expediter, an optimizer, and an innovator.

Cybersecurity, on the other hand, protects value. That is a stark difference in focus. Cybersecurity is all about risk management and IT is all about value creation. You should never have risk management report up to value creation because of the potential conflict of interest. That would be the same as having a clinical research trial for a drug being funded by the drug's manufacturer! Remember all those doctors who were proclaiming that cigarettes were safe?

Cybersecurity and IT are two distinct functions, frequently at odds (e.g., do IT faster, easier, and cheaper versus double-check it, restrict it, and monitor it). Each aligns with two different, but equally important strategies: value creation and risk management. The process of value creation is all about taking risks—falling, getting up, and trying again. It's about innovation, experimentation, and boldly going where no one has gone before. The process of risk management, on the other hand, is all about evaluation, risk assessment, threat assessment, and semper fidelis to the mission and vision of the company. These are like two parallel railroad tracks that your company's engine runs on. Thankfully, never the twain shall meet, or else your train just derailed.

Now that we have kept them separate, how do you align technology with your business strategy? Excellent question, and one that is within the purview of my next book, coming soon to a bookseller near you. The question we plan to answer in this book is how to align your cybersecurity with your business strategy.

## Addressing the Alignment Problem

Many years ago, I had an amazing geometry professor. The man ate, drank, and breathed geometry. In his apartment, there was a big room, filled floor to ceiling with filing cabinets labeled with numbers. A bunch of us students used to go there to train for the university geometry entrance exam (don't even ask ... ). When I saw these cabinets, I asked him about the labels. He replied that those were filing cabinets filled with geometry problems classified by the amount of time needed for a solution. If you wanted a five-minute problem, he'd walk up to the corresponding cabinet and pull one out. A two-hour problem? No worries! Even a five-day problem? Easy. There was even a cabinet with his forever problems—theorems that remain unsolved to this day.

He had a great piece of advice for gauging the difficulty of any problem: the length of its definition. He told us that if you see a problem whose definition is a one-liner, skip it. Leave it for last. That one will be the toughest to solve because it gives you the least information to go on. You see one that has a paragraph-long definition? Easy! Tackle that first.

With that in mind, what kind of problem is aligning cybersecurity with your business strategy? Well, another way of looking at it is aligning cybersecurity with your risk appetite. Both definitions are one-liners, and short one-liners at that. Not pretty!

How do you come up with your risk appetite? Who is responsible? By now, you know the answer: It's the board of directors (read: owner, partner, shareholders, etc.). Only the board can accept risk, and therefore only the board can set the risk appetite for the company. This appetite may change over time, but even the changes are governed by the board.

The implication here is clear: A board must understand the consequences of cybersecurity decisions and thereby set the correct appetite for what's acceptable risk and what is not. The issue is that most boards are excellent at understanding business strategy and managing business risk, but are—let's say—*challenged* when it comes to cybersecurity.

For example, a board may well understand the need to *digitally transform the business* because that is a business problem involving a response to market conditions. They may not fully understand the technologies necessary to achieve this transformation, but they understand enough about the environment to be able to navigate it. They place their trust in their CIOs and CTOs, monitor the transformation progress based on business (not technology) metrics, and depend on their C-level execs to make sure that the appropriate technologies have been evaluated, vetted, and implemented in accordance with board strategy.

Similarly, a good board knows how to manage risk. Depending on the size of the organization (and the board), there are risk committees and risk officers involved that inform the board. The board weighs all the recommendations and sets the risk appetite for the best interests of the business. In short, the board exercises their "due care" responsibilities. In the absence of a board, the owner(s) perform the same function. They set the risk appetite and accept the residual risk.

Enter cybersecurity risk. Now, we're talking a foreign language. And I don't mean Chinese, Greek, or Spanish—I'm talking Klingon-level foreign! You walk into a conference room and start throwing around *threat landscape* and *brute force* and *man-in-the-middle* attacks, sprinkle in a bit of *network worms* and *ransomware,* and the room goes eerily quiet. The vast majority of business-people can't even begin to weigh risk with this information.

That's when they can fall into what I call the *compliance trap.* It is a common pitfall—people confuse cybersecurity with compliance. Boards do it. Executives do it. Even middle managers and employees do it. But don't *you* do it! Being compliant doesn't mean you're cybersecure! It means you're compliant. That's all. Don't associate risk appetite to equal *minimum required compliance.*

You need to do cybersecurity correctly.

This is where you, and this book, come in. Your job is to align the board's strategy with the right cybersecurity program. You will need to educate in plain business language what the risks are (operational risks, reputational risks, regulatory risks, etc.) and explain what the options are to mitigate all of these risks with their associated costs.

You will also need to show how one decision about one control can affect the performance of others and how it may affect your defense-in-depth strategy by either strengthening it or weakening it.

When all is said and done, you'll need to leave the board with a set of recommendations on what you think best aligns their vision, strategy, and risk appetite with your cybersecurity program, and let them do their job. You've done yours!

## CASE STUDY: HOW IMPROVING CYBERSECURITY SAVED MONEY AND IMPROVED BUSINESS RESULTS

*An interview with Mark Thomas, president, ESCOUTE Consulting*

### The Situation

"We were facing an identity crisis," says Mark Thomas, former CIO of managed service provider CompuPro (not its real name). "We were entrepreneurial, with a mission to grow, grow, grow."

When Thomas joined as CIO, an external audit had just shown an extremely poor cybersecurity posture. This meant the company's core business—providing outsourced IT services such as a helpdesk, application support, and infrastructure support to clients—was at risk. Thomas was tasked with fixing CompuPro's cybersecurity problems without compromising growth.

The company's imperative to grow and grow fast was driven by the business climate. "We could hear our competitors' footsteps behind us," says Thomas. At the same time, others in the space were small and weak. CompuPro wanted to acquire these failing companies' customers and consolidate their position in the market.

But what CompuPro was discovering was that its main goal, aggressive growth, was at threat because of the lack of attention to cybersecurity standards. In short, its core business was at risk.

"We even had a chief risk officer," says Thomas, who is now a consultant and cybersecurity trainer with an alphabet soup of certifications following him name. "He looked at enterprise risk, financial risk, market risk. Everything except cyberrisk."

Cybersecurity was not the company's only weak point, Thomas soon learned. Customer satisfaction scores were nosediving. Multiple incidents on CompuPro's systems were causing the company significant downtime. Some of these events put them in violation of their service level agreements (SLAs). "If you can't meet the SLA, then you're in breach of contract," says Thomas. That meant chargebacks.

One cause: Deployments of changes to the production environment such as feature enhancements, application changes, OS-level changes, and patches both critical and scheduled, were often unsuccessful. The "failed change rate"—the rate at which modifications to the production environment didn't "stick"—was up to 52 percent.

A failure was defined as a change that was half-baked or had to be backed out.

Failed changes, particularly ones involving security patches, obviously create cybersecurity vulnerabilities. So, in addition to the fact that such failures were delaying or compromising new customer-facing features and functions, or needed system improvements, they were also significantly amplifying cybersecurity risk.

In the face of all this, there was a tendency for the IT department at CompuPro to kick the can down the road. "The technical environment in those days was so complex," admits Thomas. "We had several configuration management databases to try to manage it all, and we knew that every one of our changes created a potential for a vulnerability." Making sure every "I" was dotted and every "T" crossed would be overwhelming.

But if IT doesn't accept its role as the first line of defense, then the burden transfers to enterprise risk management and finally lands on audit.

"Blaming audit for one of my failures is like blaming the goalie for losing the game," says Thomas.

When CompuPro's flagship customer left for a competitor, it was a blow to the company's reputation as well as to its bottom line.

## What They Did

### Step 1: Decision by Leadership

One day, in a meeting of C-level executives, the CEO slapped his hand on the table and declared enough. "The company was at the point where leadership was willing to balance performance with conformance." In other words, growth at all costs was unsustainable.

### Step 2: Choosing the Right Framework

Thomas and his team modified the COBIT framework to meet CompuPro's needs.

CompuPro was in a state of "framework exhaustion," says Thomas. They had Prince2, Zachman, MODAF—the list went on. As each framework was introduced, everyone said, "This is the framework that is going to save us."

COBIT became the framework to manage frameworks. "COBIT helped IT. Internal audit and the risk organization speak in the same vernacular," says Thomas.

Next, Thomas and his team dove deep into the risk register to fully enumerate risks and to determine the cost and benefit of every risk and its mitigation strategy.

In some instances, the cost-benefit analysis indicated the need for only a "detective control," which finds where there are problems, but it accomplished nothing more. In other cases, CompuPro upped the ante and put in place a "deterrent control," which warns an attacker that they should not attack.

Preventative controls, those that can actually ward off attacks, carry higher price tags. These were instituted less frequently.

### Step 3: Linking IT Risk with Overall Business Risks

The COBIT framework helped CompuPro look at more than just the cybersecurity issues the company faced. The process also exposed other areas that were causing the company significant pain.

"We didn't just focus on a cybersecurity checklist," says Thomas. They instead linked each risk to a business goal and a cost if that business goal were compromised or not achieved. They evaluated each risk, weighed its likelihood of becoming real, and determined its impact to corporate objectives. This figured into the cost-benefit analysis described earlier.

Based on the linkage of risk to the business goals, CompuPro determined what its response should be to each risk. In other words, how much it was willing to spend to address each risk.

What had started as a cybersecurity effort became a corporate-wide evaluation of risk, using the COBIT 5 framework.

Thomas and his team pointed out to other business stakeholders the following proposition:

If an IT risk becomes real, here are *your* business goals that won't be met.

The obvious conclusion: What we're talking about here is not solely IT risk. It's business risk.

## Step 4: Understanding Enablers

Thomas's team introduced the COBIT concept of enablers into the conversation at CompuPro.

Enablers are those things that help a business succeed. The COBIT framework identifies seven:

1. Principles, policies, and frameworks
2. Processes
3. Organizational structures
4. Culture, ethics, and behavior
5. Information
6. Services, infrastructure, and applications
7. People, skills, and competencies

Enablers are interdependent. Recognizing the interconnectedness of enablers is a necessary prerequisite to successful decision making.

For example, if a certain IT service is not available (enabler 6), another business process (enabler 2) will not perform.

Similarly, because the company viewed itself as entrepreneurial, people were apt to break the rules if they felt it was justified by a growth goal.

Yet a compromise of ethics such as bending or breaking a rule around security policy (enabler 4) will put the company's information at risk (enabler 5).

## Step 5: Institute Proper Governance

Governance at CompuPro was absent, unevenly applied, or left up to the business units themselves.

Thomas recalls one IT incident that resulted in a 22-hour fire drill. Afterward, exhausted, he was called to a meeting of the board of directors. The chairman asked, "What can the board do to help?"

"I need to be governed better," Thomas answered.

He went on to explain that he, in IT, was effectively being told, "Govern yourself." The situation was similar in other business units.

It left him, he told the board, to make up his own guidelines as well as decide the consequences when rules were broken.

It's like a home with kids. In the family, the parents are the "governing body." Consider what happens if, when they go out, they give the vague directive, "Kids, while we're away, behave yourselves."

What does that mean? What are the kids to do and not do?

"The kids don't know what you mean until you say, 'Don't stay out late. No big parties,'" says Thomas.

But even that's not enough. What does "out too late" mean? Midnight? Eleven p.m.? And what defines a "big party"? Three kids? Ten?

When you start to get into the details of the parents-away example of governance, you begin to understand the concept of risk acceptance. "By telling the kids a big party is ten people, I am giving them the risk I'm willing to accept, which is nine kids or fewer in the house while I'm away," says Thomas.

The scenario also helps businesspeople understand the idea of establishing tolerance thresholds, another aspect of governance. Most kids know if they arrive a few minutes past 12 on a midnight curfew, they're good. If it's 12:30, they're grounded.

The business-level equivalent of parents in a household is, of course, the board or other governance bodies. They need to establish the main governance principles as well as risk acceptance and risk tolerance guidelines.

Thomas and team asked the board to provide the proper level of governance, and they responded.

### Step 6: Get a CISO with the Right Reporting Relationship

CompuPro did not have a CISO, chief information security officer. The security function was embedded in the networking group—"the old-fashioned model," says Thomas.

CompuPro hired a CISO, which was good. But the company had him reporting to Thomas in IT. This was the wrong reporting structure.

According to cybersecurity best practices, the CISO needs to be independent of IT. Because how can you audit your boss? Soon, on Thomas's recommendation, the CISO was moved out of IT into a separate organization with a separate budget and reporting relationship.

## Results

This kind of organizational realignment and risk assessment didn't take place over a weekend. It was a two-year "expedition," Thomas says. In that time, they looked at processes, obtained board-level guidance, and effectively showed the linkages between IT risk and enterprise risk. They then took steps to reduce the risk.

It affected metrics across the whole organization.

- The "failed change" rate dropped from 52 percent to 13 percent.
- Outages and SLA violations decreased drastically.
- The time to understand and respond to a cyberevent was cut in half.
- Governance and process changes resulted in cost efficiencies throughout the business.
- CompuPro went from a point at which their core business was at risk to strong performance and ultimately a lucrative purchase.

## Lessons Learned

One key lesson to be found in the CompuPro experience was the role of the rewards structure in the success of the program.

First, it was important to understand and acknowledge that the word "reward" does not always translate to "money."

"It could be—how do I get recognized in the organization?" notes Thomas.

The existing CompuPro rewards structure looked only at growth, not at other organizational behaviors such as violations to policy.

By making the cost of risk visible, it was easier for those in the organization to see how their rewards might be compromised by risk. "We could say, 'Excuse me, Mr. VP, if that risk becomes real, here are your goals that don't get met. And here is how your rewards will suffer as a consequence in terms of recognition, promotion, and compensation.'"

Those kinds of conversations—directly tying behavior to rewards—are how you get cooperation inside the organizations. Individuals are influenced to make decisions favorable to themselves as well as to the organization. "People will always be biased toward their own success," Thomas says, at all levels of the corporate ladder.

Another revelation involved the importance of what Thomas calls the "Silent Killer." That's Thomas's term for culture and organizational change. He says, looking back, he would have focused more on it.

"The people who break the rules the most are the ones who create the rules," says Thomas. If you have this going on, good governance structures and good policies don't help.

There's hardly a control in the world to keep a VP from saying, "Bring down this environment." From a leadership perspective, leaders must be the first ones to follow the rules. If they don't—that's a cultural issue.

Say you have a control that you cannot go into a system and put in a patch before 6 p.m. "I could simply have directed someone who reported to me to do it and they would have done it. There's not a control to stop it," says Thomas.

Because leaders may be apt to break the rules as a matter of culture, what's needed are escalation procedures, which Thomas says CompuPro eventually put in place. It gave the team a way to evaluate which requests are out of bounds and also gave them the escalation point.

Escalation procedures are necessary, especially for those unusual situations in which a policy really needs to be bent. The employee can say to herself, "Mark is asking us for this, and he's our boss. But there's a procedure that says we have to get approval from this other level." The next level may be another executive, an advisory board, or a steering committee.

# CHAPTER 5

# Your Cybersecurity Program: A High-Level Overview

W hen it comes to designing a cybersecurity program, what is the most important thing to know before you begin? You need to know where you are right now. If you don't know where you are, the first step you take may be over the cliff, so please don't do that. You haven't even finished the book yet!

For every business there is a vision, a mission, and one or more goals. This may seem trivial, but it is very important to put those down on paper. If it is your business, then you already know them. You may need to develop them a bit further, but in essence, you do know them, even if you think you don't.

## Vision and Mission Statements

A mission statement is your company's *raison d'être*. It's as existential as it gets. It tells the world why you exist. A vision statement, on the other hand, is more directional than it is existential. One is *who and why we are*, the other is *what we are*. The website TopNonProfits.com has collected the top vision and mission statements for several nonprofits. I have taken a few and paired them up to show the difference between mission (top) and vision (bottom) statements:

### ASPCA

- *Mission*: To provide effective means for the prevention of cruelty to animals throughout the United States.
- *Vision*: That the United States is a humane community in which all animals are treated with respect and kindness.

**Cleveland Clinic**

- *Mission*: To provide better care of the sick, investigation into their problems, and further education of those who serve.
- *Vision*: Striving to be the world's leader in patient experience, clinical outcomes, research, and education.

**Creative Commons**

- *Mission*: Creative Commons develops, supports, and stewards legal and technical infrastructure that maximizes digital creativity, sharing, and innovation.
- *Vision*: Our vision is nothing less than realizing the full potential of the Internet—universal access to research and education, full participation in culture—to drive a new era of development, growth, and productivity.

**Feeding America**

- *Mission*: To feed America's hungry through a nation-wide network of member food banks and engage our country in the fight to end hunger.
- *Vision*: A hunger-free America.

**Smithsonian**

- *Mission*: The increase and diffusion of knowledge.
- *Vision*: Shaping the future by preserving our heritage, discovering new knowledge, and sharing our resources with the world.

Now, there are those who will argue that mission and vision statements are a waste of time. There is one goal, and one goal only: Make money. The end. After all, as one executive director of a national nonprofit told me, *"No money? No mission."* I agree. There is truth to the "make money" imperative. But is it your—or your company's—true mission? Does it reflect your company's vision? (If so, write it down.)

From our perspective, this is the starting point of establishing what's of value to you. This will be vital later, when we establish the right level of protection for it.

## Culture and Strategy

With your mission and vision statements in hand, the next thing you need to understand is your company's culture. To clarify, we're talking about organizational, or corporate, culture. This is not about any ethnic or societal culture (although it may well be influenced by them). This is business. And as such, it has been studied within an inch of its life. I'll spare you the diatribe, and focus on David Needle's definition from his 2004 *Business in Context: An Introduction to Business and Its Environment*. He writes:

> *Organizational culture represents the collective values, beliefs, and principles of organizational members and is a product of such factors as history, product, market, technology, strategy, type of employees, management style, and national culture; culture includes the organization's vision, values, norms, systems, symbols, language, assumptions, beliefs, and habits.*

What he didn't write—and actually no one did, despite misattribution to Drucker—is: "Culture will eat strategy for lunch any day of the week," or some variant thereof. This statement appears in the literature in various guises (e.g., in Thomas W. Lloyd's 2000 monograph in the form of "Culture beats strategy," and so forth) but although the source of the idea is mysterious, the wisdom is real.

The bottom line here is this: In a fight between culture and strategy, culture always wins. Always. That's why you need to spend some time understanding your corporate culture. Without that understanding, your cybersecurity and risk strategies will fail.

Are you in an entrepreneurial "damn the torpedoes" culture or more of a risk-averse environment? Are you in a highly regulated industry? Are you in the armed forces? Whatever the case, you'll need to identify the culture and understand it. There are some things that your culture will allow that others will not. For example, if you try to institute strict authentication and access controls in an entrepreneurial, no-risk-is-too-big environment, you are guaranteed to fail. The staff will not follow suit; they will bypass the controls, and you'll have to deal with a staff revolution (and we know how those end: Chop! Chop!) On the other hand, if you are too lax in an environment that is expecting safety through rigorous controls, you'll be dismissed as irresponsible and too dangerous to work with.

How do you determine culture? Let's say you just walked through the door day one in your job at a new company and you're somehow charged with reviewing cybersecurity risk and making a recommendation. You don't know anyone yet and it will take some time for you to assimilate into your new company's culture. What can you do to determine the culture of your new home? Why, you ask, of course! It will take more than asking a couple of people by the water cooler, though. It will take a survey.

As luck would have it, Kim Cameron and Robert Quinn wrote *Diagnosing and Changing Organizational Culture* in 2005 (second edition in 2011) and in it you will find their "Organizational Culture Assessment Instrument"—a short but very useful survey that, when followed, will provide you with a cultural profile for your company. Their survey assesses a company across six dimensions:

1. Organizational dominant characteristics
2. Organizational leadership
3. Employee management
4. Organizational glue
5. Strategic emphases
6. Criteria of success

Each one of these has four rankings in the spectrum of personal versus controlling, nurturing versus results-minded, teamwork versus conformity, trusting versus policing, humanistic versus efficiency-first, and people-centric versus company-success.

## Off to See the Wizard

Save your cultural survey results—you will be needing them later. Now you are ready to talk with the people in the IT department. Why the jump to technology first? To be sure, there are many departments, profit centers, etc. that you could focus on first, so why IT? Because cybersecurity and IT are inseparable. IT doesn't own cybersecurity (the organization does), but consider this: No information technology? No cybersecurity. It's simple. The word *cyber* by definition is about information technology. One cannot exist without the other. IT and cybersecurity are twins. Sometimes opposing twins, to be sure, but twins nonetheless.

What happens if there is no IT department in your company? Then you should talk with the vendor who's responsible for supporting IT. What happens if there is no such vendor? Well, figure out if there is anyone charged with IT in the company and ask her. What happens if she doesn't exist?

Let's cut to the chase: Companies come in all sorts of shapes and sizes. Some are totally virtual, whereas others are multinational behemoths. Even those we call virtual have tremendous variation in their use, adoption, and support of technology. You may be in a company in which all technology is provided as a service (remember infrastructure as a service, software as a service, etc.? If not, maybe zip back to the "cloud" definition in the Cybersecurity Primer). Alternatively, the company may be operating under a bring-your-own-device (BYOD) IT model, so you—the individual user—may be responsible for maintaining your own devices. On the opposite side of this spectrum are the IT stormtroopers: a humorless bunch walking about stomping on any electronic device they don't recognize.

The majority of companies are somewhere in between these extremes. They have one or more people in their IT department—sometimes they are employees, other times they are vendor-provided—and they maintain a set of technologies that are hybrid (on-premises, cloud, and a mix of company-provided and BYOD), and have some degree of control over what kind of software is running where and doing what. We'll talk about them, and we'll call them: *the IT department*. What happens with the fringe cases? You'll still need the information; it's just that the way you go about it will differ. In the virtual company case, you'll determine who the vendors are and what services they provide, and so on. Think of them as your virtual IT department. In the stormtroopers case, bring your papers and make an appointment. Besides, if the stormtroopers are in the building, I'd hazard a guess that the company has a formal risk and audit function, and they'll need to be included in all this as well.

No matter what, no matter who, this is an excellent opportunity for you to build a bridge with the IT department, irrespective of structure and delivery. In most cases, you'll be welcomed. It isn't often that non-IT professionals take an interest in what's behind the black door and all those blinking lights. Connect with the IT leadership and get a good understanding of the role of technology in your company.

What does that typically look like?

To begin with, IT in organizations is manifested in more than one way. Many different analysts and research firms have given the phenomenon different names. For example, Gartner Research has coined the term *bimodal IT* to describe the *keep the lights on and trains moving* version of IT, and the *go wild, innovate, and experiment* version of IT. Then there is *shadow IT*. That's the version of IT that springs up as a result of unanswered (or frustrated) user needs. For example, let's say corporate policy prohibits more than 5MB email attachments, and to get to the company's file-sharing server, you have to jump through all sorts of hoops. The user, acting out of urgent need or defiance, opens up a Dropbox account and shares the credential with colleagues and clients. Each one of these modes will have its own cybersecurity considerations, with shadow IT being particularly tricky to support and secure.

For example, there are companies whose infrastructure (the stability part) is absolutely critical to operations. For example, think of a trading system. If the system goes down during trading hours, the company loses business, with potential losses in the millions. Alternatively, there are companies whose infrastructure is not as critical when compared with their ability to deliver an answer quickly. In this case, think software development. A firm could be running on a distributed infrastructure all over the world with little worry about any one component of it being unavailable, and yet it must be able to deliver a necessary fix to an application as fast as possible because, say, there may be lives depending on it, as in the case of a hospital management system.

Going back to your discovery needs, your IT team will be able to provide you with their specific assessment. They can identify their systems, the locations, what's critical, and what's not. They'll supply you with exciting documentation like network diagrams, systems inventory, application inventory, licensing documentation, and they'll cap it off with the disaster recovery and business continuity plans. Depending on the size of your organization, these assessments will fit in a neat little binder, or the mailroom will drop off a pallet. Either way, you'll be good to go.

The IT department will also give you their views of what's at risk and when they do, take careful notes—especially on the intersection of technology and business operations. This will prove very useful as you move forward with asset valuation, business-impact analysis, vulnerability, and risk assessments.

So far you have gathered the following pieces of information:

1. Mission and vision statements
2. Cultural assessment findings
3. IT documentation and assessment

Now, you're ready to understand what's at risk.

## What's at Risk?

This is the part where you get to walk around and pose this question: "How much is *this* worth to you?" *This* is the asset you're interested in protecting, and the only one who can determine its worth is the person who owns it.

Without getting overly complex here—after all, this is only the overview chapter!—the asset owner is the person who, one way or another, is responsible for the asset. For example, the CFO is responsible for the financial assets of the company. What are those? They can range from simple things like Excel spreadsheets, access to the bank accounts, and the accounting system files all the way to massive ERP (enterprise resource management) applications. The CFO is the one who is responsible for all of this, and she's the one who can tell you how much these assets are worth to her. By *worth* I don't really mean monetary value. I mean things like: How long can she be without those assets, how much data can she afford to lose, and, in cases of loss, how quickly does she need to be back in business?

Where do you start this risk assessment? First, identify your business managers. Each one will typically be responsible for a line of business or a department. Sit down with each one and ask him or her to identify all the things that are absolutely necessary to do their jobs. The list is likely to include multiple assets, both hard (computers, facilities, etc.) and soft (software, work-flows, etc.). You should work with each manager in ranking and prioritizing each asset. At the end of these meetings, you will have a very clear idea of each department's assets, and the corresponding impact of each asset's loss.

If you want to get formal about this, you can ask for a department-by-department business-impact analysis, and from the results, you can derive both the assets and the business impact of their loss or disruption. But what fun is that? Make it personal and get in there! Roll up your sleeves and work with your colleagues in getting all this done. You'll certainly gain a better under-standing of what's going on with the business, and make a whole bunch of new friends. (Or, enemies, if they don't want to be bothered … but hey! You're the one trying to cover their assets! They'll see the light eventually.)

Okay, you're almost done. You've made tremendous progress in gaining an understanding of your organization, more than most employees or even managers ever do. You should celebrate. Go have a nice lunch. Nothing crazy, though: There is still work to be done. Skip the martinis.

## Threat Assessment

So, what's left? Well, the next step in the process should be a threat assessment. Now, that can be really intimidating, but it needn't be. Here's why:

Performing a threat assessment requires skill and expertise that you may not have readily available. It requires up-to-date threat intelligence access, and it requires understanding the threat behavior. As an example, consider a house on the top of a large hill. The owner has done all the work up to this point, recognizes the asset at risk (the house), and is getting ready to deploy controls to protect the asset. One of the controls he chooses is a sump pump. Now, sump pumps are wonderful and really, really useful if you're flooded, but the house is at the top of the hill. Is the threat of a flood realistic? Wouldn't it be better to invest in a lightning rod? Don't get me wrong, you may still want the sump pump in case one of the pipes burst, but what's the priority here?

That's exactly why you should not be intimidated by performing a threat assessment: You are armed with common sense, and you are ready to take this on! You also need to remember you're not alone in this. There is a whole community out there watching, analyzing, and sharing all sorts of threat intel-ligence and best practices. In the United States, the Department of Homeland Security is running the United States Computer Emergency Readiness Team (US-CERT), whose mission is to "strive for a safer, stronger Internet for all Americans by responding to major incidents, analyzing threats, and exchang-ing critical cybersecurity information with trusted partners around the world."

You will find them at: https://www.us-cert.gov, and you'll get all the alerts and tips you need to get a very good feel of what's going out there in cyberspace.

According to a recent ISACA cybersecurity snapshot, the top three threats facing organizations are social engineering, insider threats, and advanced persistent threats. I'll go out on a limb here and predict that these rankings will stay around for a few more years. Could there be new, disruptive technologies that would alter these rankings? Certainly, but consider that both social engineering and insider threats are people-centric, not technology-centric. People will always be both the biggest asset *and* the biggest threat in cybersecurity.

Finally, of these threats, I would suggest that most organizations would need to seriously consider and address the first two: social engineering and insider threats. The third category, advanced persistent threats (APTs), is particularly nasty and typically focuses on big multinationals, governments, physical infrastructure (think power grid, water supply, etc.), and the military. That's not to say that your firm should not consider APT. It always depends on who you are and what you do. Again, I trust that you know best.

Social engineering threats tend to be planned well ahead of time. The attacker harvests information about the target from publicly available sources (social networks, professional networks, corporate websites, public records, even data aggregators) and then uses that information to impersonate and compromise the target. How common are social engineering attacks and how likely are you to be targeted? Extremely and very. And the more public information you have openly available and accessible on the Internet, the easier it gets. If, for example, your corporate website has photos and bios of the executive team, then a hacker already knows who does what at the company, as well as some information about each person's background. If you happen to be working in finance, even better. And, if your company is big, indicating a potentially large accounting department, even better yet! Any leftover blanks can easily be filled in with a quick visit to LinkedIn. From there, on to social networks, school alumni associations, and public records. In short order, a solid profile of an executive has been formed and it can now be used to gain access to processes and workflows controlling money movement, intellectual property, deal secrets, etc. In extreme cases, the profile could even turn into personal extortion, turning the executive into an insider threat.

Speaking of which, insider threats are your basic good-people-doing-bad-things threat. Yes, there are bad people doing bad things, too, but hopefully you minimized that risk (remember *deter*?) by doing your pre-employment due diligence, including a thorough background check.

For our purposes, an insider threat is any employee who attempts to use his or her position of privilege to commit illegal acts. The reasons vary: family emergencies, divorce, unexpected medical bills (the good-people-doing-bad-things part), or thrills, espionage, and kleptomania (bad-people-doing-bad-things part). These reasons top my list. Bottom line, and whatever their excuse may be, the result is the same: data exfiltration. Perhaps a fake vendor is created and invoices are sent to the employee who approves them, or expense reports are fraudulently submitted, or something similar with one goal: money! If it is corporate espionage, then the employee steals data, which she either sells to a competitor or gives away in hopes of a procuring a better position with the competitor. (Obviously, if the employee is not working for a corporation but for a government, we go from corporate espionage to Bond. James Bond. You know the rest.)

Advanced persistent threats are the stuff of migraines. The "advanced" part speaks to the incredible sophistication and technical skill involved, from crafting payloads to delivering them, and from finding zero-day vulnerabilities to exploiting them. The "persistent" part speaks to the *I-will-not-stop-until-I-succeed* commitment of the attacker against the target. Any which way you look at APTs, they are nasty, painful, and expensive. If you have serious reason to believe that you may be the target of an APT, take this book and walk over to your cybersecurity department and ask them what are they doing about it. If you don't have a cybersecurity department, walk over to the CEO's office and, kindly yet firmly, suggest to her that you need to create one. Yesterday is good.

Have we exhausted the possible threats? Not by a long stretch! There are zero-day threats, end-point threats (computers, tablets, phones being compromised), and Internet of Things (IoT) threats (such as your car deciding to turn off when you're driving at 75 mph). There are operational technology (OT) threats (hacking industrial control systems), threats of new forms of fraud (crowdfrauding, rent-a-hacker, hactivists), denial-of-service threats, and all the other fun stuff we defined in Chapter 3.

As we move forward with our cybersecurity program development we may need to drill deeper and consider the threat landscape in more detail. But for now, we're ready to continue framing our overview.

## At the Club House Turn!

At this point, you have:

1. Mission and vision statements
2. Cultural assessment findings
3. IT documentation and assessment
4. Asset valuations
5. Business-impact analyses
6. Threat assessments

Now you need to think about your vulnerabilities, the kind of controls you need to put in place to plug them, your processes, and your people.

Let's start with the vulnerabilities. Every system has them. Every single one. If someone tells you otherwise, he is lying. The goal here is to identify them and apply controls to protect them. Some vulnerabilities you may be able to eliminate altogether. Others, you may have to live with. Those are the ones you need to worry about. And finally, there are the vulnerabilities you don't even know about. Those will keep you up at night, but even for those, there's usually something you can do.

Step one: discovery! We have to uncover those vulnerabilities. There are several ways of doing this, starting with vulnerability and penetration tests. Testing will identify most vulnerabilities and dictate necessary steps to eliminate or remediate. We'll discuss all this in detail in the chapters that follow, but suffice it to say that when we're done, we'll need to apply a whole set of controls.

At this point in the game, though, having finished with asset valuation, business-impact analysis, and threat and vulnerability assessment, you're ready to bring everything together. You are ready to conduct your risk assessment.

A risk assessment is always company-specific; there is no standard risk assessment or template. You have to create it for your own specific environment. Now, I recognize that this assessment soup can get confusing. We have threat assessments, vulnerability assessments, business impacts, risk analysis, risk evaluation, risk registers, and finally, risk assessments! That's a lot of assessing! What's what here?

Let's recap, and make it personal:

- *Threat Assessment*: Who's out to get you? Why? How likely is an attack? How bad can it get?
- *Vulnerability Assessment*: How easy is it to get you? What's stopping people from doing it? What tools might they use?
- *Risk Analysis*: Combine equal parts of threat assessment and vulnerability assessment. Mix, cook, and serve in the form of risk probability over time and potential business impact.
- *Risk Register*: A go-to menu of your risks, listing as much information as possible, including risk type (e.g., what, who, why), evaluation date, description, probability, impact, classification (e.g., low, medium, high), response (e.g., accept, insure, run for the hills), and risk owner (who's on the hook for it?). It's fine to go all in when creating your risk register, but keep in mind that throwing everything and the kitchen sink in a risk register will make it difficult to maintain and update. Think comprehensive, but not overwhelming.

- *Risk Evaluation*: Compare your risk analysis to business-specific reality. Deal only with pragmatic, real, and present risk. Avoid paranoid thinking and rabbit holes. To wit: Accept meteor strike as "risk I won't worry about," and sleep easier.
- *Risk Assessment*: Using all of the preceding, identify the issues, rank them, and answer what happens if you stick your head in the sand and ignore them. I like my risk assessments to be short and sweet. For each identified risk, think *Name, Rank, and Serial Number*. Rank, of course, is the key here. Other than that, that's it. If I want the details, I can always refer back to the source documents.

Now that I have all this information clear and prioritized, I can start thinking about what controls to place where.

## Mitigating Risk

Controls, as we discussed earlier, do stuff. You know the drill by now. They are *preventative* (think: Stop signs), *detective* (think: cameras), *corrective* (think: backup), and *compensating* (think: failover sites). Now that you understand both your assets and the threat landscape, you can start making intelligent choices about which controls to apply to protect yourself. The goal to remember is: *defense in depth*. You want your controls laid out in layers. You want the ability to thwart an attacker at all the different stages of an attack, across various systems, and you need controls to mitigate all the vulnerabilities you discovered.

The last factors to consider in developing your cybersecurity program are processes and—again—people. In a sense, we've come full circle: We started with people, and we are ending with people, only this time we're adding a crucial link. Processes. They are absolutely critical in your program's success. Processes are the essence of *how* business is done. They link assets, connect people, and create value. Some processes cannot be disturbed and must be protected as is. Others have more flexibility and can bend to accommodate controls.

To find out which is which, you'll have to map all key processes in the company. This may not be fun, but it is essential that it be done and done correctly. Your work in this may brush up against bigger issues like overall information security, not just our favorite subset of cybersecurity. For example, consider a credit card processing workflow. It's not only the systems that need protecting. The whole process—from the moment your client gives you a credit card number to the moment the transaction is complete and filed—must be carefully thought out and appropriately protected. You may discover that you may need a different set of controls, which are not necessarily cybersecurity controls, to protect these mission-critical processes and people.

People, of course, is what this is all about.

People are the ultimate value creators, the true engine of creativity, innovation, and the spirit of your company. They are your biggest asset, and as such your top priority in ensuring their protection.

People can also be your largest liability. They can be a liability if they are not aware of the threats, if they are ill-prepared to deal with the environment, or worse yet, if among them there is a "bad apple" who is intent on compromising everyone else's hard work.

You can apply controls to protect assets and systems, but you cannot control people. That should not be confused. Ever. Interestingly enough, well-trained, sensitized, cybersecurity-aware people are the best way for the company to survive and thrive. That makes them one of your most effective controls, since through their training and awareness they actually do stuff to protect the assets! We will review how to develop the right cybersecurity awareness program in the chapters that follow.

## Incident-Response Planning

At this point, you have:

1. Mission and vision statements
2. Cultural assessment findings
3. IT documentation and assessment
4. Asset valuations
5. Business-impact analyses
6. Threat assessment
7. Vulnerability assessment
8. Risk assessment
9. Process and workflow maps
10. Control and defense-in-depth deployment
11. Cybersecurity awareness program

What's missing?

There used to be a saying that there are two certainties in life: death and taxes. This book is not about either. It's about the third certainty: a cybersecurity incident. What's missing, therefore, is our incident-response plan.

Based on your work so far, you have created the necessary foundation on which to build an incident-response plan. You have put in place the processes and controls to *deter, identify, protect, detect,* and *recover.* You've got one more step to go: *respond.*

No two incident-response plans are alike: The variables alone are overwhelming. For one, you can't define beforehand what type of incident you'll be dealing with. Second, no two businesses are alike, no two systems are alike, and no two workflows are the same. We do payroll one way; you do it another way. We use LINUX; you use Windows. And so on. So, how can you create an incident-response plan? By preparing for surgery!

Like cybersecurity incidents, no two surgeries are alike. But all surgeries have a checklist to be followed, such as: premedicating the patient against infection (preventive control), having enough blood in place (corrective control), having imaging and diagnostic equipment ready (detective controls), and so on. It's the same with cybersecurity incident response.

You should develop a checklist that you practice, refine, drill, refine some more, test, tweak, and so on. Depending on the size of your company, you may create a red team and a blue team and practice simulated cyberwarfare in which one team attacks while the other defends and recovers. You will develop an arsenal of tools to use throughout the operation—from forensic capabilities to data recovery. You develop communication plans for the company, its clients, the press, vendors, and even the authorities. All of these become part of your incident-response plan, a living document that should be constantly reviewed and adjusted as circumstances change.

Now you're done! You have your response. The board has reviewed your program and approved it. Everything is in place. You can sleep more easily—until tomorrow, when you have to review the whole thing all over again, making sure that your program remains current and reflects your changing business and the changing world. Cybersecurity program development is not a once-and-done. It's not a date; it's a marriage. And you'll need the commitment and effort to keep it thriving.

For now, let's take stock of where we are after this whirlwind of a chapter: This is what we have so far:

1. Mission and vision statements
2. Cultural assessment findings
3. IT documentation and assessment
4. Asset valuations
5. Business-impact analyses
6. Threat assessment
7. Vulnerability assessment
8. Risk assessment
9. Process and workflow maps
10. Controls and defense-in-depth deployment
11. Cybersecurity awareness program
12. Incident-response plan

That's a lot of work! For me, it feels like we've been riding a bullet train. Have you ever stared out the window of one of those speeding trains? In the far distance, you can see the countryside, but up close? Everything is a blur. That's pretty much the speed we traveled in this cybersecurity program overview chapter. You should have been left with a sense of landscape, and lots of blurry details.

We'll get to the details one step at a time, and when we're done, we'll discuss item 13: cybersecurity program management.

# CHAPTER 6

## Assets

We are now getting into actually *doing* your cybersecurity program. If the previous chapters gave you the 40,000-foot view, the next will take you straight down into the weeds. I've divided the doing part of the work into several phases:

1. Assets
2. Threats
3. Vulnerabilities
4. Environments
5. Controls
6. Incident-response planning
7. People
8. Living cybersecure

We will deal with each phase separately, breaking down the various steps needed to build your cybersecurity program. We'll start with assets.

In Chapter 1, we defined *assets* as *anything of value*. So, what exactly are these things of value in your world? Always remember the basic rule: If it is of value to you, it is of value to someone else, and it will need appropriate care and protection.

Of course, all things in context, and our context is cybersecurity. It may well be true that your most valuable asset is a physical product, well worth considering and protecting, but in our case, we need to look at that physical asset from a cybersecurity perspective. We are looking at cyberassets! Those are typically digital assets, but not always.

Even if your most important asset is a physical thing of great value, the question to ask is: Is this asset a risk from a cyberattack? If yes, then that needs to be considered. If not, then the thing itself won't be considered, but the processes, data, systems, etc., that are involved in its creation still need to be looked at very carefully.

Let's consider a firm that makes a high-end analog watch. Each watch costs $30,000. The company lives or dies based on the sales of this very expensive analog item, so in that sense the watch is the firm's most important asset.

From a cybersecurity perspective, however, it is not the watch itself that is the asset, but rather, all the data relating to the watch, such as its design, manufacturing plans, marketing strategy, etc. If the design is stolen, then someone can replicate the exact watch and flood the market with knockoffs, causing enormous damage to the company.

So, what are your cyberassets of value? The category can include your company's data and the supporting (curating and controlling) systems, processes, workflows, and people. Other examples of cyberassets of value include all intellectual property (designs, product information, research, etc.), personally identifiable information, personally identifiable health information, strategic plans, financial plans, merger and acquisition plans, tactics, etc. If in doubt whether a cyberasset is of value, ask a few simple questions:

What happens if this asset is destroyed? Corrupted? Unavailable?
What happens if it becomes public? Or, falls into the wrong hands?

If the answer is nothing, scratch your head as to why are you maintaining worthless cyberassets, and move on. Those assets are not worthy of protection, much less your attention! If, on the other hand, you discover that all sorts of things happen if the assets are exposed, then ... start cataloging!

How exactly do you go about doing this? What are the questions you need to answer to have a complete picture of the value of these digital assets? First things first: asset classification and valuation. This is a fairly existential exercise! You will need to understand and document the true essence of your company. Depending on size and product or service offerings, your work will range from interviewing the executive team and the board all the way to having an honest talk with just yourself if you're self-employed. Your work may take you down a complex path. One interview may lead you to dig further and interview more people at different layers of the organization. But at the end of the day, you will have come up with a list of valuable assets for your company.

## Asset Classification

A good first step will be to get a grip on the total universe of our cyberassets. What is included in our definition? Cyberassets would typically fall into one of the following categories: data, hardware, software, systems, processes, and workflows.

### Data

It is important to differentiate between *information* and *data*. Frequently, people use the terms interchangeably, and that's okay for everyday use, but we should be clear on the distinction because the implications can be significant.

Data, in one sense, is information that has been captured, stored, and represented in some medium. Data is often an expression of information, but that doesn't mean that data is a complete representation of that piece of information. Consider a pot of boiling water. I have a sensor in the pot that measures the temperature of the water and transmits this datum, which is stored in my system in a field called "water temperature." That's data! But there's a lot beyond the number that we could notice about the actual physical event of boiling water: the magic of phase transition from liquid to gas; the beauty of the rising bubbles; the mathematics of turbulence of the water's surface, and so on. That's all *information* about the boiling water … but it's not data.

## INFORMATION SECURITY VERSUS CYBERSECURITY

Before we go further down the "rabbit hole," let's stop and discuss why the difference matters in cybersecurity.

You'll remember that cybersecurity is part of information security. Information security does indeed care about all kinds of information (e.g., events) and all forms of data, not just digital. But the scope of this book is more limited, to cybersecurity only. As such, we need to stay focused on digital data. Specifically, on how data is stored, processed, and transmitted. We are interested only in the three-plus-one pillars: confidentiality, integrity, availability, and safety. That's it.

That said, I cannot emphasize enough the importance of overall information security and its direct impact on the success of a cybersecurity program. As an example, consider the potential data loss from printouts left unattended on a printer in an unsecure area—while that data loss is not in digital form (and consequently outside the purview of this book), it still matters and should matter to you. *Cybersecurity should never be treated in isolation.* It should always be addressed in the context of people and the environment, especially in the age of the Internet of Things and the Internet of Everything. After all, one unsecured wearable device brought into a secure network is all a hacker needs to gain access.

## Hardware

Hardware is all the electronic equipment that stores, processes, or transmits data. It's also the stuff that controls other stuff, such as thermostats, and all the fun gizmos that make the Internet of Things possible. Why did I limit myself to "electronic" just now? Okay, you got me! Computer hardware can also be mechanical or even quantum. But unless you're Charles Babbage building the Difference Engine or you work at an advanced computing facility, electronic hardware is the only kind you need to worry about.

## Software

Software is the applications—from operating systems to apps—that use hardware to get things done. This includes, of course, software that runs in the IoT.

## Systems

A system is a collection of hardware, software, and networks that processes data. Systems can be internal or external, and they are frequently a combination of both.

## Processes and Workflows

Those are the sequence of steps involved in the creation, transformation, processing, storing, and transmitting of data across systems. The definitions for process and workflows can be confusing, but as far as we are concerned, processes and workflows are assets that contribute value to the company, and as such, are worthy of careful consideration and protection.

How exactly do you protect processes and workflows? It depends! The first step, no matter what, is knowing about them, that is, documenting and cataloging them. This step will reveal any dependencies on systems that these processes and workflows may have. Your thinking about protection starts there, and it cuts both ways: How does the process affect the system and how does the system affect the process? We'll look at this closer when we discuss controls. For now, keep this in the back of your mind and think about concepts like business continuity and disaster recovery.

## Asset Metadata

Now that we've listed our universe of assets, what do we need to know about them? When I do an asset classification and valuation, I insist on knowing at least the following 10 pieces of information. I call these the *asset metadata*:

*Owner:* Who is the owner of the asset? If we're talking about a root-level digital asset, like a finalized product (e.g., a product design, a filing for litigation, financial statements, etc.), then the owner is the enterprise.

If, on the other hand, we're discussing a value-generating system such as an e-commerce website, a medical records system, or a content management system, then the owner may be a business unit. More on this when we discuss business-impact analysis further on.

*Custodian:* Who is the custodian of the asset? The custodian cannot be "the enterprise" in general. It's always an identifiable person, department, business unit, or vendor. You need to be able to say, "Fatima is the custodian—go get her!"

*Location:* Where is the asset geographically located? This is key, especially if the asset ends up living in the cloud. Again, be specific.

*Confidentiality Classification:* Rate the asset 1 through 4: public, confidential, secret, or top secret.

*Criticality Classification:* Rate the asset 1 through 4: nice-to-have, optional, essential, or mission critical.

*Impact Classification:* This is a pain measurement on the asset's unavailability, corruption, or destruction. A rating of 1 through 4 works here, too: If the asset were suddenly unavailable or damaged, would the pain be none, minor, moderate, or severe?

*Maximum Tolerable Downtime (MTD):* This is the point in time at which if the asset is not recovered, the impact becomes severe.

*Recovery Point Objective (RPO):* This is the particular point in time you'll need the asset to recover to.

*Recovery Time Objective (RTO):* How long you are willing to wait before getting the asset back into production?

*Resources:* Who will be needed to bring the asset back to life within the RTO and at RPO? Remember, be specific. Use names!

I am going to let you in on a little secret. Those are exactly the same 10 questions that I want to know when I am doing a business-impact analysis, business unit by business unit.

The difference? When I am doing an asset classification and valuation, I am looking at root assets—assets of value at the enterprise level. When I am doing a business-impact analysis, I am looking more at systems—specifically, systems that are critical for each business unit to contribute to the production of the root assets. Some might argue that the distinction is artificial, and they would be right. But I like to think of the whole exercise as a continuum. Asset classification and valuation feeds into business-impact analysis, which feeds into business continuity and disaster recovery, all of which contribute to a solid cybersecurity program.

After you have collected all of the data for the assets, you are ready to take the next step. Like peeling an onion, you need to perform the same exercise on a business unit by business unit level. This in turn may lead you down even more levels as you discover system and workflow dependencies.

Notice that I have avoided mentioning any specific asset valuation at this point. So far what we have is a spreadsheet of valuable assets whose owner is the enterprise, and a few whose owner is a business unit. We haven't assigned any dollar value; we have only accomplished a listing of important stuff that we'd be loath to lose. Before we start talking dollars and cents, we have to perform the business-impact analysis work.

## Business-Impact Analysis

At this point, we move away from looking at enterprise-wide root assets to looking at business units. You could apply the same exact methodology with each business unit, and you would be right. You'd also be tired. Very tired. That's because if you attack a business-impact analysis (BIA) from the start by creating that unit's asset listings, you'll be spending endless hours cataloging and cross-referencing assets into systems, and so on.

I recommend going at it from the top, and digging down only to the point that is useful to your specific cybersecurity program. To do this, you'll need to look at the world from the point of view of systems, not assets. Systems, in this context, encompass all assets: A system, in this case, is defined as the collection of hardware, software, processes, workflows, and people that act to create, preserve, modify, disseminate, and curate data throughout its life cycle.

Say that three times fast, and notice: We added *people*. That's important in a business-impact analysis because when it comes to resources you will need to consider the people necessary for recovery and operations. Now, let's take this definition, and business unit by business unit, identify our top 10 properties, expanded in more detail further on:

- *The owner*: We are now moving past the enterprise as the owner. We're looking at humans! We need to find the one true subject-matter expert when it comes to a specific business unit, system, and assets. No one will know it better than the owner. He or she will know what it takes to run it, where the possible vulnerabilities are, what the impact of its loss may be to them, and by extension, to the company. This is why the owner must lead this identification and classification effort for the particular business unit, systems, and assets. They are also very invested in the longevity and health of their world, which makes them even more in tune with the threats against it.
- *The custodian*: Just as the owner is critical in helping you understand all the nuances about the business unit and its systems, the custodian is critical to providing an ecosystem context. Think of a horse and a barn manager. The barn manager doesn't get to decide who rides the

horse (that's the owner's job), but the barn manager is responsible for providing a safe environment, food, water, coordination with the vet, and so on. The custodian is important to you because he or she can provide information that's critical to understanding what it takes to keep the owner's business viable, which in turn will define all sorts of priorities and criticalities (e.g., No hay? No horse! Or at least a very hungry, cranky horse! Don't ride that horse.)

- *Location:* The location of a business might sound like a painfully obvious detail, but keep in mind that location is not just a real estate question anymore. Of course, you need to know the physical location of the business unit, especially if there are multiple locations all over the planet. This information will also provide valuable context ("What do you mean you can't find the CFO in India?") and exposes all sorts of vulnerabilities that are specific to geography, time, and local regulations.

But beyond real estate, our particular interest is locations in the cloud. Forget the obvious (where *is* the cloud, exactly?), and start thinking about new and exciting terms like *co-tenancy* (your stuff has roommates that you didn't know or approve), *transborder data flow* (your stuff lives on servers in multiple countries), *regulatory* and *compliance* issues (e.g., data in Europe is regulated differently from data in the United States), right-to-audit issues (the cloud provider must agree to your ability to audit), certifications, and so on.

Do remember, please, that if your stuff is in the cloud, then by definition, you are a tenant. This matters because the landlord may have different priorities than you do. For example, imagine that there is a robbery in the building, but not in your apartment; the landlord may or *may not* notify you. Now translate that into digital terms: If your cloud is breached but your specific data is not affected, will you even find out the breach occurred? Wouldn't you want to know? Bottom line: If your stuff is in the cloud, you will need to do additional homework to make sure you're protected.

1. *Confidentiality Classification:* Like before, I recommend that you use a scale from 1 to 4, with 1 assigned for "public," 2 being "confidential," 3 for "secret," and 4 for "top secret."

   Two tips: First, avoid the trap of having more classifications than necessary. Keep it as simple as you can.

   Second, use an even number of classifications to avoid giving anyone the option to pick the middle number as a safe bet. Since you're doing all of this work in partnership with the asset's owner, insist that both of you think this classification through and through. You'll be surprised at the dividends down the line.

If in doubt, use scenarios. Ask what-if–type questions. What would happen if this data was leaked to the public? What is the impact of a payroll report mistakenly being circulated company-wide? Can you identify groups of users with clear delineations for information access? Who needs to know this data, and who should not know? Are there policies in place that delineate access rights to the data?

2. *Criticality*: Again, I recommend that you use a scale from 1 to 4, with 1 assigned for "nice-to-have," 2 being "optional," 3 for "essential," and 4 for "mission critical." These are applicable across the spectrum, from business units to assets, and you need to be as objective as possible when assigning them. Not all assets are critical. They may all be *valuable*, but that doesn't make them critical. You may be able to operate okay for months without the music server streaming, but be forced to close your doors if accounting can't pay vendors or meet payroll.

    Scenarios are very helpful in establishing criticality, especially when framed by a specific business unit function, that is, limited in scope. If you start talking criticality at the enterprise level, that is, which business unit is more critical than another, then you had best do so only in the presence of the executive committee and the board—otherwise all these friends you worked so hard for are going to be looking at you sideways (e.g., "What do you mean 'facilities management' is not as critical as 'finance?' Let me see you work with no heat!").

3. *Impact*: This is the measurement of pain on a scale from 1 to 4, from "none," to "minor," to "moderate," to "severe." How painful is the outage going to be in terms of business impact? Are you out of business? If so, the impact is severe! Are the fees associated with the outage so high that the business will lose money for the year? I'd call that "severe," too. The quarter? Let's go with "moderate." You wouldn't even notice the charge in the P&L? I'd call that "minor." You should feel free to come up with your own terms, but my advice is keeping it down to no more than four, and to avoid colorful language. Other people, potentially of sour disposition, may read the document someday, and you don't want them raising any eyebrows as they contemplate litigation, especially if the outage will cause a public relations nightmare for your company.

    An interesting side note: The business unit owner will assign their version of impact. Then, the executive team may assign a different version of impact for the unit. And finally, the board, which is the ultimate decision-maker on all matters of risk, may choose to accept an impact classification of severe as not worthy of a set of controls, despite your advice to the contrary. Crazy, I know, but these differing points of view are entirely appropriate.

The business unit owner will justly consider a system's failure impact as severe for their unit while the CEO may consider the business unit's inability to contribute value as moderate, and the board may very well accept that risk and elect not to apply any controls toward that moderate or severe impact assessment. There are times when yours is not to reason why.

4. *Maximum Tolerable Downtime (MTD):* Let's assume the business unit is out of commission for some reason—cyberattack, power outage, whatever. Ask the question: "How long can the business unit owner tolerate the outage?" That's the amount of pain that the business owner is willing to accept before things turn ugly. What's ugly? Ugly is going out of business. That's pretty ugly. Less ugly is finding yourself unable to comply with a contract or regulation while more ugly is loss of life because of the outage. You get the idea. The MTD provides a baseline for building disaster recovery and business continuity plans.

5. *Recovery Point Objective (RPO):* The RPO tells you the *when* in time you need to be able to recover to. Think of it this way: Let's say you have an accounting system. The thing goes south on you. It's out. Gone. Nothing is running. Can't pay invoices, can't process receivables, and can't run payroll. The natives are starting to get restless. The IT department and the accounting vendor look at the situation and they tell you that the system will be back in two days' time, and the data will be restored from last week's backup.

   Here's the question you should be able answer to *before* the failure: Is that okay? If so, it means that once you get the system back (in two days) you'll have to reenter all transactions that happened between the last good backup and the day you have the system back. If you agree, that means that you have implicitly accepted two values: One is the recovery point objective of one week.

   The second is:

6. *Recovery Time Objective (RTO):* Your RTO is the maximum amount of time that you're willing to wait to be back in business, or—to put it in a more positive light—RTO is, ideally, how fast you'd like to have the problem go away and you back in business. In the preceding example, you accepted an RTO of two days. This is different from the MTD, which you may have set as one month, because with no payroll for a month, you'll be left with no employees and no business. Hence: maximum tolerable downtime.

   Now, consider that instead of an accounting system going down, you're a brokerage firm, and your brokerage system crashes. No more trades. No more reconciliation. No more portfolio management.

You have no idea where the orders that were in the pipeline are, what's executed and what hasn't, what the values are, etc.

What's your recovery time objective? If you said a few seconds, you would be right! Anything more could put you out of business. And your recovery point objective? Right up to the last second before the outage. You can't afford to lose any transactions. (To say nothing about those "men in black" from the regulators who will want to have a friendly chat with you about the outage.)

7. *Resources:* This is one of the most important pieces of information you'll collect. What are the resources (always per business unit per system) necessary for recovery? They need to be accurately identified and be cataloged in an actionable, meaningful way. You'll need not only the "Who is doing what?" question answered, but also how to get in touch with these resources, including backup plans if the resources are not available.

For example, if your can't-live-without-it custom application was written in Etruscan by Molly, who has since retired to Oahu, it is probably a good idea to: (a) have all of Molly's up-to-date contact information, (b) have identified the last few remaining Etruscan speakers, and (c) reflect on the lesson-learned about keeping mission-critical systems up-to-date and not in dead-and-gone language.

Similarly, you need to keep in mind that resources will be placed in contention if more than one system goes south (a likely event in the case of a cyberattack).

Now, the good news: You will be pleasantly surprised at how easy it is to collect these 10 pieces of information from a business unit owner. But you will be unpleasantly surprised at the difficulty of collecting same if you have not found the right business owner! In other words, don't necessarily look at the organizational chart and expect that a department head is the right owner of a business unit. That person may be the administrative head, but the *real* owner is someone who not only *takes action*, but has the experience and expertise in the running of the unit.

This is not as unusual as it may sound, nor is it necessarily a problem. There may well be cases, for example, that the vice president of finance is an excellent strategist and an invaluable member of the management team, but it is the controller who is the business unit owner because she knows everything there is to know about it. You need to engage the vice president, be deferential to her, and include her in the process, but roll up your sleeves with the controller by your side.

There are also software applications that you can use to help you with BIA, asset classification, and so on. One important safety tip: Bring your wallet! They tend to be expensive, and frequently part of a bigger business continuity management solution. Don't get me wrong; some of them are excellent, and if the size of your company warrants an enterprise-grade solution, you should look at them. But as far as mid-sized and small-business markets are concerned, at the time of this writing, my recommendation is to stick with my one-spreadsheet-to-rule-them-all solution, which comes next.

## One Spreadsheet to Rule Them All

Start by creating one spreadsheet per business unit. The name of the spreadsheet file itself is the name of the unit. All spreadsheets live in the same directory to make linking easy. Your spreadsheet should look something like Table 6.1.

Each row is taken up by a system owned by the business unit. Owner, Custodian, Location, and Resources can be initials or spelled out. Classification, Criticality, and Impact are numbers 1 through 4. MTD, RPO, RTO are numbers in hours (or minutes, or seconds, depending on the situation; just make sure you're consistent across all spreadsheets).

Additionally, I recommend that you make System, Owner, Custodian, Location, and Resources links to other spreadsheets that contain more granular data, all the way to a single asset. Where do you stop? Wherever it is appropriate for your firm! Remember, no two companies are alike. For example, for one mid-sized company, you may have something that looks like Tables 6.2 through 6.7.

**Table 6.1** Example of Business-Impact Analysis Table

| Asset/ System | Owner | Custo- dian | Loca- tion | Classi- fication: | Criti- cality | Impact | MTD | RPO | RTO | Resour- ces |
|---|---|---|---|---|---|---|---|---|---|---|
| | | | | | | | | | | |

**Table 6.2** Example of Business-Impact Analysis Table for Finance

Spreadsheet name: **FINANCE**

| Asset/ System | Owner | Custo- dian | Loca- tion | Classi- fication: | Criti- cality | Impact | MTD | RPO | RTO | Resour- ces |
|---|---|---|---|---|---|---|---|---|---|---|
| The Books | CM | AM | NY | 3 | 3 | 3 | 40 | 24 | 48 | IT |
| Payroll | CM | AM | NY | 4 | 4 | 4 | 40 | 24 | 48 | IT |
| Time Track | CM | SL | CA | 3 | 4 | 4 | 20 | 8 | 16 | IT |

**Table 6.3** Example of Business-Impact Analysis Table for an Accounting Application

Spreadsheet name: The Books

| Asset/ System | Owner | Custo- dian | Loca- tion | Classi- fication: | Criti- cality | Impact | MTD | RPO | RTO | Resour- ces |
|---|---|---|---|---|---|---|---|---|---|---|
| FIN SERVER | IT | IT | NY | 3 | 3 | 3 | 40 | 24 | 48 | IT |

**Table 6.4** Example of Business-Impact Analysis Table for a Payroll System

Spreadsheet name: Payroll

| Asset/ System | Owner | Custo- dian | Loca- tion | Classi- fication: | Criti- cality | Impact | MTD | RPO | RTO | Resour- ces |
|---|---|---|---|---|---|---|---|---|---|---|
| PAY SERVICE | IT | IT | MO | 4 | 4 | 4 | 40 | 24 | 48 | IT |

**Table 6.5** Example of Business-Impact Analysis Table for a Time Tracking Application

Spreadsheet name: Time Track

| Asset/ System | Owner | Custo- dian | Loca- tion | Classi- fication: | Criti- cality | Impact | MTD | RPO | RTO | Resour- ces |
|---|---|---|---|---|---|---|---|---|---|---|
| TM SERVER | IT | IT | CA | 3 | 4 | 4 | 20 | 8 | 16 | IT |

**Table 6.6** Impact/Criticality Systems Spreadsheet

| Impact/Criticality | Nice to Have | Optional | Essential | Mission- Critical |
|---|---|---|---|---|
| No Impact | Lunch ordering | Online 401K review | Building lease and drawings | |
| Minor Impact | Ad hoc reporting | Expense reports | Travel advance | Inventory control |
| Moderate Impact | Online ticketing | HR appraisals | HR hiring | Financial systems |
| Severe Impact | Policies and procedures | Fixed assets | Payroll | Fulfillment |

Clicking on the second-level spreadsheet's system entries (**FIN SERVER, PAY SERVICE,** and **TM SERVER**) would take you to another spreadsheet that contained the specific information about that system. This could be configuration information, vendor information, warranty information, etc., or contact and account information for the services in use.

**Table 6.7** Systems/Criticality Spreadsheet

| System/Criticality | Nice to Have | Optional | Essential | Mission-Critical |
|---|---|---|---|---|
| System 1 | X | | | |
| System 2 | | X | | |
| System 3 | | | X | |
| System 4 | | | | X |
| System 5 | | | X | |
| System 6 | | | X | |

When you are done, you can choose to combine these spreadsheets into an enterprise-wide one that, instead of listing systems, lists business units. Where do you get the classification, criticality, and impact numbers? That's a bit tricky. Yes, you could theoretically apply a formula based on the individual business units' impact assessments, but you would be off. As I am sure you realize, any one business unit may have one or more systems scoring high on classification, criticality, and impact while the business unit itself would score low at an enterprise level. That is why assigning those numbers is best left to the executive management team and (if necessary) to the board. Your goal for that spreadsheet is to arrive at a prioritization by business unit for business continuity and disaster recovery purposes. This prioritization will filter down to your cybersecurity program work as you tackle the creation of an incident-response plan in case of a cyberattack.

You can also separate out different components of these spreadsheets for easier review and presentation. For example, you can separate out Impact and Criticality by creating an impact-specific spreadsheet per system. That table could look like Table 6.6.

Of course, as much as I wanted to put in *"CEO Blog"* as *"Mission-Critical"* with *"No Impact,"* I was advised against it, and left the entry blank. After all, how many mission-critical systems do you know that have no impact? (The rest of the examples are also to be taken with a grain of salt. Or two. Used only for demonstration purposes. Please don't send hate mail. Thank you.)

Another example of a table you can derive is shown in Table 6.7.

You can derive any combination you need, and many you don't: Criticality by Location, Impact by Asset/System, Resources by MTD. Each one can provide different insight on how to best manage the overall risk to the organization.

There is one more thing left to do. You need to assign a financial value to all of these assets (systems, and others) that you have so painstakingly cataloged, indexed, assessed, inventoried, and reviewed. Typically, this solicits the response: "Good luck with that!" Unfortunately, that won't suffice here. We need to get some sort of valuation in the books.

Now, before you start running for the hills, consider this: We're not really looking for a formal, accounting, audit-proof valuation. Sure, that would be very nice to have (and in some cases required), but we can make do with an informal valuation. You may also ask "Why now?" Why couldn't we do this as we spent all those hours of uninterrupted fun doing the asset classification and business-impact analysis work? Well, the truth is that you *could* do it then, but I recommend that you don't. Instead, I recommend that you take the opportunity to do a presentation of your findings to date to all those involved. This will give you valuable feedback (in case something was missed), and give them a unique view of their world as seen through your eyes. That is when I feel is the best opportunity to talk dollars and cents.

So, corral your business unit owners and executive team and don't let them leave the room until they give you what you need: a number per asset. Some sort of quantifiable dollar value that answers the question: How much is the asset worth to you?

Replacement value is an easy starting point for most executives to grasp. What would it take to replace a particular asset? Think about it holistically: purchase or lease, equipment, licenses, expertise, staff time, the works. It's not that crazy of a calculation, really.

When you're done with the first pass, let's talk damages. What kind? Which assets or units are affected? All? Some? Which contracts? What services? Any products? Any regulatory implications? What about reputation? You should assess those costs as well. For example, your team will know the value of the contracts and the corresponding penalties and losses associated with failure to fulfill. They also will know any regulatory penalties that may ensue as a result of a loss or breach. Finally, you can estimate with the team the cost of rebuilding the firm's reputation when those emails that you called people all sorts of names leak out. You got this!

That's it. Now, you're done. You added the last field on your spreadsheet: Impact, expressed in dollars. Take a well-earned break, and get ready for the next step.

# CHAPTER 7

# Threats

Before we start, we need to briefly review a few key concepts: threat, attack, vector, and payload.

- *Threat* refers to the potential of an agent to cause adverse effects on an asset.
- *Attack* is the realization of a threat.
- *Vector* is the pathway that a threat takes to compromise an asset.
- *Payload* is the actual way that the compromise is effected.

And, as per the wise people at NIST: The threat source (agent) initiates the threat event (attack); the threat event (attack) exploits one or more vulnerabilities that cause adverse impact (you got hacked!); the end result produces organizational risk. And migraines. Painful, splitting migraines.

As we discussed, a cyberthreat has three core attributes: the kind of threat agent, the probability of occurrence, and, of course, its impact. During our threat assessment, our goal is to determine all three attributes on a per-asset basis. To do this, we'll need to know what the assets are (which we have already accomplished), what their value is to us (our definition of impact), who the threat agents might be (the bad people out to get you), their motives, and any pertinent threat intelligence and historical data out there.

Regarding the part about people out to get you: As you recall, anything that is of value to you, is of value to someone else. If it is your personal data that is of value, then yes, in that sense they are after "you." Your digital "you." If it is corporate data that is of higher value, then they're after that. The higher the value, the more attractive the target.

## Types of Threats

Ultimately there are two, and only two, kinds of threats: external and internal.

An external threat originates outside your organization. We have a nice long list of those later in the chapter. An internal one? Well ... remember the

1979 cult classic, *When a Stranger Calls?* That's your best example of an internal threat: *"The call is coming from inside the house!"* Not surprisingly, though, both external and internal threats can and do share the same motives, which include ideology, ego, and money.

What makes an internal threat particularly dangerous is that it has already bypassed your perimeter defense. The attacker is already in the system, and needs only to bypass the internal controls in order to wreak havoc! Internal attackers also know where all the bodies are hidden: in other words, what's of value and what's not. Who are these internal threats? What makes them so dangerous?

## Internal Threats

There is no typical profile for internal threat actors except that they have the *means*, the *motive*, and the *opportunity*. They can be employees, either full-time or part-time. They can be contractors. They may be vendors that require temporary access to your system (e.g., a telephone system vendor). And, God help you if they are "power users" or some sort of "administrators" of systems. Anyone who has access, whether onsite or remote, presents the possibility of an internal threat.

Their means can be many. They can physically exfiltrate the data by removing printouts of sensitive information, even taking pictures of screens with their mobile phones. If they have the right (or wrong!) privileges, they can copy data onto USB drives or transmit data to cloud storage. There have even been cases in which "administrators" removed terabytes of data on removable hard disks!

Motives are equally varied. Internal threats are usually motivated by the same things that motivate external actors, only internal threats have easier access to your systems. Many are motivated by money. Indeed, they may have a pressing need for money for any number of reasons (e.g., family emergency, debt, drugs, etc.). Others may be motivated by ideology (e.g., a disagreement of company or state policies, a sense of right versus wrong, self-righteousness, etc.). Others still may be motivated by personal reasons (e.g., disgruntled employees, various psychopathologies, just "the thrill of it," etc.). They may be recruited by the competition, a nation-state, or any other organization. Or they themselves may be the victims of a crime, such as blackmail. No matter what the motive, they will always find a way to rationalize their actions—be it to save the world, to save a loved one, to save themselves, or because "they deserve it."

There is one exception to the motives list, and that is the accidental insider. Someone who sincerely "didn't know any better" and copied half the database to his private cloud so he could work from home! Or the one who fell for the phishing scam and clicked that link, or answered the fake call from "Microsoft" when that big-bad-red-alert sign popped up while surfing, and so on. Regardless of whether the breach was deliberate or accidental, the damage is very real. But that doesn't mean you should apportion blame in precisely the same way. Yes, you can trace the data exfiltration to accidental credential leakage, but is it really the victim's fault? Is someone whose wallet was stolen responsible for the thief who used the access card? To be sure, a stolen card should be reported it in a timely way ... but in the cyberworld, access is instantaneous. There is no "timely reporting" when you are a victim of social engineering and you click that link! Moreover, shouldn't you be looking closely at your own policies and procedures, your own training protocols, and your data loss prevention systems? I would!

This brings us to the final requirement: opportunity. Internal threat actors, whether intentional or not, require opportunity. How do they get it? If the organization has poor internal controls, that's all the opportunity they'll ever need. What do I mean by "poor internal controls"? The list is long! For example, if the employer has poor onboarding procedures, lax physical security, no training, etc., then the employee may well be able to access data that they shouldn't. Similarly, there may be poor implementation of technical access controls, segregation of duties, even nonexistent data classification. Or the employer may have poorly trained or inexperienced managers in human resource–related matters (e.g., performance reviews, employee behavior monitoring and support, confidential employee help resources, etc.), or be lacking a sophisticated human resource function altogether. Who fits this last profile? The majority of small and mid-sized businesses that are focused—day in, day out—on simple survival. Unfortunately, it is these same businesses that frequently cannot even afford to retain cybersecurity expertise, much less rolling out a data loss prevention system (DLP). They are the firms that need it most.

There are sets of controls that can be deployed against insider threats, accidental or not. For now, we need to focus on the threat itself. How does it manifest? What are the things we need to know about the threat going in? These are similar questions that we need to ask about all threats, but the human element of the insider threat makes this analysis unique.

The first question to ask is how can someone turn an employee into an insider threat? As it goes in the spy novels, so it goes with cybercrime: Nefarious agents turn your employees into assets. How are these employees identified and compromised? What are the signs you need to watch for?

Well, Mr. Bond, you need to think like a criminal to catch one! How would you go about it? You'd identify the weakest links. Employees who are having problems would be on the top of the list, followed by disgruntled ones. How do you identify them? Just monitor their social media! People offer all of this information for free and to all. Someone's getting divorced, someone else has cancer, a third person complains about her boss (you?) .... You'd be amazed what you can learn from people's blogs, Twitter feeds, poorly secured Facebook pages, and so on.

Need to get more sophisticated? Buy the information from any of the major data aggregators. They will gladly sell it, showing everything from credit status to health status and purchase trends.

As we continue to think like our enemy, consider that you must pick your asset wisely. You need someone with enough privileges to get you what you need. Targeting the marketing associate because he just happened to be going through a nasty breakup won't do: You need to target the right asset for the job. Think: Find the privilege, work the motive, ensure the opportunity.

Now, reverse this strategy to protect yourself. Sensitize your employees to abnormal behavior. Is someone who never worked late spending endless nights in the office? Or surfing the file server in areas outside their work scope? Is somebody constantly making backups on USBs or accessing cloud storage? Perhaps somebody with no history of working at home is suddenly accessing the site remotely all the time?

What about an employee who jumped ship from your competitor? Is the person still a bit *too* close with ex-colleagues? Could he or she be a "plant"?

Does an employee seem stressed out of his mind, or exceedingly paranoid of the boss or others? Is someone living large on an associate's salary?

These are just a sampling of behaviors that may be signs of impending trouble. Some of these you can turn into controls by institutionalizing them, for example, access controls, segregation of duties, multifactor authentication, geolocation sensitivity, behavioral patterning. Others are a matter of proper training and sensitivity toward your environment. All are important in managing the insider threat.

## External Threats

According to a recent ISACA estimate, around 40 percent of the threats you may face will be internal, which leaves us with 60 percent coming from the outside. And, just like for their insider counterparts, you'll need all the intelligence about them that you can get. Who are they? What are their motives?

As we discussed in Chapter 3, the main external threat actors have fairly predictable corresponding motives (Table 7.1).

All the preceding are human actors (okay, there is some debate if they represent the *best* of the species, but still ... ), and well within the scope of your cybersecurity program. If you were looking at this from a business continuity or disaster recovery perspective, you would include accidents, and the only nonhuman actor: Mother Nature.

**Table 7.1**  Threat Agents and Motives

| Actor | Motive |
| --- | --- |
| Cybercriminals | Money |
| Online social hackers | Money |
| Cyberspies | Espionage |
| Hacktivists | Activism |
| Cyberfighters | Patriotism |
| Cyberterrorists | Terrorism |
| Script kiddies | Curiosity, thrill, fame, money |

How does motive drive an actor in your case? This question is as simple as recognizing your place in the world.

Are you a country? It's a safe bet that the threat agents are motivated by espionage, terrorism, activism, and right-out warfare. Wouldn't it be fun, for example, for one country to hack another country's elections? Crazy talk, I know, but one can speculate!

Are you a utility or part of the national infrastructure? Same drill! Crippling a utility can cause warfare-scale chaos. Nation-states and cyberterrorists would jump at the opportunity. As (bad) luck would have it, Ukraine's electrical grid suffered just this kind of attack in 2016. It caused all sorts of chaos, as you'd expect, but to our knowledge no fatalities. The culprit? Well, the culprit remains, officially, unknown.

Are you a Fortune 5000, a multinational, or massive conglomerate of some sort or another? You are fair game for espionage, sabotage, extortion, activism, and terrorism.

Are you in health care or education? Then the motive is more than likely data exfiltration for identity theft, and money, although terrorism can't be ruled out, especially in large health-care institutions and major universities.

Everyone else? Show me the money!

There is no specific order based on industry or motive du jour. Clearly money is a major motivating force, with cybercrime expected to fetch upward of two trillion dollars by 2020. For that matter, now that we are in the era of cybercrime-as-a-service, your competitor, or a nasty nation-state, can buy the services of hackers to achieve their ends. They may want to steal your intellectual property, sabotage your operations, or to commit an act of terror—the hackers don't care as long as they get paid.

Given the absence of any other meaningful ranking, let's look at the main motives alphabetically.

*Activism/Terrorism.* This is very tricky. After all, one man's activism is another's terrorism and vice versa. Is Edward Snowden a patriot? A traitor?

An activist? Or a terrorist? What about Julian Assange and WikiLeaks? What about Anonymous? Or what about the Guardians of Peace, who hacked Sony Corporation?

They all framed their actions in some type of social justice narrative, but we don't always know the true motives. In many big hacking cases, experts suspect that lurking behind motives of activism (or terrorism) is a nation-state, terrorist organization, or clandestine service that funds and directs the attacks.

Are you a *likely* target of activists or terrorists? There's actually no easy answer. You need to weigh carefully your industry and your role in the world. Even then, what makes terrorism horrific is that they prey on unsuspecting civilians, who all too frequently pay the ultimate price.

*Espionage.* Tinker, tailor, soldier, spy? No more—those days are over. Today, most acts of espionage, be they corporate- or state-sponsored, are done over the Net. The motives behind espionage have not changed, but the methods have. The type of attack motivated by espionage is typically advanced and persistent. The skill sets involved are many and complex. And the effects, when successful, can be catastrophic for the victims. Are you at risk? If your intellectual property is of value at the international level, then yes. If you are involved in critical infrastructure, communications, energy, or government, then absolutely.

*Money/Extortion.* From internal threats to ransomware to denial-of-service attacks, take your pick, money ranks as the highest motive behind the majority of cyberattacks. The methods are many, the barriers to entry low and getting lower, especially with cybercrime-as-a-service. Are you at risk? One guess: Yes! You are.

*Patriotism.* Whether they are called "resistance fighters" or "commandos," the result is the same: These hacker armies perform what they believe to be their patriotic duty by developing and unleashing sophisticated, advanced, persistent threat-type attacks at "the enemy." Their activities are typically funded—overtly or covertly—by nation-states. If you have any nation-states that consider you the enemy, then, of course, you're at risk. But if you're even perceived to be "working with" or "working for" someone else's enemy, you are also at risk. For example, a small manufacturing facility that makes those pretty camouflage uniforms is definitely on the list.

*Revenge.* It's not business, it's personal—and frequently, very ugly. Hell hath no fury like an employee scorned, or one who is, as Freud might put it, a bit "kooky." Who is at risk? Anyone with employees. In 2016, ISACA ranked insider threats second only to malware. Revenge, by the way, doesn't have to mean destruction of property. It may well mean data exfiltration and sale to your competitor, or leaking it out to the public. Be afraid; be very afraid.

*Trolling/Cyberbullying.* A very dark motive, indeed. These are typically individuals who target other individuals, frequently (but not always) famous or prominent in some way, and deliver attacks designed to besmirch their reputation or cause outrage. There have been cases in which this has jumped from the cyberworld to the physical world, just as there have been cases of cyberbullying among young students with horrifying results. Are you at risk? There is no easy way to tell—worse yet, there aren't many effective controls against a personalized troll attack. If you are in the public eye, and depending on the extent and role, the chances are that you may fall victim of trolling.

*Vanity.* Typically, these are hackers who want to make, or maintain, their name and status in the media. Their goal is fame and notoriety. Their targets are not picked based on some ideology, although they may claim otherwise. The target is picked on their potential for making news, or some real or perceived hacker challenge. Are you at risk? It depends on your visibility as a business or institution, or—worse—personal fame. If your company or its staff is frequently in the spotlight, you should expect to attract vanity-driven hackers.

*Warfare/Sabotage.* Stuxnet was the first and best-known cyberweapon, used against Iran's nuclear facility, but there is little doubt that there are many more just like it in the arsenal of most nation-states. The Ukrainian infrastructure, for example, was another victim of such an attack in December 2016. Obviously, these are acts executed by well-funded, state-sponsored and -controlled hacker armies. You are at risk if you're in any business supporting critical infrastructure, and, of course, if you are working in any government institution.

## Threat Rankings

Your next task is to rank the preceding list in terms of which actors and motives are most likely to be engaged in your world. You have a good sense of your assets, both at the enterprise level and at the business unit level, so spend some time and think: Who on this list is the most likely agent for an attack? Assign a numerical value from 1 to 4, ranging from "least likely" to "somewhat likely" to "very likely" to "extremely likely." Regarding my bias and recommendations, I'd consider the insider as a very likely agent, and money or extortion as the primary motive.

You now have an understanding of the threat agents and their motives as they might apply to your organization. This is an excellent first step, but you're far from finished. Knowing the *who* and the *why* of cyberattacks is not enough. You also need to know the *how* and the *when*.

First, the *how*. One of the best places to look for this type of information is the European Union Agency for Network and Information Security (ENISA). They have been putting together an annual threat landscape and

**Table 7.2** ENISA Table: Overview and Comparison of Cyberthreat Landscapes 2015 and 2014

| Top Threats 2014 | Top Threats 2015 | Change in Ranking |
|---|---|---|
| 1. Malicious code: Worms/Trojans | 1. Malware | Same |
| 2. Web-based attacks | 2. Web-based attacks | Same |
| 3. Web application/ Injection attacks | 3. Web application attacks | Same |
| 4. Botnets | 4. Botnets | Same |
| 5. Denial of service | 5. Denial of service | Same |
| 6. Spam | 6. Physical damage/theft/loss | Increasing |
| 7. Phishing | 7. Insider threat (malicious/accidental) | Increasing |
| 8. Exploit kits | 8. Phishing | Decreasing |
| 9. Data breaches | 9. SPAM | Decreasing |
| 10. Physical damage/ theft/loss | 10. Exploit kits | Decreasing |

trends report since 2012. At this stage in your process, this is required reading. The reports are excellent, succinct, and easily understood by both executives and cyberprofessionals alike. At the time of this writing, the most recent report was the 2015 edition, published in January 2016. In it, ENISA ranks the top 15 threats and compares them year over year with 2014. The top 10 are shown in Table 7.2.

These reports and others like them offer you an understanding of what were the prevalent *hows* in the previous year. You can extrapolate from that (who was at play last year, using which tool?) and make reasonable assumptions and decisions that will affect your choice and tuning of your cybercontrols. What these reports do not give you is a sense of what is happening right now.

You need the *when*.

# Threat Intelligence

To get that information, you will need real-time threat intelligence. This intelligence will provide you with clues about the types of likely payloads and who is currently using them. For example:

- What kind of malware has just been released?
- What new vulnerabilities have been discovered, and what's being done to address them?
- What attacks are in progress?
- What's the current buzz on the dark web?

Threat intelligence will also gather information from inside your organization and provide insight on everything from the state of equipment to who is accessing what, when, any abnormal behavior and traffic, etc.

As you can imagine, the amount of data involved in threat intelligence is massive. Moreover, processing and making sense of the threat intelligence data requires expertise and dedication. Someone in your staff with cybersecurity and technology training needs to be charged with making sense of the data and providing the necessary feedback and recommendations.

Doing this involves threat intelligence tools and feeds (both private and public). I highly recommend picking one of the top-tier vendors, installing (or subscribing to) their solution, and dedicating the right personnel to monitor and advise. Otherwise, you may find yourself trying to empty the ocean one teaspoonful at a time.

If you really want to take a crack at threat intelligence on your own, you will find many places with public feeds.

- LookingGlass Threat Map: https://map.lookingglasscyber.com
- AlienVault's Open Threat Exchange: https://otx.alienvault.com
- Threat Intelligence Review's Cybersecurity Intelligence Feed Reviews: http://threatintelligencereview.com

Furthermore, most cybersecurity vendors produce free threat intelligence reports on a regular basis. For example:

- CISCO's Security Advisories and Alerts:
  https://tools.cisco.com/security/center/publicationListing.x#~Threats
- McAfee's Threat Center:
  http://www.mcafee.com/au/threat-center.aspx
- Symantec's Security Response:
  https://www.symantec.com/security_response
- Bitdefender's E-Threats Landscape Reports:
  http://www.bitdefender.com/site/view/e-threats_reports.html

If a formal threat intelligence solution is not appropriate to your size company, then, at a minimum, I recommend that you review these reports on a regular basis.

## Threat Modeling

Is there some sort of organized methodology for all this? You bet! In fact, threat-risk modeling is a vast discipline. It's PhD-level stuff, with some of the best and brightest minds in risk management, cybersecurity, and technology working on it day and night. The following is a very, very small sampling of their work.

- Several years back, Microsoft developed STRIDE to replace their older threat classification DREAD. DREAD stood for: *Damage Potential*, *Reproducibility*, *Exploitability*, *Affected Users*, and *Discoverability*. But STRIDE stands for *Spoofing* (of a user's identity), *Tampering*, *Repudiation*, *Information disclosure*, *Denial of Service* and *Elevation of privilege*.
- TRIKE, which doesn't stand for anything in particular, is an open-source threat-modeling tool created by Brenda Larcom and Eleanor Saitta. Their claim to fame is its granular, risk-based approach. TRIKE's great spreadsheet and help file are free to download from octotrike.org.
- Carnegie Mellon University's Software Engineering Institute, in collaboration with CERT, developed OCTAVE, which is currently considered to be one of the best threat-modeling frameworks and toolsets. OCTAVE comes in three sizes: the original OCTAVE for large enterprises, OCTAVE-S for smaller companies, and OCTAVE Allegro, which is a narrower, information-asset-focused version.

When it comes to the total universe of frameworks, tools, and resources available for threat analysis, this list doesn't even begin to scratch the surface. The subject matter is vast, and unless you are at a minimum a cybersecurity professional—or better yet, a threat researcher—you can quickly become overwhelmed. Even the well-meaning, beautifully curated open-source community sites with the latest threat intelligence can quickly make you feel like you're trying to drink from a fire hose.

So, what do you do? Take it a step at a time, use the resources at your disposal appropriately, and trust yourself.

I am hoping that by now I don't need to tell you that threat assessments are dynamic: What is a threat today may be moot tomorrow. You need to remain vigilant in your efforts to stay current with what is going on in cyberspace. Money and effort spent to protect yourself from one threat must be redirected to protect you from the new threats that have surfaced.

Cybersecurity will never be something you can do once and forget. It must always be present in your thinking and your planning. Much as we consider healthy living to include proper nutrition and exercise, good cyberliving includes proper cybersecurity practices.

Both are a way of life.

# CHAPTER 8

## Vulnerabilities

A s we've discussed, the ugly truth about vulnerabilities is that every system has them! Every single one. And we're not just talking about a couple of issues here and there. Think thousands upon thousands, with more being discovered every day. Our goal is to identify the ones applicable to our environment and deal with them. To do that, we'll need a list.

So, off we go searching for vulnerabilities listings. It should be no surprise that one of the first entries that comes up is NIST's National Vulnerability Database (NVD). At the time of this writing, the NVD contained the following information.

- 79,261 CVE vulnerabilities (CVE: Common vulnerabilities and exposures from MITRE, a nonprofit that operates several R&D centers)
- 368 Checklists (Detailed guidance on operating and application security settings)
- 249 US-CERT Alerts (U.S. Computer Emergency Readiness Team)
- 4,455 US-CERT Vuln notes (U.S. Computer Emergency Readiness Team Vulnerability Notes)
- 10,286 OVAL Queries (Another MITRE-coordinated effort on standardizing reporting on machine states for computers)
- 115,051 CPE Names (Common platform enumeration: A structured naming methodology for information technology assets)

## Who Is Who in Vulnerabilities Tracking

Keep working the list and you'll run into all the usual suspects: MITRE, OWASP, CERT, and several security vendors. The situation can quickly become confusing and overwhelming. If you thought threat assessment was a bear, welcome to vulnerability assessments!

It is worth your while to understand the sources of vulnerabilities data because you will need to refer to them as you apply them to your specific business.

Before we take the plunge, let's make sure we know what we are looking at. What exactly are these vulnerabilities? It's useful to refer back to NIST's definition once more: *Vulnerabilities are weakness in an information system, system security procedures, internal controls, or implementation that could be exploited or triggered by a threat source.*

The good news is that the vulnerabilities you need to be concerned about are limited to your world and your world only. In other words, we care only about your information system, system security procedures, internal controls, or implementations, not the universe of vulnerabilities out there. You have enough headaches as it is! More good news is that since you've done your asset classification, you know exactly which systems and so on need to be tested against known vulnerabilities.

Of course, *your world* is a rather expansive term, one whose boundaries you'll need to decide ahead of time. Think about the now-famous hacking of Target in late 2013—the largest hack of a retail company to date. What's important for our purposes here is that it wasn't the *actual* Target systems that were hacked. It was instead a Target vendor that was compromised—a so-called trusted partner. The question therefore is: What constitutes Target's cybersecurity world? If you answered, "Their own systems *plus* all the vendor partner systems," you get a cookie! You are correct!

The problem is, doing a vulnerability assessment on such an expansive definition of my world becomes impossible, not to mention legally tricky. For example: Do you, as a procuring organization, have the right to test the seller's systems? It depends on (a) what you are buying and (b) how good your lawyers are. What if you are buying *something-as-a-service?* What kind of vulnerability testing can you reasonably demand? Again, those are very tricky conversations.

What most organizations have settled on, and my recommended approach, is for the buyer to do the following: First, request that the seller complies with a reasonable cybersecurity operational standard (e.g., "Have you implemented *<insert your favorite standard here>* in your organization?"); and second, demand the right to audit the vendor.

Whether you have the right to audit or not can be a matter of dispute. For example, what if the vendor serves multiple clients, some of which may be your competitors? If you have the right to audit, the other clients may object on the grounds of data confidentiality. You could descend into a legal rabbit hole defining exactly what system you'll audit, how you'll audit, and so on, but you get the picture.

*Audit* is a five-letter word that is best used sparingly and with profound respect. Fortunately, there are workarounds. For example, you may be able to demand the results of an independent audit as opposed to performing one yourself.

How do you decide which vulnerabilities apply to your world? You start by matching your systems to known vulnerabilities. You know your systems. Now, you need to find the list of applicable known vulnerabilities.

What about the unknown ones, you ask?

## Zero-Day Exploits

Obviously, you can't test against an unknown vulnerability any more that you can vaccinate against an unknown virus. But, just like in medicine, you can monitor your systems closely for any signs of abnormal behavior and respond accordingly. Most importantly? You are not alone in this! Thousands of dedicated cybersecurity professionals and cybersecurity companies make it their mission in life to scan for-as-yet unknown vulnerabilities, publish them, and recommend patches or mitigating controls.

Referencing back to our cybersecurity primer, you'll remember that *zero day* refers to nasty little bugs that exploit vulnerabilities in existing systems that are known only to the hacker. So, your goal with zero day exploits is simple: Stay alert, stay informed, and have in place a defense-in-depth strategy that protects your organization as much as is practical.

The choice of the word *practical* here is key. It's not about protecting your organization to the outer limit of what technology allows—that would not be necessarily appropriate to your risk appetite. It is always about deploying protection in a practical and pragmatic way.

The first step is to use your asset classification to determine which type of vulnerabilities may apply. At a top level, you should be able to place your assets into the following buckets:

*Operating Systems:* These systems drive your hardware. They can be manufacturer-specific, like Apple's and Microsoft's, or they can be open-source based like LINUX. Operating system conversation and choices can be extremely polarizing and I advise you to avoid them like the plague. The thing you need to know is which ones are deployed in your organization. Leave the question of which one is better to be debated by the corresponding high priests of each tech religion. If you are interested in market share of operating systems, browsers, search engines, platforms, etc., I recommend you visit the Global Stats site (http://gs.statcounter. com)—a free website of statistics happiness.

*Servers:* These are essentially applications that host (or enable) other applications. For example, database servers or web servers. You will need to know how many, what kind, the manufacturer, version, etc. Remember the one spreadsheet to rule them all from Chapter 6? If you have gone granular enough, all this information will be in it.

*Applications:* These run either directly off the operating system (like a word processor), or in combination of operating system and some server (like a website). For example, your accounting system is running both on an operating system, using a database server, and is itself an application for which you need to know all the fun stuff we've been cataloging (manufacturer, version, etc.).

*Services:* When will the fun stop? It stops with services. Those are any services that your company consumes from a third party. It could be storage. It could be infrastructure. It could be anything-as-a-service. And, yes, you need to know about it in as much detail as possible. In the case of as-a-service you will need to consult the agreements you have with the vendors, as well as contact their cybersecurity personnel to determine what their baseline posture is. Assuming you're dealing with a reputable vendor, they will be able to provide you with all the documentation you need.

## Vulnerabilities Mapping

With your spreadsheet in hand, you will now research and develop a current known vulnerability list for each of the four buckets. To do this, you will need to consult with the following amazing, free, and hard-to-imagine-anything-more-useful services:

*MITRE.* According to their website:

> *The MITRE Corporation is a not-for-profit company that operates multiple federally funded research and development centers (FFRDCs). We provide innovative, practical solutions for some of our nation's most critical challenges in defense and intelligence, aviation, civil systems, homeland security, the judiciary, health care, and cybersecurity.*

I am here to testify that yes, they do, and I am one of their biggest fans! One of their many projects is the Common Vulnerabilities and Exposures Details website at https://www.cvedetails.com. This is an amazing tool, in which you can search by vulnerability, product, vendor, or anything else you can imagine and get meaningful, up-to-the-minute, actionable information. For example, searching for Microsoft SQL Server will return a table by year, number of vulnerabilities, type, etc., all of which are links to more specific information. So, in the same example, if you click on year 2015 "Code Execution" vulnerabilities, you will get two of them: *CVE-2015-1763*, and *CVE-2015-1762*. Clicking the second one, you'll get all the details about a remote code execution vulnerability for the specific product, and what to do to mitigate it. What's not to love?

*The National Vulnerability Database (NVD).* If you thought MITRE was hot, you haven't seen NVD yet! Originally the brainchild of the National

Institute of Standards and Technology's (NIST) Computer Security Division, these days the NVD is brought to you by your friends at the Department of Homeland Security's National Cybersecurity Division. According to them, *The National Vulnerability Database (NVD) is the U.S. government repository of standards-based vulnerability management data represented using the Security Content Automation Protocol (SCAP). This data enables automation of vulnerability management, security measurement, and compliance. The NVD includes security checklists, security-related software flaws, misconfigurations, product names, and impact metrics.*

When you visit their website (https://nvd.nist.gov) and click on the Vulnerability Search Engine link, you'll have a very powerful research tool at your disposal. For example, entering the *CVE-2015-1762* vulnerability from our previous example, you will get a detailed report including description, impact, and references to advisories, solutions, and tools, to say nothing about all the technical details you can eat. Personally? You had me at *References to Advisories, Solutions, and Tools*.

*OWASP.* Last, but not least, we have the *Open Web Application Security Project.* OWASP is an international open community *dedicated to enabling organizations to conceive, develop, acquire, operate, and maintain applications that can be trusted. All of the OWASP tools, documents, forums, and chapters are free and open to anyone interested in improving application security.* Their claim to fame is the periodic publication of the OWASP Top 10 most critical web application security risks.

It is not only an incredibly useful and actionable tool, but it has also significantly contributed to cybersecurity awareness among developers, and computer professionals as a whole. You will find this and many other tools and guidance at their website: https://www.owasp.org. Entries for their 2017 OWASP Top 10 2017 release candidates have the perennial favorites of Injection, Broken Authentication and Session Management, and Cross-Site Scripting, adding two new ones: the Insufficient Attack Protection, and Underprotected APIs.

Is that it? Are these three sources all there is? Not even close. There are many more sources and resources out there for vulnerability research. Many are free; some are subscription-based. The three listed here are simply a good start: They are all free and they will suffice for most organizations' vulnerability identification needs. The trick to all this is vigilance. Like all things cybersecurity, this means you do it once and recheck at regular intervals. How regular? It depends on your systems and assets: No two companies are the same.

Having identified and mapped the known vulnerabilities to your systems, the next step is remediation. Known vulnerabilities have, thankfully, known remediation steps. If you can, follow them to the letter!

Why did I say, "*If* you can"? Crazy as it may sound, you may not be able to plug a known vulnerability, because some application or workflow may actually depend on it. Now, you have a real problem: You know you're vulnerable, and you also know you can't fix it. What do you do? You apply controls around the known vulnerability to mitigate the risk until such time as the genius who wrote the application that depends on the vulnerability issues a fix.

Following your vulnerability remediation is to confirm them as fixed. Your next step, therefore, is to perform a vulnerability test.

This is not to be confused with a penetration test, or "pen test" for short. A pen test, simply put, is a simulated cyberattack against your systems or company. Pen tests are used to assure that a cybersecurity program is working as intended. A vulnerability test, on the other hand, is a diagnostic test that will help in the development of your program.

## Vulnerability Testing

Best practice, and my strong recommendation, is to retain a reputable third-party vendor to run vulnerability tests on your behalf. They would get the list of your assets and create sets of tests to check against all known vulnerabilities against those assets. Once done, the vendor will present you with a list of holes you need to plug.

A typical vulnerability test follows the steps discussed here:

1. *The vulnerability test vendor will use your asset classification work as input:* This is a critical step, and it's where the quality of your earlier work gets to shine. The more detailed and prioritized it is, the easier this step becomes. For example, if your list of systems and assets is long, you may be forced to prioritize and segment the test. You will do this based on the criticality of systems and assets that you established earlier on. I strongly recommend that you test all systems, but I do understand that time and budgets may force a tiered testing approach. That's fine, insofar as you don't make the mistake of thinking that the least important system doesn't need the test. In their attempts to be frugal, too many firms approach cybersecurity like it's the Maginot Line—France's "impenetrable" defense against Germany that didn't extend along the Brussels border, enabling the Nazis to simply go around it. That is exactly what hackers hope you'll do with your security. So even if you can't test everything at once, make sure you do test everything eventually. Otherwise, attackers will simply go around your hardened systems and compromise the least important one, using it as a staging point.

2. *Compare the list of assets against known vulnerabilities:* With the assets prioritized, the tester will use external resources to match each asset to known vulnerabilities of that asset. For example, one question might be: "What are the known vulnerabilities for the asset, Windows Server 2008?" There are automated applications that do these comparisons, making life easier for all. Nevertheless, that doesn't absolve you, or the tester, from double-checking that work, especially on all critical assets. You want to make sure that any automated system is picking up the most up-to-date vulnerability list, and does so from multiple sources and feeds.

3. *Test each asset against its identified vulnerabilities:* This can get tricky. In some cases, testing for the vulnerabilities is as easy as making sure that a security patch has been applied, or the system is running the most current version of software. In other cases, you may need to take the system offline and check the underlying hardware for one specific vulnerability or another. Either way, you'll need the help of at least two technical experts: the vendor performing the test and your in-house (or outsourced) IT team. Both must be in alignment about the goals, the methodology, and the end result. A critical thing to remember here is to avoid pointing any fingers at the asset's custodians (e.g., the IT team). You need to look at this exercise dispassionately—you simply need to know the truth of the matter—but also with empathy toward the people charged with supporting the asset. Think of a patient going for a CAT scan: The radiologists are not there to judge whether you smoked or not. They want to perform a test and get a result. Even in an adverse diagnosis, one should never berate the patient. What's done is done. The goal after the diagnosis is only to apply the cure and the lessons learned.

4. *Recommend specific steps to either eliminate or mitigate vulnerabilities:* The results of the vulnerability tests tend to be fairly black and white: Either the asset is vulnerable or it is not. If it is, then you hope that there is a clear path to eliminating the vulnerability. Like we discussed earlier, that may not always be the case, and the reasons may surprise you. There may not be a fix available for the vulnerability…*yet.* The manufacturer or developer may be currently working on it. A worse situation is if your system is no longer supported and there are no plans to fix the vulnerability (but in this case you might well wonder what you're doing running an antique!). Another common problem is when the vulnerability does in fact have a fix, but if you apply it, your systems downstream may not work properly. The list goes on and on, but the good news here is that you have an answer: You either fix the vulnerability or you take mitigating action. Be aware, however, that the answer may be different for each vulnerable asset.

## Prioritizing Vulnerability Remediation

Managing your vulnerabilities can feel like shoveling snow in the middle of a blizzard: Get the list of assets; research the vulnerabilities; plug the vulnerabilities; test the fix ... start all over again. Because no matter how diligent you are, there will always be new ones that are discovered designed to make your life miserable.

The failure to keep up with vulnerability assessments is one of the most common problems I see as a consultant. It is boring work. It is overwhelming. It is constantly changing. And, for many firms, the job is just not as big a priority as it should be. I know many good technologists who may well be aware of a vulnerability on a server but hesitate to apply the vendor patch. They are oftentimes worried that something else may break downstream and, all of a sudden, what is a half-hour job turns into a two-day crisis.

I understand the hesitation but I can't excuse it. According to White Hat Security, in 2016, the average vulnerability age—meaning how long the vulnerability has been around—was 339 days! And yet the average remediation rate is a paltry 42 percent. And the time to fix? 117 days! That is almost four months *after* someone knew about a vulnerability. And, that's just in the banking industry, which is supposed to be tight and regulated!

The excuses are many: overworked staffs, underfunded departments, competing priorities.... I've heard them all, and I believe them. Most cybersecurity professionals and most IT shops are truly overworked, underfunded, and drowning in competing priorities. Unfortunately, that is not likely to change anytime soon. We therefore need to reprioritize vulnerability assessment and remediation. It truly represents relatively low-hanging fruit, and we are leaving it to rot on the branch because we're too busy to go get the stepstool?

My recommendation is that you engage with your IT department (be it in-house or outsourced) and make sure that vulnerability identification and remediation, along with frequent testing, is someone's explicit responsibility. You should further insist on a monthly report that shows you the vulnerability status per system, and the remediation timeline. It is silly for us to be trying to secure the fort if someone keeps leaving the side entrance unlocked!

Speaking of locks, those are controls! The time has come for us to take a real close look at controls: how to select them, how to deploy them, and how to manage them.

# CHAPTER 9

## Environments

I use the term *environments* to mean three things:

1. *Computing Environments.* There are four basic types:
   a. *On-premises* or *onsite* (the servers are in your office).
   b. *Private cloud* (the servers are in someone else's building, but you have the only key to your own private office in that building).
   c. *Public cloud* (the servers are in someone else's office, many people have keys to that building, and you don't have a private office there).
   d. *Hybrid cloud* (the servers are all over the place. Some in your private office, some elsewhere in the building).
2. *The Internet of Things (IoT).* For our purposes, IoT means every device that is connected to the Internet, regardless of its location or function—from nanny cams to SCADA (supervisory control and data acquisition) systems. If it's not part of our standard endpoint definition (computers, phones, tablets) but it's connected to the Internet, it's IoT.
3. *Distributed Workforces.* I like huddling over a good watercooler conversation as much as the next person, but modern workspaces seem to be doing away with the concept of the "office." More and more people are taking advantage of the Internet to collaborate from locations all over the world. Sometimes, these arrangements mirror employer–employee relationships. Other times it's a collection of freelancers coming together for a project. The fact is, the way we work is changing in a fundamental way, and the way we view cybersecurity over a distributed workforce needs to reflect this new and dynamic environment.

Each of these environments will have different cybersecurity needs, so let's take a closer look at each environment in turn.

## On-Premises (Onsite) Computing Environments

Most people are familiar with an on-premises computing environment. Depending on company size, this is basically your typical business office with a server room. These server rooms range in size from a cramped, dusty closet, to a large, raised-floor, air conditioned, fireproofed data center. The commonality is that the server room is in the same physical space where the information technology services are being consumed. That said, a larger company with multiple buildings will still be considered to have an on-premises environment if they house their data center in one of their own buildings, despite distributing the services to multiple others, potentially across cities and countries.

On-premises environments afford you total control. You control access, you control what equipment is deployed, what software is installed, how the infrastructure is monitored, etc. It's all yours, no questions asked. If you want to decommission a server, you go right ahead. If you want to install a new firewall, knock yourself out! If you want to let your six-year-old kid bike around the environmentally controlled room, you can do that, too. Of course, total control comes with the corresponding price-tag. More than just dollars, euros, or yen, the price-tag also reflects the responsibility of maintaining this infrastructure from an IT point of view (installations, management, maintenance, etc.) and, of course, protecting it.

Ay, there's the rub! Yes, you have total control on how you can protect the equipment, and as such you can be sure that it is always safe and sound, with the best and most appropriate controls at all times. But on the other hand, you're paying for all this infrastructure and associated headaches—including the likelihood of underutilizing your technology during a downturn, not to mention the challenges of scaling it up during a rapid growth cycle. If you're a businessperson, you'll loathe both the expense and rigidity. If you're a cybersecurity professional, you'll probably love it. But! If you're an IT professional with vision—one who recognizes that you always need to align technology with business goals—then you will always recommend that choices about IT architecture align with business goals as much as possible … even if that meant you'd miss looking at the blinking green lights of a traditional server room.

So, is an on-premises computing environment worth the headaches? How to decide? And who decides?

Remember, this entire book is based on this question: "What's it worth to you?" The only people who can answer that question are the business owners or their legal representatives. No one else. Not IT. Not cybersecurity.

IT must inform and advise on how best to generate value for the company by aligning with its business goals. Cybersecurity must inform and advise on risk and how best to protect company assets. The business will evaluate and adopt the most suitable IT strategy, and accept the appropriate risk. If that means 100 percent on-premises, that's what it will be, and if that means 100 percent carrier pigeons, so be it!

## Private-Cloud Computing Environments

Whatever its downsides (and there are more than a few!), an on-premises computing environment does provide IT professionals with lots of something they simply adore: control! Once you switch to cloud environments, that control starts to fade away, and that can make some IT folks nervous. One of the ways to talk a cybersecurity professional off the ledge when you're discussing the cloud is to promise that you'll be moving the IT infrastructure into a private cloud. What that means is the infrastructure will at least be located inside a dedicated, secure, access-controlled, and likely ISO-certified data center, and only you and your team will have access to it.

Private clouds try to deliver the benefits of scalability and on-demand provisioning of a public cloud solution while maintaining the sense of ownership and control of an onsite architecture. In other words, private clouds attempt to deliver the public-cloud advantages, but they do so in an exclusive way for your organization. You are still responsible to maintain the resulting IT services footprint, just as you are responsible for protecting it, but now you have the advantage of not actually owning the infrastructure. You are, in essence, leasing on demand whatever it is you need at any one time. You can provision and deprovision as much and as often as you like, thereby gaining the flexibility that on-premises infrastructure denies while maintaining the tight control that a highly secure or mission-critical infrastructure demands.

It is important to note here that you should not think of a private-cloud infrastructure as a bunch of dedicated physical computers. Although that may be a possibility, it is unlikely. The probability is that your private-cloud solution will be virtually delivered to your company just as with a public cloud, but with one key difference: The delivery of this infrastructure-as-a-service is done through proprietary, dedicated, single-tenant pipes, in essence creating a physical separation tenant-to-tenant.

When you're running a private cloud, much like running your own on-premises infrastructure, you are entirely responsible for your private cloud's security needs. It's all you. Essentially, what you have gained is the flexibility of cloud infrastructure-as-a-service and perhaps software-as-a-service while you have retained total control over cybersecurity. If that's worth it to you, then great! The answer lies in aligning business goals to IT value delivery, and nowhere else. If that alignment results in a private-cloud implementation, then cybersecurity will step up to the plate and protect it.

The catch is, of course, that any cloud choice, private, public, or hybrid, will introduce additional cybersecurity considerations to any on-premises infrastructure. For example, before you even contemplate procuring the service, you'll need to make sure that the provider of your private cloud is in compliance with several standards. These include all the usual suspects like CSA STAR, HIPAA, ISO27001, PCI-DSS, SAS-70, SOC-3, and TRUSTe, to name a few. If you must pick one certification, you should pick Cloud Security Alliance's STAR certification (it integrates ISO27001 with their own cloud controls matrix CCM). CSA STAR comes in three flavors: a level-one self-attestation, a level-two certification, and the in-development level-three continuous monitoring implementation. Then, once you have that, you can investigate additional requirements like Privacy Shield (if you're concerned with the European Union's General Data Protection Regulation (GDPR), which you should be), PCI, or HIPAA.

## Public-Cloud Computing Environments

The very idea of a public cloud makes most cybersecurity professionals hyperventilate. Sure, there are tons of certifications, the marketplace is maturing, there are appropriate controls, and so on and so forth, but we're talking risk-minded computer scientists. No matter what you say, for them the risk is just too much. Why is it too much? Because, we're not a trusting folk! In a public cloud, cybersecurity is the responsibility of the provider, and, simply put, we don't trust them. Some will call this paranoid and inappropriate. We call it prudent. Go figure!

So, how can we all get along here? For one, you (as the acting cybersecurity executive) should fully understand the provider's policies and controls across several key variables: What are their privacy policies? Where are they compliant and where are they not? What are the issues with global data flow? And what is their transparency policy?

You should insist that your cloud-solution provider be able to articulate, demonstrate, and make available to you for audit-on-demand their security strategy, their controls, their business continuity and disaster recovery plans, staffing expertise and security clearances (including background-check policies), staff training and certifications, cloud facility certifications and past audit results, their incident-response plan, and communications policies. If they comply, then we're good. If they don't, then the risk is yours to accept or not. What is that risk?

There are a few. If you don't know how your data is actually protected, then you may also not know if it has been stolen or altered until it is too late. Or, consider the fact that since you're in a public cloud, an attacker may be targeting your roommate and trash your servers in the process. Or, imagine that another tenant is hacked, but the landlord chooses not to communicate this fact to you (or anyone else), because it is not in their best interest to expose the breach. And so on and so forth.

There are also serious technical considerations that you will need assurances on: issues such as co-tenancy, parallel processing, and process-memory segregation. We don't need to get into the weeds with this stuff here—that's why you should retain a cloud security certified professional. Suffice it to say that since everyone is in the same pool, you want to make sure that if the kid in the corner has an accident, you don't end up swimming in it!

## Hybrid-Cloud Computing Environments

You already have a hybrid cloud, even though you may not be formally acknowledging it. I think I am safe in assuming that everyone in your organization has some sort of a smartphone or tablet. If so, they are already using the cloud whether you like it or not. All these devices typically connect to the cloud for backup and storage. If your users are using these for corporate email, it is possible that, it, too, is stored in the cloud. Of course, one can apply strict controls to all this, but then you're starting a war you can't win: a losing war with shadow IT.

Shadow IT is defined as any information technology solution employed by your users that has not been approved nor is it maintained by your IT department—hence the shadow. Shadow IT frequently results from user frustration with the rigidity of IT and their approved solutions. So, the users, in an effort to be more efficient, faster, or seeking ease of use and convenience, will open up a Dropbox account, or use a work or private email address to bypass organizational controls that they perceive as onerous.

Smart organizations recognize this and get in front of it by training the users and allowing some (if not all) of the flexibility that this "IT on demand" allows. It's all about training and control. To the degree that the users understand the risk and the implications, and to the degree that appropriate controls are in place, let them go forth and conquer! Who knows? They may discover a solution that disrupts the company for the better, and that solution becomes the adopted standard. But they can also discover the pits of Hell, which is why the controls are there so that only a few users get scorched and the organization as a whole remains unharmed.

This brings us to the more conscious choice of a hybrid-cloud solution. The typical scenario is one in which a set of applications cannot be delivered over the cloud, requiring local infrastructure, while other sets can. Equally common is to see an on-premise private cloud–public cloud deployment.

That's the ultimate hybrid! What does that look like? You have a set of applications that must be on-premises (let's say, for example, your accounting system). You have a data application that you need to scale on demand, and that's on a private cloud. You also have the company email coming from a public-cloud provider. There you go! Full-bore hybrid!

The security considerations, of course, don't change much. But they are additive. You need to make sure that each one of these environments is addressed properly, has its own cybersecurity strategy and controls, and is assessed regularly. You know all about the on-premises requirements, and now you have some sense of what you need to look at for both public and private clouds. Put them all in the mix, and you've got yourself the hybrid-cloud cybersecurity considerations.

Before we wrap up our computing environments review, I would like you to consider two things: First, evaluating a *cloud* solution is not about evaluating a *technology* solution. You're evaluating a business solution. The work you need to do to satisfy yourself on its fit and applicability is closer to a business acquisition due diligence issue than a technology assessment.

Second, it is highly probable that as you're starting down your cybersecurity journey, one or more cloud solutions will already be in place. Now, we are adding not just a business due diligence exercise, but an asset discovery one as well. There's data up in those clouds! And you need to discover them and treat them like the valuable assets they are.

## CLOUD SECURITY QUESTIONS

Our friends at ENISA have a wonderful publication that can help you with the first part: *ENISA's Cloud Security Guide for SMEs—Cloud computing security risks and opportunities for SMEs—April 2015*. I urge you to download and read it. There you will find an appendix labeled: *E.3 Security Questions Form*.

Their questions, repeated here but edited by me, should be your go-to in getting a sense of where your cloud provider stands:

1. How does the cloud provider manage network and information security risks?
2. Which security tasks are carried out by the provider, and which type of security incidents are mitigated by the provider?

3. How does the cloud service respond to natural disasters affecting data centers or connections?
4. How does the provider ensure that personnel work securely?
5. How is the physical and logical access to customer data or processes protected?
6. How do you ensure software security?
7. How is the physical and logical access to customer data or processes protected?
8. Which national legislation or foreign jurisdictions are involved—for example, because of the physical location of data centers or cables?

It's important to not fall in love with the provider's promises. Stay vigilant. If you don't like the provider's answers, look for a different provider.

When it comes to understanding what's already out there, you need to use all the asset discovery and classification skills that you already learned in our Assets chapter. You'll need to engage with stakeholders, identify the assets, understand the corresponding workflows, and document the full life cycle of the assets. What services are being used on the assets? Where from? Who controls them? Who monitors for incidents? What's the reporting like? What happens in regard to business continuity and disaster recovery? Who are the asset's custodians? Who's responsible for compliance? Who's responsible for any cross-border issues? And so on. By now, you're an old hand at this!

## The Internet of Things (IoT)

In July 2016, *Business Insider* predicted that by 2020 there will be 34 billion devices connected to the Internet, with a corresponding six-trillion-dollar spend. In the business world, the primary drivers of this expansion will be operating efficiency and increased productivity. Meanwhile, a day doesn't go by when you don't read about the new smart home or smart office, the new smart cities, the connected cars, and, of course, the wearables like FitBit, Garmin, Apple Watch, and the like.

Why is this important to you in our cybersecurity context? Because if you have a smart thermostat in your office that is connected to your network and the device is not secure, then you might as well leave the door unlocked with a big neon sign welcoming anyone in.

The unfortunate reality is that these devices crept into corporate use while no one was looking. Certainly, the cybersecurity department wasn't informed that a smart refrigerator was being plugged in at the company cafeteria. IT wasn't notified, either. Why would they be, right? Somebody at facilities spoke with the vendor and gave the vendor the Wi-Fi password, and they were razzle-dazzled by the pretty colors on the refrigerator's screen.

Given their pervasiveness, IoT devices represent a clear and present danger to your cybersecurity program. You will need to follow a rigorous set of steps to make sure IoT doesn't come back to haunt you later. Namely:

- *Extensive inventory of all IoT devices.* You'll need to get with both IT and relevant departments (for example, facilities, security, audiovisual, and so forth) and go through every device that is Internet-enabled. What do they do? Why are they there? And, of course, where are they?
- *Configuration analysis of all IoT devices.* Depending on the number of devices in play, this task alone can be hours of uninterrupted fun. You'll need to know what exactly is running in your environment, but that's just the beginning. You also need the gory details, like: What sorts of data are going through the devices, what are the corresponding data-loss profiles, what are the risks of compromise to the devices, and how do these IoT devices fit into your incident-response, business continuity, and disaster recovery planning.
- *Securing the IoT devices.* Now that you know the nature, location, and configuration of the devices, you'll need to secure them. This sounds a lot easier than it is. Some of these devices do not have any security capabilities at all because the manufacturers, driven by low margins, couldn't care less about security, patching, and software configurations. That leaves you holding the bag. If the software on the device cannot be secured, you'll need to seriously think about either eliminating the device altogether, or air-gapping it (not connecting it to the network).
- *Rinse, lather, repeat.* Granted, doing this exercise once sets the baseline IoT posture for your company. But that is not enough. You will need to stay on top of this. Devices are introduced all the time. Some are even brought into the organization by unsuspecting users. Consider, for example, some newfangled wearable (but unsecured!) device walking through the door and immediately connecting to your Wi-Fi through the user's cell phone credentials. It's like Bring Your Children to Work Day, but with electronics! You therefore must constantly be

scanning the network for any unauthorized attempts to connect. Your default should be to deny all unless authorized at the media access control (or mac) address level. Moreover, as part of your cybersecurity awareness program, you need to make sure that people understand the implications of IoT and how it can potentially become the company's *Kerkoporta*, which, unless you were really paying attention to your Byzantine history lectures, you may not know what it is!

Kerkoporta (*Greek: Κερκόπορτα*) was a small, unattended doorway along the fortified walls of Constantinople, which was allegedly left unlocked and unchecked, thereby allowing the Ottoman troops to enter and sack the city. Thus, no more Constantinople! We have Istanbul instead. Lesson learned: Keep all your gates attended and locked!

There are currently a lot of efforts by industry groups—such as the Industrial Internet Consortium (IIC), which has rolled out the Industrial Internet Security Framework (you guessed it: IISF)—and by both domestic and international regulators, all voicing their concerns about security and privacy in the IoT. For example, the U.S. Senate introduced (and later reintroduced) S.2607, the *Developing Innovation and Growing the Internet of Things Act*, aka *The DIGIT Act*. We can't make this stuff up, but there you have it!

Bottom line? Expect to see a lot more action on this, especially as the growth path of IoT makes the infamous hockey-stick curve look limp by comparison.

## CASE STUDY: HOW A SECURITY PROFESSIONAL'S HOME WAS HACKED. LESSONS ABOUT THE CLOUD AND THE INTERNET OF THINGS

### An Interview with Frank Downs, Senior Manager, Cyber and Information Security, ISACA

Frank Downs calls his home "one big living experiment."

His Internet of Things setup is "hedonistic," he says. About the only thing not connected to the Internet is his shower. Thanks to the Internet of Things, he no longer has to get out of bed to turn off the bedroom lights, but says, "Alexa, turn off the bedroom lights." He can lock and unlock his door from anywhere with an Internet connection.

Consequently, when he goes on long runs in the neighborhood, he doesn't have to take his keys with him. He just unlocks the door from his phone. Even better, his house knows when he gets back from a run, and opens the garage door for him. "I haven't needed to touch a light switch in my house for several years," Downs says.

His prize accomplishment was his personal cloud. Downs became so fascinated with the power of the cloud that he built his own.

A Defense Department–trained security professional, hired out of college by the Department of Defense for his ability to speak Arabic, Downs had done cybersecurity deployments in war zones. So, creating a cloud in his suburban home was a cinch.

"I took my personal router, made a few tweaks to it, connected a 3-terabyte hard drive, and proceeded to connect it to the router," Downs says. With this system in place, he could access the data on storage devices in his house from anywhere in the world.

"For several blissful months, I felt like the king of my digital castle," he says.

Until he got hacked.

A short while after he connected his home, Downs decided to check in on things. "I logged on to make sure that all the files were there, make sure everything was in the right folder, and used my admin privileges to make sure that each user had access to only their files."

As he poked through directories, he noticed something strange. "I discovered a file on our cloud drive that wasn't put there by me, my wife, or our roommate," he says.

The note read as follows:

*This is an automated message being sent out to everyone affected. Your Asus router (and your documents) can be accessed by anyone in the world with an Internet connection. You need to protect yourself and learn more by reading the following news article: http://nullfluid. com/asusgate.txt*

*The following is a list of all the vulnerable IP addresses that have been leaked. If you are reading this, you are vulnerable too: http:// pastebin.com/ASfYTWgw*

*Solution:* Completely disable "ftp" and "aicloud," immediately.
*I hope we helped.*
*Sincerely,*
*/g/*

Downs immediately recognized the signature, /g/. It's the handle used by individuals from 4Chan's gaming forum—a known virtual hangout for the notorious hacktivist group, Anonymous.

The effect was chilling.

"Few things are more unsettling than getting a note from 4Chan and knowing you are vulnerable," says Downs.

"I overreacted," Downs admits. As a cybersecurity expert, he knew that the router was the absolute worst device that could be compromised. It gives access to literally everything else that is connected.

"It's worse than exploiting the computer," says Downs. With access to a router, a hacker can look at all the communication across a network. He or she can retrieve usernames and passwords. With that, the hacker can figure out how to hack anything and everything else.

Downs yanked the router from the wall and the hard drive from the router. Then he went on a spree that he calls a mixture of MacGyver and Sherlock Holmes, "if both of them [had] suffered from ADHD and had an understanding of cybersecurity" and understood that if their routers were compromised, the cloud and all of their devices were also compromised.

"I proceeded to spend the next week conducting forensic analysis against both devices, looking for any additional compromise."

Then he went about disassembling and analyzing all the things in his Internet of Things, trying to understand what further damage might have occurred. He went so far as to disassemble light switches and reread the manual of his door lock. Afterward, he slowly began to reconnect his home.

With one key difference: "This time, I did it behind the firewall," Downs says.

### The Lesson

"I wanted to have my cake and eat it, too," Downs says. In his enthusiasm to network his home, create a private cloud, and connect it all to the outside world, Downs had taken shortcuts. "The problem was, the router *was* the firewall."

Downs had put the router in the "demilitarized zone" (DMZ), like a web server. But that meant that part of his internal network was on the local area network (LAN), which can also be accessed on the wide area network (WAN), which means by the outside world.

What was worse, a factory setting on the router Downs had purchased made it vulnerable. "Someone had forgotten to turn off the file transfer protocol (FTP) by default." That meant anyone could jump on to this open FTP, exploit the router, access his files, and compromise any connected device in his house.

Downs has done away with the DMZ and has a proper firewall in place. He's given up on the idea of a personal cloud as too risky. "I pay $3 a month to Google for a higher-level drive account," he says.

"Just because I know how to do these things doesn't mean I'm going to spend all day every day making sure my cloud is secure," he says.

Google, he says, is better than he will ever be at protecting data. That's because data security is core to their business so that, unlike himself, they can focus on it 24/7. It's the same concept as using a financial advisor, he says. "These are people who spend all day every day reading financial analysis. I can do it on my own, in the five minutes I think about it. Or I can go with the person who focuses on it eight hours a day."

The irony, says Downs, is that even Hillary Clinton would have been more secure using Google than a personal server for email.

### A Better Way to Connect

Through his experience, Downs has become more careful and sophisticated. At the same time, the Internet of Things (IoT) is growing up as well.

At first, Downs says, IoT devices were simple. They were like older computers. "If you wanted to spend enough time, you could find a way to hack them," he says. Since these old-style devices were seldom updated, the hack would work for a long time.

Now, there are newer, sophisticated, and powerful devices like the thermostat from a company called NEST.

To change the temperature in his home, Downs communicates with the servers at NEST. Those servers then send a message to his home thermostat. The communications to and from the server are all encrypted, thus secure in all directions.

It will take awhile for all IoT devices to catch up with this approach.

"Not all IoT devices are created equally," Downs says. Take his webcam and baby monitor. That device doesn't speak through a server. Many will remember reports in the media a few years ago when live feeds of infants started appearing on the Internet. "You could just log on and see people's babies," Downs says. In some cases, there was two-way communication. "Not only could you see the baby, but you could yell at the baby."

For his own baby monitor, Downs had to engage in some "roll-your-own" security. He set it up with a secure connection going through the router.

Not everyone is going to know how to do that. Downs's in-laws had no idea how to create a secure connection for a vulnerable baby monitor, so he set theirs up through a secure virtual private network (VPN).

**The Role of Language**

Downs says part of the problem has to do with marketing-style terms like *cloud, Internet of Things* and even *Wi-Fi*.

The buzzwords obscure what the terms actually mean. Downs admits that during one of his first jobs, he heard the term *cloud*, but didn't know what it was and was afraid to ask. He was working at the Department of Defense at the time, and he understood the cloud icon on PowerPoint slides to mean "just another data path."

Later, on an army base, he and a friend started talking about their night courses. The friend was taking advanced programming for security. His assignment: to produce customized programs that would encrypt data in a way for which there were no known decryption technologies.

"Wow, that sounds like a lot of code," Downs said to his friend, and asked him if he had to invest in extra storage.

"Not really," his friend responded. "I'm just putting it up in a shared Dropbox folder that our professor has set up—and he has a subscription, so there's no concerns about space." The friend went on to describe how he kept all of his semester projects in his professor's Dropbox and, as a result, didn't have to use any of his personal space. "Well, that's the cloud for you," the friend concluded. "You're just putting your stuff on someone else's computer."

It was at that point two light bulbs went off for Downs simultaneously. First, he understood in the concrete sense exactly what the cloud was. Second, he was horror-struck that encryption-decryption programs were being casually uploaded to it.

"The power of buzzwords is that they get people to swallow computing concepts they really should challenge," Downs says.

The real definition of the cloud would go something like this:

*The cloud is a term referring to accessing computers, information technology (IT), and software applications through network connections, often by accessing data centers using wide area networking (WAN) or Internet connectivity.*

"But you get tired halfway through the sentence," say Downs. So the term *cloud* was invented to capture it all.

"It becomes a friendly icon on a PowerPoint slide and nobody analyzes the word anymore," he says. "The cloud is, like most things, just a bullshit description of a capability or technology that has existed for years. For myself specifically, I would sit in briefings and presentations, day after day after day, wondering what everyone was talking about when they mentioned 'the cloud.'"

The "Internet of Things" is yet another buzzword for small, every-day items that happen to connect to the Internet.

"It was the same with Wi-Fi," Downs says, which was originally known as IEEE 802.11, a reference to a radio frequency policy. This term was used "until a group of marketers realized the word 'Wi-Fi' rolled off the tongue better."

## The Future

Despite his home hack and initial feeling of horror about the cloud, Downs believes individuals and businesses need to embrace new tech-nologies, not run from them.

Downs's own information was accessed in the infamous hack of the Office of Government Accountability. "It was literally the most sen-sitive information you could get on an individual. Information on my security clearances, on my family, on *their* Social Security numbers. It was all compromised."

What could he have done differently? Downs can't think of a thing he would have changed. "I guess you could say, 'You don't have to take that kind of job or work for the government.'" But where does that end?

A friend of Downs, who has a paving business, simply does not use a computer. Part of his argument is security. "He struggles with having to deal with literal paper on matters such as invoicing and if he gets audited."

A person could take the same attitude toward IoT, Downs says. You can try to resist it. But we're getting to the point at which it won't be up to us. "How much longer do we have until doors are automatically enabled and you can't buy a door without it being connected? You already can't buy a digital watch without it being connected," says Downs.

And then, there's the pure life-enablement offered by IoT. "I don't really need all my devices. Really. But do I really like them? Sure, I do," says Downs.

**A Final Caution About Cybersecurity Pros**

Downs advises that businesses understand the nature of cybersecurity professionals.

"When it comes to cybersecurity, you're taking the two most conservative person types and professional types, audit and IT, and putting them together," Downs says. The fact that these individuals are risk-averse is to be expected. That's their day job.

But as businesses and individuals look to the future, they must harness the expertise of cybersecurity professionals, and, at the same time, decide for themselves what risks they will and will not accept.

## Distributed Workforces

Once upon a time, people used to get up and physically transport themselves to an office where they performed work. When they were done, they did the physical transport routine in reverse. Endless hours were wasted in transit, with tons of pollutants dumped into the environment. People toiled for years and years under these conditions, until Alexander Graham Bell invented the telephone, and Mr. Watson started to phone it in. Things went south from there.

According to Gallup, from 1995 to 2015 the percentage of workers in the United States telecommuting for work rose from 9 percent to 37 percent. That is more than one third of the workforce of the United States telecommuting at some point during the month, with 9 percent of those telecommuting half the time or more. There's some debate about whether the trend is leveling off or increasing, and also about whether it's smart or counterproductive. Regardless, one thing remains clear: Telecommuting is real, it's increasing, and it is likely to continue in one form or another, especially if work entails getting into an office and working on a computer. Hence, your headache.

Why? Because, unless your company is providing and controlling the equipment used to access corporate resources, you have a problem. A big problem. If your organization's corporate policy is BYOD (bring your own device), then it implies that a private piece of equipment is connecting to the corporate network, working with corporate assets, and doing so over potentially unsecured connections, which could include someone's home, hotel, coffee shop, airport … anywhere they go. Moreover, neither your IT nor cybersecurity departments have any legal standing with regard to accessing and controlling an employee's private computer or phone. That causes a serious legal headache if, for example, the employee is terminated and IT and cybersecurity want to ensure that no corporate data is walking out the door. You cannot exactly take over the system remotely and wipe it! The individual may have personal data (for example, his or her personal contacts), which, of course, are commingled with their corporate contacts. And if the employee was in, let's say sales, and if you have reason to assume the employee may seek a new job with your competition, you can see how this can quickly become a serious problem.

What is a cybersecurity czar to do? Assuming that you cannot persuade the company to provide equipment for all employees (local and remote), then your options are limited to creating a set of policies and standards to which employees must consent in order to access the network. These policies and standards, translated into some form of an employee agreement or consent form, will not guarantee that your data won't fly out the door. But they may set minimum security standards and corporate rights that survive separation. It is absolutely critical that your attorney is involved in drafting these. It is the only way you can maximize your chances of making the policies enforceable following an event. Even then—I won't lie to you—enforcing these rules can become very time consuming and very expensive.

Remember our guiding principle to date: "What is it worth to you?" You must have a heart-to-heart talk with your executive team and your board to determine how far is far enough in regard to writing and enforcing security policies. It is only they who can accept the risk. There is no "best practice" when it comes to these issues. It's all about your risk appetite: What are you willing to accept, and what are you not?

There are companies that will not accept this risk. They recognize the reality of a distributed workforce. They even welcome the savings in physical plant costs, but they are not willing to accept the risk of their network being accessed by noncompany equipment. And so, they provide everything: the equipment, the policies governing its use, and extremely tight controls on who, how, where, and when is accessing the corporate network and assets. If an employee is separated, they immediately *brick* the equipment (a slang term meaning to render the equipment as useful as a brick), and provide for a mechanism for the equipment's safe return. Of course, all the corporate data across the board, local or remote, tend to be encrypted both in transit and at rest.

Obviously, this level of control does not come easily or cheaply. The systems, workflows, and personnel training required are complex and expensive in both time and money. Moreover, the message to the company is that Big Brother is watching. Therefore, when discussing with your board such an approach, make sure that you sensitize them to all aspects of such an implementation. In some cases, there is no choice (e.g., you're working for the NSA for crying out loud! What did you expect?). In others, there may be some give and take. As always, your role is to be there and inform the board, owners, or executives charged with accepting risk, with all the pertinent details, and then accept their decision.

On the other hand, there are other companies that fully, and perhaps cavalierly, accept the risk. Their position is that even if data is exfiltrated, it is useless without the company know-how with regard to generating value, so the corporate attitude is: "Let them have it!" In terms of the gaping cyber-security hole that this allows (e.g., access by an infected computer), well ... as we've discussed: "Ours is not to reason why ...." You have informed the stake-holders of the risk, you made sure they understood it, and they have accepted it. Move on.

Then there are the companies that fall somewhere in between. Yours probably—hopefully!—is one of them. These companies are very concerned about the risks introduced by BYOD and distributed workforces, and as such, they mitigate the risks as best they can through their defense-in-depth strate-gies. In practice, that looks something like this:

1. Create legally binding agreements between employees and their use of equipment accessing corporate assets.
2. Create and communicate clear policies, standards, procedures, guide-lines for all information technology use and corporate systems access.
3. Have clear and timely onboarding and offboarding processes for all employees.
4. Provide cybersecurity awareness training to all employees, at least quarterly, and maintain awareness throughout the year.
5. Deploy a wide range of controls, including a well-tuned security information and event management system and a data loss protection system.

Like it or not, distributed workforces, freelancing, telecommuting, BYOD, and so on are here to stay, likely to grow, and likely to have significant impacts on our definition of the workplace. The impact of these develop-ments on IT and cybersecurity is equally profound: The concept of perimeter security is completely redefined. Indeed, some argue the perimeter no longer exists at all.

As for me, I argue that your current perimeter does exist, but it's not one or more campuses or offices.

Your perimeter is planet-wide. Plan accordingly.

# CHAPTER 10

## Controls

I n Chapter 3, we defined the four broad types of controls: *preventative, detective, corrective,* and *compensatory.* Some analysts include a fifth type, called a *targeted control* or a *countermeasure,* which addresses a specific threat or a specific vulnerability. But for simplicity's sake, I'm going to include targeted controls as part of the four categories, depending on how they function.

Keep in mind that the examples that follow are just that, examples—not an exhaustive list by any means. New controls are developed almost daily as part of the constant arms race between hackers, cybersecurity vendors, developers, IT companies, end users, and governments.

## Preventative Controls

Preventative controls are the road barriers of the information highway. They are designed to stop an attacker from getting to an asset. If the asset involves physical protection, then a good example of a preventative control would be security guards. Digital equivalents of the security guard include:

- *Antivirus and antimalware applications.* Typically lumped under end-point protection systems, these are mostly signature-based applications that scan traffic, compare it against a known database of threats, and decide accordingly. What I mean by signature is that these viruses and malware programs, once discovered, are found to have a unique look, like a signature. That makes them identifiable to the antivirus and antimalware applications. They now know what to look for. These applications are as good as their signature databases and their frequency of update, although the best-of-breed versions employ heuristic analysis to predict possible malware as well as sophisticated interfaces across applications (such as email, web browsers, mobile apps, and so on). My recommendation: Don't turn on a computer without one installed and up to date.
- *Cybersecurity awareness training.* Discussed earlier, employee awareness is one of the most effective preventative controls. Training consists of

onsite and on-demand training for all employees. The most effective versions employ a blend of delivery methods, repeat at least twice a year, and include followups such as short quizzes to keep everyone on their toes.

■ *Data loss prevention (DLPs)*. Designed to ensure that sensitive data stays where it belongs, these systems operate across several layers in an organization. Depending on configuration, a DLP will look for specific types of data (credit card numbers, Social Security numbers, account numbers, etc.) and make sure they are being accessed by authorized users only. A DLP can also inspect traffic to make sure that sensitive information is not on the move, be it on a network, an external storage device (e.g., a USB drive), or even a printer. DLPs are as good as their configuration and upkeep, so you need to be particularly sensitive in making sure that they constantly know your data environment and your security policies. When correctly deployed, they can be a powerful preventative control, which plays well with others, and is one of the few that can alert you to a possible insider threat.

■ *Firewalls*. These are appliances meant to segregate the inside (company) network from the Internet. They come in several flavors ranging in capabilities, configuration options, and complexity. There are firewalls that encrypt data as well as monitor traffic. Others monitor traffic and compare it against malware signatures. Still other firewalls do all of the preceding and more. Keep in mind that a firewall is as good as its configuration. An erroneously configured firewall, or one that is poorly maintained, is useless. Your specific control requirements will dictate which kind and how many firewalls to deploy, as well as how they are configured.

■ *Gateways*. Gateways monitor and control Internet traffic coming and going from your company servers. Let's say you call up a web page on a company computer. You can have a gateway that senses your request for a web page, segregates it from other traffic, disguises it, even encrypts it, and then sends it out. Why do this? Because if the request is intercepted, the intercepting person doesn't get your address; he or she only sees the gateway instead. In this example, this gateway would be called a (web) proxy server: a device designed to hide the other internal devices from the Internet by managing each session and exposing only itself to the outside world. You can have an application-level gateway, which is focused on services, or a circuit-level gateway that monitors, for example, a specific communications protocol across all services. Most firewalls and proxy servers perform network address translation (NAT), which is a way to map internal nonroutable device addresses (that cannot be used on the Internet) to external Internet-acceptable addresses.

- *Intrusion prevention systems (IPSs).* These systems complement the panoply of firewalls, antivirus and antimalware systems by introducing a systems monitoring layer. Unlike IDS, which looks for a signature, an IPS will be tuned to what constitutes normal behavior on your networks. The moment something happens outside that frame, an IPS raises the alarm. An alarm in this context includes not only logging the event but also the ability to terminate connections. An example of a well-tuned IPS response would be the immediate termination of file encryption activity taking place unexpectedly, usually the result of a ransomware attack. Of course, if your *normal* is all over the map and no baseline can be established, then the IPS may become difficult to tune and could produce many false positives as a result.

## Detective Controls

If the preventive controls are the road barriers, the detective controls are the motion sensors that let you know that someone is in the room. The idea behind them is to detect abnormalities and raise the alarm. Some controls listed as examples under preventive controls work here as well—for example, antivirus and antimalware systems and intrusion prevention systems can be considered both preventive and detective. Other examples of detective controls include:

- *Intrusion detection systems (IDSs).* These are essentially antivirus and antimalware systems on steroids, using a combination of signature-based analysis (comparing traffic not only to known signatures of viruses and malware but to specific attack patterns), and anomaly analysis (comparing expected normal system behavior to current state). IDS can vary in intelligence and efficacy, depending on which system you deploy. Some use artificial intelligence applications to learn from their environment and therefore become better at detecting an attack. IDS integrates into the larger suite of controls by providing extensive event logging, automated responses and triggering of downstream controls, and organization security policy enforcement. That last one is a set of rules that your cybersecurity department has painstakingly established to address control and notification behavior across systems. Heady stuff.
- *Security information and event management systems (SIEMs).* These are applications that combine both detection and response management. They combine analysis of event logs across multiple systems, event correlation, abnormal event detection, notification, automated actions, and response event tracking. As you can imagine, the volume of logs

and events has risen exponentially and can be properly managed only by a good SIEM. If forced to choose, I would deploy a SIEM before an IDS, because as far as I am concerned, a solid SIEM will provide greater insight and coordination across the enterprise than any IDS will.

## Corrective Controls

Like the name implies, these are controls that focus on repairing damage during or after an attack. Many targeted controls fall in this category: For example, vulnerability patching is a corrective control. Keeping your systems current—meaning, most recent operating system release as well as application releases—also represents corrective control, because it patches (corrects) known vulnerabilities.

But the ultimate corrective control is backup, and that's worth spending some time on. There no substitute to the feeling of relief that you will have when you know that you have a good, solid, backup set from which you can restore your data. To get there, you need to understand the kinds of backup that are available to you, and when to use which kind.

There are three main kinds of backup: *full backup*, which as the name implies is a complete and total copy of all of your data; a *differential backup* copies only the data that has changed since your last full backup; and finally *incremental backup*, which involves only the data that has changed since the last backup of any kind. Which backup you use and when depends on the size of your organization, the amount and type of data, and the values that you established for your recovery time objective (RTO), and recovery point objective (RPO). Speaking generally, small organizations do a daily full backup while larger organizations tend to employ periodic (e.g., weekly) full backups as well as a combination of differential or incremental backups.

A full backup has the benefit of the most rapid restore time, since all the data is in one place and you don't have to go hunting among differential or incremental backups for that one file that's missing. On the other hand, if you're backing up several terabytes worth of data, then, irrespective of method, you're using multiple and complex strategies to ensure timely restores.

There are additional considerations when it comes to your backup and restore strategy, most of which need to be covered by your business continuity and disaster recovery plan. There are different methodologies—such as mirroring, disk-to-disk-to-cloud, continuous backup, and hot failover—that may make sense given your specific requirements.

The one thing you need to be concerned about, no matter your size or strategy: Make sure that your backups are absolutely solid and 100 percent verifiable. Check often! Trust me on this! You'll thank me later.

## Compensatory Controls

These are the types of controls you put in place when you know that all your other controls cannot mitigate one or more risks all the way down to a desired level—be that a level required by regulators or simply your own peace of mind.

In a perfect world, every company would address every vulnerability in a perfect way with perfect timing. But that's not our world. You may find, for example, that you cannot apply a necessary security patch or upgrade because doing so will cause havoc with your systems downstream. Or you may have a recovery time objective that's so short that no backup strategy can meet it. Maybe you are dealing with such highly classified data that your system must be completely "air-gapped" (i.e., no Internet access ever).

Typical examples of compensating controls include hot failover sites (mirror sites where duplicate systems and facilities exist and can go live instantly), access controls (e.g., access depending on your clearance and the data's classification, function, geography, etc.), and the extremely important one, especially for insider threats: segregation of duties. Segregation of duties is a very powerful compensating control, and one that you can easily implement.

Consider the following example: You have a mission-critical database application. As a result, you have some version of an application/database (DBA) manager, who may be in house or a vendor. You also, of course, have a systems administrator. Again, that person may be in house or outsourced. A good segregation of duties control implementation would be for the systems administrator to not know the database password, and for the application's manager to not have system administrative privileges. This keeps everyone honest. The administrator can always report on the DBA's actions from the logs, and the DBA can never erase those logs because they don't have the privilege, and vice versa.

## Defense in Depth

The right way to use all of these controls is by deploying them across systems in a way that achieves defense in depth. This has the effect of putting multiple and diverse barriers (controls) between the attacker and the asset. This strategy looks different from case to case (e.g., cloud-based versus office versus mobile), but has proven to be the best way to protect yourself and your assets.

If you translate all the creative ways people used to protect their castles into the electronic realm, you've got your basic defense-in-depth concept down pat. (Of course, most things can trace their roots to antiquity, and, I assert with no evidence or significant bias, to the ancient Greeks!)

Back in March 2010, the NSA published a paper called "Defense in Depth," in which the authors pointed to three critical elements for success: people, technology, and operations. In my view, they nailed it! But not everyone agrees. There are many cybersecurity experts who question the approach. Some argue that defense in depth is dead and can no longer address the current asset realities and threat landscape. Their argument centers on two main—and very valid—points: first, the rapidly expanding network perimeter, and second, the rapid adaptation and availability of attackers, attack vectors, and payloads.

What does this mean? Now that everyone has a mobile device, and using applications and storage that are increasingly consumed as cloud services, this new Information Age reality blows out the traditional notion of concentric castle-type defense-in-depth ideas. In other words, we can't build walls tall enough and encompassing enough to cover our users and their diverse technologies. Making things worse, attackers are faster, meaner, and their tools (and themselves) are available as a service with guarantees! To say nothing of the insider threats (willing or not) who are already inside the castle, so ... defense-in-depth *that!*

I disagree. The arguments about the perimeter breakdown are sound, but I don't interpret defense in depth as simply meaning the creation of a multi-layered perimeter.

Quite the opposite: My view is that defense in depth applies at all levels and across all perimeters. It applies as much to the organizational perimeter—location by location, end point by end point—as it applies to its providers, partners, and clients, and as it applies to individual users, no matter where they may be.

In other words, defense in depth is not just a top-level "let's build a castle with five walls and three crocodile-filled moats" strategy. It is also a practice that needs to be applied at each asset point. Firms need to develop defense-in-depth strategies for physical (and virtual) offices, both local and remote, plus they should expect a defense-in-depth approach from their cloud-services providers (trust but verify, always), and, depending on scope, they need it from their trading partners as well. If you doubt the last one, talk to the folks at Target, who suffered a spectacularly bad hack in 2013 that was made possible by vulnerabilities at, of all things, a heating and ventilation company with a Target service contract.

That is why I firmly believe that the NSA has it right. Defense in depth is not about any specific technology or topology. Defense in depth is truly about people, technology, and operations, no matter where, no matter how.

## People, Technology, and Operations

Of this triad, the *people* component is in my view the most critical element of a successful cybersecurity program. Support from the board on down is essential. This support must be emphatic, clear, and actionable. There can be no doubt anywhere in the company that cybersecurity is a mission-critical organizational practice: It needs to be supported with clear policies, standards, procedures, and guidelines.

At each level of the organization, these policies, standards, procedures, and guidelines must be actionable, complied with, measured, tested, and reevaluated at least annually. All members of the organization must receive regular cybersecurity awareness training, with mandatory attendance and followup quizzes. Specifics of compliance, metrics, and reward and penalty policies will vary from company to company, but ultimately one thing must be unambiguously clear to all: These cybersecurity policies are mandatory, and just like any human resource policy (e.g., nondiscrimination), are enforced rigorously across the board.

When it comes to the *technology* part, things can be both complicated and complex. Anna Murray, in her excellent book, *The Complete Software Project Manager*, explains the difference between simple, complicated, and complex projects—her example is the difference between shoveling snow (lots of hard work but relatively simple), assembling an IKEA desk (It's complicated. Trust me!), and performing open heart surgery (Complex. Really complex!). In our case, developing and deploying a defense-in-depth strategy for the technology component, we will have to deal with both the complicated and the complex.

I'll go on record by saying that I believe that you can deal with the complicated: I am confident that you can put together an IKEA desk. I do, however, feel that you'll need to partner up with a surgeon for the open-heart surgery part. There is no escaping it. The subject matter becomes very specialized and it requires experience and expertise.

Your role will be to review and prioritize the assets that need to be protected by criticality. The role of your surgeon will be to match those up with a set of controls based on threat surface (how vulnerable is the asset) and control resilience (how well can the control protect it).

The goal is to have several controls protecting each asset. These controls will be placed either in sequence (Control-A -> Control-B -> Control-C -> Asset, that is, the concentric-circle view) or layered across system function (User Controls -> Operating System Controls -> Application Controls -> Database Controls -> Hardware Controls).

You will also need both to think about using overlapping controls. What this means is that you want to place different controls in parallel, protecting the same asset.

Then you should consider asset segregation. That is when specific assets "live" segregated from one another. The accounting systems are on an isolated server on an isolated network segment from the file servers, and those are separated from the human resources systems, etc.

When you're done with asset segregation, you need to think about segregation of duties. This is very important. You should confirm that the custodians of your critical assets do not have unnecessarily elevated privileges. For example, there is no reason why the database administrator needs to have system administrator privileges, and vice versa.

Speaking of privilege, the same kind of thinking applies for your users. At a minimum, you should implement least-privilege, role-based access. For instance, the accounts payable person cannot run the accounts receivable module. Different roles mean different access privileges. The more secure and sensitive the site, the more elaborate this can become. For example, there are mandatory access controls, context access controls, discretionary access controls, rule-based access controls, location-based access controls, and so on and so forth. The majority of businesses will be well served with clearly defined and religiously maintained simple role-based access. The religiously maintained part means that when the aforementioned accounts payable employee gets promoted to accounts receivable, her role is to be immediately changed by first eliminating the accounts payable rights, and then granting the accounts receivable ones. Were you to simply add the additional rights, you would have a user with unnecessarily elevated access privileges, creating an opportunity for mischief!

Finally, be aware that the introduction of controls themselves may introduce unplanned vulnerabilities. After all, you are introducing all sorts of technology layers, and we all know that not all technologies play well with one another. There are cases that one control rendered another one inoperative or ineffective. Make sure you test, check, and retest. Avoid the deployment of any control that depends on another one.

And don't forget: What happens when a control does fail? (Yes, think in terms of *when*, not *if*.) You need to decide how they behave not only while working, but also while dead. Do your controls fail open or fail secure? As an example, consider that failing secure can be life-threatening in certain circumstances: if, say, your access doors to the computer center fail secure (i.e., all doors automatically lock) while there is a fire!

Ideally, all these practical considerations need to be addressed before any control is turned on. But this is not an ideal world. The possibility exists that you are not starting from a blank slate and that some, or many, controls are already in place. You will therefore need to examine each control and how it measures up both to the defense-in-depth strategy and to the practical considerations previously discussed. Learn from what you discover and adjust accordingly. Repeat this review at least annually. Controls become obsolete, threats change, systems and people change, and so does risk appetite, strategy, and company needs.

The thing to always remember, your go-to safe bet, is to have as many independent and automated controls as necessary. Nothing more and nothing less. The main reason you should strive for automation and independence of controls is the third item in the people-technology-operations triad.

No two companies operate alike, but across companies operations share a common set of responsibilities that ensure the smooth running of the value-producing engine. Operations are the heartbeat of your company. You always want it to be nice and steady, never erratic, and God forbid never arrested!

For your defense-in-depth strategy to be an operational success, you need to keep things as simple as possible, not overburdening operations with anything more than what they are already doing, and make sure you have the following one key ingredient.

## Communications

As you can imagine, operations people have a tall order to fill. Depending on the size of your company, and in terms of cybersecurity always, operations will include members of risk management, audit, IT, cybersecurity, and HR.

If you are a company of one, well ... the good news is your environment is simpler. The bad news is, you still need to make sure you have your finger on the pulse of all this, which will typically mean being diligent with the vendors that provide you all these services.

The larger the company, the more complex the operational food chain. The more complex the operations, the more essential the need for proper change management, strong communications, and cross-departmental engagement. If there is one takeaway that I can offer you from my experience evaluating different companies' operations, it is this: The minute you uncover a communications block in operations, pull the emergency break and address it. If you don't, your attackers will.

In the absence of communications, there can be no successful business strategy implementation, much less a successful cybersecurity defense-in-depth strategy. You need to be comfortable in sitting down with your operations teams and discuss options, explain issues, and engage them directly in developing your specific defense-in-depth strategy.

Once that is done—once you are confident that the people-technology-operations triad has been properly engaged, issues addressed, and concerns satisfied—you are ready to document your defense in depth and let your people know what's expected of them.

## Policies, Standards, Procedures, and Guidelines

Remember all that fun stuff in our management, governance, and alignment chapter? This is where you put all that great knowledge to work!

First, please note the absence of the word *training*. Training is not communicating; it is educating. It is critically important, no doubt, but at this stage of your program development, we need to communicate what the program is all about, and how it will be governed. We'll do this through our policies, standards, procedures, and guidelines.

As always, we'll start with our definitions:

- *Policies* are the highest-level directives in any organization. They originate with either the board or the top management. Policies are both definitive and general. For example, a policy might be: "This company is always headed north." It's definitive (we're going north) but it's also general (we're heading north, but not necessarily on I-95).
- *Standards* set the ecosystem of a policy. They create a mandatory and meaningful framework for understanding and implementing the policy. In our northward policy example, the corresponding standard would specify which modes of transportation should be used (plains, trains, and automobiles), what types of compass are acceptable in determining true north, and any other metrics that can be used to verify that the policy is being followed.
- *Procedures* are listings of actions that, if and when they are followed, satisfy the standards and thereby implement the policy. People frequently merge standards (which are mandatory) and procedures (which are optional) into a mandatory procedure—hence the frequent reference to policies and procedures. An example of a procedure would be: "When using a car to go north, you must: (a) make sure you have fuel, (b) make sure you have insurance, (c) make sure you have your license with you, (d) make sure the GPS is on ... " and so on.
- *Guidelines* further clarify procedures. They, too, are optional, and may be specific to a department or function. In the example we have been using, a guideline would be: "You can only use the mail room truck if you are transporting boxes; otherwise, you should don your leather jacket and use the facilities' Harley."

When it comes to cybersecurity program development, you're on the hook for developing and disseminating policies and standards. They must, of course, be approved by the executive team and, ultimately, by the board or its equivalent.

Procedures and guidelines will be the responsibility of each department downstream. As the one charged with developing the cybersecurity program, you will advise and consult, but you cannot—and should not—be drafting departmental procedures and guidelines. Ownership of those must be local, or they will be unenforceable.

The first policy you will create is the one that announces the existence of the cybersecurity program, along with its standards. I recommend that the structure of all your policies and standards follow a consistent format. You should always check with your HR and legal departments to make sure that you are following internal templates, but in the absence of one, I'm partial to the following list as an excellent starting point:

1. *Policy title:* This is where you announce to the company what this is about. My recommendation, across all these fields, is that old standby, "less is more." Keep it short and to the point. For example, cybersecurity policy is enough. (No, your company name is not needed. If the people reading this don't know which company they are working for, you have a much bigger problem than cybersecurity.)

2. *Policy description:* What is this policy about? Be specific without being verbose. For example, "This policy establishes the intent, provides direction, and sets expectations of conduct regarding cybersecurity."

3. *Why are we doing this?* This question and the next have proven extremely helpful for two reasons: Answering the questions will force you to communicate a well-thought-out policy, and second, answering the questions will help set transparency expectations. Everyone needs to understand why a policy has been created and why it makes sense for the organization to have it. Finally, providing this information goes a long way in creating buy-in by all involved, and trust me, without buy-in, there can be no cybersecurity program. A good entry in this field should read something like, "We take the security of our people, our clients, and our data very seriously. As a direct result, we have decided to create and rigorously maintain our cybersecurity program which we have based on basic practices and proven cybersecurity frameworks."

4. *Why does it make sense?* As I mentioned already, the great Peter Drucker wrote, "There is surely nothing quite so useless as doing with great efficiency that which should not be done at all," and this is your opportunity to explain why this cybersecurity program does makes sense.

Keep it brief. For example, "Having evaluated our assets, threats, and our risk tolerance, we understood that unless we take concrete, measurable action in cybersecurity, we would be exposing everyone to unacceptable risks. This program is our answer in minimizing and mitigating this risk as much as possible."

5. *Whom does it impact?* The answer here is simple: everyone. Cybersecurity affects everyone in an organization. It is also everyone's responsibility. It should be no surprise to hear that my recommendation in introducing a cybersecurity policy would be to answer this question in exactly that way: "Cybersecurity affects everyone in the organization. Moreover, cybersecurity is everyone's responsibility."

6. *What are the applicable standards?* Here you have some choices. If you prefer to stick with just policies and procedures, then skip this entry altogether, replacing it by a list of mandatory procedures. My recommendation is to stay with the standards because the idea behind a policy is that it rarely changes. It is a top-level directive. For example, you wouldn't expect our go-north policy to change anytime soon, but you might expect the occasional change on the standards supporting the policy (for example, the addition of GPS to acceptable compasses). And you certainly expect the procedures and their guidelines to be changing as often as necessary. If you do choose to implement standards, then this is where you list them. For example, because you're all over the NIST cybersecurity framework, you could say, "The standards supporting this policy are: identify, protect, detect, respond, and recover." You would then produce and publish each standard, allowing for each department to develop procedures to support it. So, for example, accounting might set their own procedure for user access while the IT department would determine their procedure for endpoint protection.

7. *What is your responsibility under this policy?* This is where the rubber meets the road. Remember all the buy-in talk earlier? This is where you find out if it worked or not. If you have done a great job in getting everyone's feedback, incorporating their concerns, responding to their questions, engaging with them across levels, then they will be happy to integrate this policy into their lives and operations. If not … nothing you write here—even if it's blind and unquestionable obedience—will help. I suggest something like, "You are responsible to understand, disseminate, and comply with this policy, its associated standards, and the specific procedures and guidelines as applicable to your job function in the organization."

# Regulatory Compliance: The European Example

Before we go any further with our controls and defense-in-depth strategy, we need to discuss compliance. Not policy or employee compliance, but regulatory and legal compliance. Regulations will certainly affect the way you write your standards, and in some cases, they may dictate them.

Every business, no matter where located, is subject to local laws. The operative word here is *local*. You'll need to always account for local law, especially when it comes to cybersecurity, personal identifiable information, data storage, and data movement. The laws in Germany, for example, are very different from the laws in the United States, and those are very different from the laws in Singapore. What happens when you are a U.S. corporation with offices in Germany and Singapore? Therein lies the rub!

Analyzing all the different regulatory frameworks is beyond the scope of this book, but let's take a brief look at the European Union (EU) as an instructive case study.

In 1995, the European Parliament and Council issued Directive 95/46/EC "on the protection of individuals with regard to the processing of personal data and on the free movement of such data." The directive laid down the law on how data can be lawfully processed; the goal was to protect the rights and freedoms of EU citizens.

Touching only on the top-level highlights here, 95/46/EC went on to spell out that data processing would be lawful only under particular conditions: If the data subject has unambiguously given consent, the processing of data was necessary to fulfill contractual and legal obligations, or necessary for carrying out a task in the public interest. The directive went into substantial detail about data quality, fair and lawful data processing, and the rights of citizens to obtain information about who is processing their data, why and how that processing is occurring, the right to access their data, and the right to object to the processing of their data.

It also introduced a clause about the transfer of personal data from an EU member state to a non-EU country. In essence, if the EU considered the outside country to have adequate levels of data protection, then the transfer of the data would be allowable. But if not, and barring a list of exceptions, then the data transfer is not authorized.

These regulations sent lawyers on both sides of the ocean into a tizzy, with lots of back-and-forth about how to define adequate levels of protection, who can store data where, and the like. Five years later, in 2000, the EU adopted what was called the "Safe Harbor Adequacy Decision," which recognized the U.S. Department of Commerce principles as adequate data protection.

But the situation took a bad turn around 2010 when the German regulators started requesting proof of safe harbor compliance in transatlantic data transfers. Things really went off the rails when the EU Commission Vice President, Viviane Reding, said, "The Safe Harbour agreement may not be so safe after all. It could be a loophole for data transfers because it allows data transfers from EU to U.S. companies—although U.S. data protection standards are lower than our European ones." After lots of back-and-forth between countries and an Edward Snowden–versus–NSA scandal, in 2014, the EU Parliament called for the immediate suspension of Safe Harbor because its principles were not adequately protecting EU citizens.

The death knell of Safe Harbor was the 2015 decision of the European Court of Justice on the case of Mr. Max Schrems, who sued Facebook, arguing that the United States does not provide adequate protection. The court agreed with him (and then some), and for a few days there were thousands of executives and lawyers walking around looking blue in the face from holding their breath. No one knew exactly what the next step was, so everyone pretended that existing laws covered all business already in place, until the EU issued revised data protection laws, and the EU and the United States worked out a Safe Harbor replacement.

That didn't happen until 2016 when the European Commission issued the General Data Protection Regulation GDPR (EU) 2016/679, finally replacing the 1995 directive. Also in 2016, the EU and the United States proposed the Privacy Shield arrangement to replace Safe Harbor. As of this writing, these new regulations are, of course, being challenged by dozens of civil rights organizations, and no one knows exactly how or when a consensus will emerge. Meanwhile, GDPR is the law of the land, and if you thought that the original directive was strict, wait till you read the GDPR! Its main points are:

- *Worldwide applicability.* GDPR applies to all companies that process personal data of EU citizens no matter where they are located.
- *Fines.* If your company is found breaching GDPR, it can be fined up to 4 percent of total revenues, or €20,000,000, whichever is greater. Keep in mind, that's *per incident.*
- *Clear consent.* Remember all those endless agreements written in legalese that you had to click "agree" on? No more. Consent has to be plainly explained, easily understood, and accessible. One more thing: It must be as easy to revoke as it is to grant.
- *Notification.* If you are breached, you must notify anyone whose data you are processing within 72 hours.

- *Access*. An EU citizen has the right to access and to a copy of your own data, including an explanation of who is processing it and for what reason.
- *Portability*. EU citizens have the right to a copy of their data and the right to transmit it to anyone else.
- *Privacy by design*. What used to be a systems design principle is now law. You are expected to integrate this principle across the life cycle of all your systems that touch EU citizen data.

And my personal favorite:

- *Right to be forgotten*. An EU citizen has the right to ask for their personal data to be erased from your systems, as well as from any third-party systems that you have been transmitting the data, including the possibility of stopping any downstream processing of the same data.

## Pulling It All Together

After all this work, what have we achieved? Let's review.

You are responsible for developing an organization-wide cybersecurity program. You have done your work, you identified your assets, the threats, and your possible vulnerabilities. You thought things through, and developed a defense-in-depth strategy that has identified the necessary controls and how they must be placed to protect the organization. You have communicated all this, trained your people, and created the necessary policies and standards. You have also contributed to the creation and rollout of the applicable procedures and guidelines.

But none of this exists in isolation of geography and the local regulatory frameworks. You must take this work and tweak it so that the local applicable laws are respected. That means that it is entirely possible that your German office will have different standards from the one in Austin. They may have the same policy, but the standard needs to reflect the local regulatory constraints. If those constraints span continents, then you will need to have standards that address that as well.

Do you have to, though? Do you *really* have to meet each and every local regulation?

Well now, you rebel! It depends!

What is our number-one yardstick that we've used throughout our cybersecurity program development? What is *the* question that must always have a definitive answer?

"How much is it worth to you?"

And as usual, that's a question for the board. The board may decide not to comply with one local regulation or another. The board may decide that it *is worth it to them* to pay any fines they may incur. In short, the board is accepting this risk. You don't have to agree with that decision. And it's not yours to make.

You can, and should, advise the board on what you think is possible regarding controls, strategy, and so on, to mitigate this risk, and you should do it objectively and clearly. Terrorizing executives and boards with "Do you feel lucky?" kinds of questions never works. Stick to the facts, present alternatives, educate, and ultimately, accept their decision and move on.

And so will we. Onward to incident response!

# CHAPTER 11

## Incident-Response Planning

"You mean to tell me," complained one executive I worked with, "that after all this work, after endless hours of assessing, valuating, cataloging, classifying, testing, planning, deploying, and educating ... now I have to develop an incident-response plan on top of it all? You'd think we'd be protected to the max!" He groaned. "Can't I at least farm it out?"

"Well, that depends ...."

I call this incident-response planning despair, the dreaded IRPD! It's dreaded partly because it comes toward the end of developing a cybersecurity program, and partly because it is so anticlimactic. It is true that a lot of work, a lot of hard work, has brought you to this point. Now, you are asked to develop a plan for when all your work has failed. Despite it all, an incident has happened, and you need to have a plan to pick up the pieces.

In the 2015 movie *The Martian*, the main character teaches a group of aspiring astronauts. He tells them:

> ... At some point, everything's gonna go south on you ... everything's going to go south and you're going to say, "This is it. This is how I end." Now you can either accept that, or you can get to work. That's all it is. You just begin. You do the math. You solve one problem ... and you solve the next one ... and then the next. And if you solve enough problems, you get to come home.

Honestly, if there is a better description about what an incident-response plan really looks like, I have not found it!

## Incident-Response Planning: Not Just a Good Idea—It's the Law!

You may have heard of FISMA. It stands for Federal Information Security Management Act. It was signed into law in 2002, and it essentially requires all federal agencies to develop an incident-response plan.

I know what you're thinking—"But my company is private, so why should I care about federal regulations?" The reason is that similar legislation requiring your firm to do the same is probably not too far away. For example, New York State passed 23 NYCRR 500, a regulation requiring most financial and insurance firms to retain a chief information security officer (CISO), have a robust cybersecurity program, perform risk assessments and testing, roll out two-factor authentication, and report incidents within the first 72 hours. And, of course, develop an incident-response plan.

Why do I predict that such regulations are imminent? Consider seatbelts as an example. Once considered optional, the current policy on seatbelts is "Click it or ticket." Having an incident-response plan is like a seatbelt for your IT. It may not prevent an attack (that's what all the other stuff is for) but if one happens anyway, it will help limit the damage.

Another reason politicians are likely to get involved with requiring these plans is that insurance companies and governments are not prepared to shoulder the hits from an attack alone. And neither should you. You need the help.

The good news is that there are plenty of resources to help you develop an incident-response plan. The bad news is that developing an incident-response plan can be fairly complicated. In a sense, it's similar to building a hospital. The basics are obvious: You know it must have an emergency room, diagnostic facilities, intensive care units, operating rooms, patient rooms, offices, etc. But that's just the beginning! You also need to know the community that this hospital will be serving. Is it a metro area? Is it a small town? A group of isolated villages? Is the hospital in the tropics? The Arctic? And more questions follow: Who's funding it? The community? A wealthy donor? Is this a private company or government-owned? What kind of specialties will it have?

You get the idea. Your preexisting knowledge of minimum essential services plus demographics, geography, and budget will go a long way in deciding size and scope. For example, maybe your hospital can handle most everyday types of medical care, but when it comes to a body-part transplant, you'll need to refer the patient to a more specialized facility.

The same is true with your incident-response plan. Your firm's size, location, and budget will determine how sophisticated the plan will be. A small company may have an incident-response plan that calls for identifying an incident and immediately calling in outside expertise. A larger firm may have multiple incident-response specialists in house. As you can guess, the most critical step in developing your incident-response plan is going into it prepared to answer these questions.

## Incident-Response Plan Phases

August 2012 was, for its time, a record breaker. Much warmer than average in New England, 63 percent of the states suffered droughts while Florida was getting drowned from Hurricane Isaac and a bunch of tropical storms.

Meanwhile, back in Gaithersburg, Maryland, the National Institute of Standards and Technology (NIST) was hard at work releasing *NIST Special Publication 800-61 Revision 2: Computer Security Incident Handling Guide*. You have to hand it to them; their titles are killers! But that's nothing compared to what's inside.

Currently, NIST 800-61r2, as it's known, is required reading for anyone in the cybersecurity field. It is a beautiful piece of work, and if you plan to get hands-on with incident management, you need to get intimate with it. You should also get real close with such other captivating titles like *ISO/IEC 27035-2 Information Technology—Security Techniques—Information Security Incident Management—Part 2: Guidelines to plan and prepare for incident response*. (No, I am not kidding. That's the title. Fantastic work, too.) And while you're at it, you should also consult *ENISA's Actionable Information for Security Incident Response, Strategies for Incident Response and Cyber Crisis Cooperation*, and *NCSS Good Practice Guide—Designing and Implementing National Cyber Security Strategies*. Can't wait for more? The list is long, and sampled in this book's bibliography.

What do you need to understand from all this? What are the essential elements of an incident-response plan that you need to own in order to complete your own cybersecurity program?

The first critical thing to understand is that incident response is a program in and of itself. As such, it has its own distinct phases, and much like the overall cybersecurity program, it, too, is a living program. It's not one and done; it's a continuously managed program.

What are the phases? Have you heard of Elisabeth Kübler-Ross's five stages of grief: denial, anger, bargaining, depression, and acceptance? Many people go through them during an incident: "No! This can't be happening to us!" followed by choice expletives, then by the desire to pay to make this go away, quickly replaced by depression about having to face the music, and finally acceptance of the fact that you, like millions of others, are a victim of a cybercrime.

But the core phases of incident-response planning are less gloomy. They are: preparing for incidents, identifying the occurrence of an incident, containing the incident, treating the incident (e.g., killing the virus, disabling access, etc.), recovering from the incident, and post-incident review, aka the lessons-learned phase. That last one is key and should never be omitted.

To properly prepare for an incident you need to have in place three things:

1. A business continuity plan.
2. A disaster recovery plan.
3. An incident-response plan.

The business continuity plan is the plan that the business has prepared to ensure continuity of operations and value delivery in case of disruption. A business disruption could involve a natural disaster like a hurricane, an earthquake, or disease outbreak. Or it could a man-made disaster like a terrorist attack or a cyberattack. It could even involve a simple human failing, like what happens when Julie from Accounting gets food poisoning from the cafeteria's tacos.

The business continuity (BC) plan has all sorts of useful information that feeds into the incident-response plan. For example, it has a defined business continuity organizational structure, policies, and workflows, as well as information about who can trigger the BC plan and how that occurs, detailed contact information, including emergency contact numbers, client and vendor information, relocation strategies, recovery procedures, and the like. The benefit of the BC is that if and when it is invoked, different parts of the business execute different workflows designed to protect people, communicate effectively with all affected, and initiate as rapid a business recovery as possible.

The disaster recovery plan (DR) is technology centric. Its focus is in recovering the technology infrastructure of the company. This is where you will find all our favorite acronyms and their values per system: recovery time objectives (RTO), recovery point objectives (RPO), and the maximum tolerable downtime (MTD). All directly influence the incident-response plan.

Consider, for example, if you have zero MTD. You'll recall, we've been there before, but it's worth repeating here: Who has such zero tolerance for downtime? Trading systems. Banking systems. Air traffic control systems. Utility systems. And, for some of us, Uncle Bob's Bagel and Pastrami Paradise. How do their incident-response plans address this requirement, keeping in mind that a cyberattack on a trading system may well have strict regulatory implications, which means preserving evidence, forensics, etc.? You would need to plan for a zero MTD *and* remain compliant to regulations, which means you can't just kill the intruder, reboot the system, and you're back in business. As a matter of fact, shutting down an infected system would wipe its volatile memory, destroying any forensic data that may be there.

Do you see now why planning ahead is so important? You need to take this a step at a time.

## Preparing *Your* Incident-Response Plan

Notice the use of *your* as opposed to the generic incident response discussed earlier. No two IR plans are alike. They depend on many variables, from the size of the company (ranging from a small business to a multinational), to the scope of business, regulatory needs, and company culture. You might be surprised to hear that the last one plays a role in incident response, but it does. An active, engaged, and educated user community is an important asset in detection, in communications, and in remediation. A passive, disengaged, and generally cyberignorant culture frequently contributes to the incident and may even hinder its remediation.

By understanding your business-continuity and disaster-recovery plans, you will gain a solid footing in framing your incident-response plan. Similarly, the absence of either of these two plans speaks volumes about the company's priorities and risk management capabilities. It is your job to confront this reality head on, starting with engaging the executive team, whose active support is a requirement in all cybersecurity program development efforts, and critical in developing incident-response capabilities.

Remember back to our hospital-building analogy? All previous aspects of cybersecurity program development were akin to building the different wards and wings of the hospital. Incident response is the surgical center. Question number one, therefore, is: *Do you need a surgical center, or are you shipping your patients to a different facility altogether?* Otherwise phrased: *Do you need, can you afford, and will you keep engaged, an in-house incident-response team, or do you need to enter into an agreement with an outside incident-response provider?*

For the majority of small to mid-sized businesses, the answer will be to outsource the incident-response function (at a minimum). If this were a hospital, that would mean you keep the internists (or at least the nurses) in-house, but outsource the surgeons. It is highly unlikely that a small business will be able to both afford and to keep engaged a team of highly skilled and specialized cybersecurity incident-response people. But that doesn't get you off the hook from designing your incident-response plan! Remember, you can outsource responsibility, but you cannot outsource accountability. You still need to work with the service provider in designing and owning the plan. For your cybersecurity program development effort to succeed, you must always maintain accountability and full ownership. You are the one responsible for being knowledgeable enough and engaged enough to be able to successfully complete a cybersecurity handshake with your vendors.

For those businesses that need an in-house team for incident responses, you must also recognize that you will need to provide a complete ecosystem for them to succeed. They will need to report to the chief information security officer (CISO), and have access to the risk management teams, information technology, human resources, legal, and communications departments. The minimum size of an incident-response team will always be two: an incident-response manager and an incident-response engineer. One interfaces with the organization and directs the incident response while the other is deep in the weeds doing forensic and remediation work. The larger the organization, the larger the incident-response team and the more specialized and complex its structure.

Irrespective of size and scope of company, be it in-house or outsourced, your incident-response plan will need to address several key components, starting with a detailed description of your incident-response policies, standards, procedures, and guidelines. These, thankfully, will be derived to a considerable extent from your business continuity and disaster recovery plans, with the added input of at least risk management, legal, and communications. These policies will introduce organizational structure and will essentially define the *who-does-what-when* part of the incident response.

Regarding organizational structure, you'll need to adopt the one that best reflects the organization's needs. If you are decentralized, you may need decentralized incident-response teams. If not, perhaps a single centralized team is best. Depending on size and scope, you may decide to introduce a blended approach, where some incident-response capabilities are in-house while the rest are outsourced. This works well when there is a large headquarters-type of facility with smaller satellite offices scattered around the planet. In this case, you're probably better off having a centralized incident-response team at headquarters, with several vetted and contracted incident-response vendors at the remote locations ready to coordinate with you. All involved get a copy of the plan, typically saved in a big red binder with "Don't Panic" written all over it.

One absolutely critical part of your incident-response plan is a clear definition of communications protocols. Think of this as the *who-says-what-to-whom-when* part of the plan. This is key. For one, you don't want to instigate a panic among users by screaming through the speakerphones, "Incident Alert! Incident Alert!" And you certainly don't want to broadcast to the bad guys that you have detected an incident. So, avoid emails (they may have been compromised), avoid nonsecure messaging platforms, even unsecured telephone lines that may have been compromised. To the degree possible, stick with personal, one-on-one, need-to-know secure communications. Needless to say, this is not the time to get social! This is the time to carefully assess what exactly is happening, its impact on the business, on its clients and vendors, and, of course, the need to notify law enforcement and regulators. The last thing you want to happen is to have someone from the press calling you with, "I got a tweet about you folks having been breached.... Can you comment on that?" That's not a good place to find yourself.

The *whom* in the *who-says-what-to-whom-when* workflow can be long and dynamic. It will change regularly, and likely involve several third parties like your own insurance company, business vendors, cloud solutions providers, your Internet services providers, and a slew of information technology vendors and their incident-response teams. You may be required to notify law enforcement—my go-to is always the FBI and the local district attorney's office. If you happen to be a multinational, then the list becomes substantially longer since you may need to comply with local regulations on incident reporting country by country. On top of all these, you should consider sharing the information that you have with the United States Computer Emergency Readiness Team (US-CERT) and other industry-specific incident-response organizations.

The fun part of notifications, of course, is letting your clients know about the breach. To be clear: There is no avoiding this, and the experience will not get better with time. The last thing you want is to have your clients learn about the situation from the news media. You need to be prepared and well-rehearsed. Legal, insurance, and communications departments must all be in complete alignment on (at a minimum) what happened, who did it, why it happened, what you are doing in response, and how you're making sure it will not happen again. You may not know all the facts (e.g., who's behind it), but you need to be as proactive in your communications as due care and prudence will allow. Nothing destroys trust in a company faster than a poorly communicated cyber-incident. Get in front of it as soon as is practical—engage the news media and be as forthcoming as possible.

The next step in your incident-response plan creation is to integrate the wonderful results of your work to date in threat analysis, environments, and defense-in-depth and control deployments. The plan needs to reference all these, with specific clarity on where your threat intelligence is coming from and how you can leverage that in case of an incident, your environments at risk (clouds, Internet-connected devices, and your distributed workforce), and your defense-in-depth and controls deployments. These will be critical in both the detection of an incident and the response to it. Remember, all these entries in your plan need to be kept current. All this is dynamic, and for the plan to be useful, it needs to reflect the appropriate level of changes over time. What does this mean for you? Get comfortable with two words: change management.

To complete your incident-response plan, you will need two more entries. First, you will need to identify your incident-response toolkit. This is a set of mostly software tools (there are some hardware tools as well) that are specifically built for forensic and incident-response work. *Please note: These are surgical instruments, and they need to be handled by experts.* Moreover, the toolkit, like all else, evolves over time; in fact, toolkits are the fastest-evolving component of your response, because software is constantly updated. It is therefore critical that the plan reflect the most up-to-date toolkit in use, its locations (yes, there needs to be more than one), and any access credentials necessary. You do not want to be scrambling for USB keys in the middle of an attack. You need to know where your toolkit is, what is in it, and who are the right people to use it.

I can't emphasize enough the importance of the right people. Forensic and incident-response work is very complicated and requires highly skilled specialists. Even the best-intentioned and expert IT professional can wreak havoc if she attempts to use forensic tools without specialized training and experience. There are any number of case studies where IR professionals walked into a site under attack only to find the well-meaning IT team having turned off the servers and already restoring systems from backup. This common mistake destroys the evidence, leaving you with no way to know who attacked and why, no way to learn how to prevent it in the future, and so on.

The last component of your incident-response plan is the training. And by that I don't mean the company-wide cybersecurity awareness training I discussed earlier. Here I mean war games. Full, all-out, incident-response exercises, conducted frequently and analyzed exhaustively. Just like the old joke about how do you get to Carnegie Hall, the only way to get to be good at incident response is practice, practice, practice. The higher your dependence on your IR team, the more and rigorous your practice exercises must be—think Red Teams and Blue Teams; the works! The exercises need to be comprehensive across all your environments and include your executive team, staff, and all key vendors. Some should be well planned, rehearsed, and announced while others should be out-of-the-blue surprise drills. Everyone, from executives on down, should be aware and sensitized to incident response. They all have a role to play.

Meanwhile, your IR team should never rest. I know, it sounds harsh and too much. But, that's the job. It's what they do. Constant training and practicing is the only thing that will make the final difference during a real attack. Now, get to it!

## Identifying Incidents

Armed with your up-to-date, shiny, fire-engine-red, "Don't Panic" folder, you're ready to exercise your incident-response plan. All you need is an incident! If you're lucky, you'll wait for a nice, long time, giving you all the training opportunities your team needs. If you're not...

How do you identify an incident? You monitor your environment. And by that I mean $24 \times 7 \times 365$. Every system. Every action. Every event. Monitor. Monitor. Monitor. For the average company, monitoring will produce several thousand lines' worth of log entries and alerts from half a dozen systems (servers, firewalls, antivirus and antimalware software, switches, end points, etc.) or more. If your company is an above-average technology consumer, you will be dealing with potentially millions of log entries and events. Attempting to correlate all this, much less make sense of it all, is not something humans can manage on their own.

To be clear: Identifying an incident is far from trivial. Many have gone undetected for weeks and even months! It's not about interpreting alerts, reading logs, or processing user feedback. Hundreds of events in the course of doing business can be mistaken as a security incident. An application may modify a configuration file, and you get an alert: Is it an incident, or a normal function? A file server is slow: Incident, or just a heavy traffic load? Access to the Internet is spotty: Incident, or ISP errors? A file modification alert has been issued: Malware, or normal use? You received an email with a threat alert. Is it mere spam or a sign of things to come? Unfortunately, all these will need to be looked at through your cybersecurity glasses, even if they end up being little else than routine bugs.

Enter SIEM. Security Information and Event Management systems ingest all this information (logs, threat feeds, etc.), correlate it, and issue alerts about abnormal events in your environment. What's not to love? Nothing. Except that not all SIEMs are alike, and, like all relationships, you need to put work into it to get the benefits out of it.

First, you should do your due diligence and select the right SIEM for your environment. They come in all sorts of sizes and flavors, including SIEM-as-a-service options. Second, depending on which system you deploy, you may have to fine-tune it. Make your SIEM too paranoid and every alert issued becomes a ticket to be investigated. But tune it to apathy and you won't be notified until your data center has been pounded into fine silicon dust.

Once tuned, a good SIEM will be your best friend and cybersecurity partner. You'll be working hand in hand in processing the alerts, creating tickets, documenting trends, correlating with threat intelligence, and escalating to containment and treatment. All this beautifully orchestrated work will also be feeding into your cyberdocumentation tools, which your reporting workflows can use to notify authorities, incident information-sharing organizations, wikis, and late-night glee clubs.

The catch, of course, is that to reach this level of incident-detection bliss will require not only the right, and properly configured, SIEM choice and the right systems management practices (e.g., documentation, normalization, synchronization, etc.), but the right defense-in-depth strategy to begin with, which—you will recall—is the one that resulted in the deployment of the right controls that are being monitored across your environment in the first place.

And how did you get to the right defense-in-depth strategy? You got there because you did all the hard work during the asset, threat, vulnerabilities, and environments phases.

Who's better than you? No one, that's who!

## Containing Incidents

ALERT! ALERT! This is not a drill!

You have an alert that was identified as legit, was pressure tested, checked, and escalated to containment. Something is truly up! Now what?

Step one: Heed the advice on the front of your binder! *Do not panic!* You've got this.

Step two: Identification. What are you dealing with? What are your detective controls telling you?

Step three: Analysis. This is elbow-grease work requiring unique skills and specialized tools.

Step four: Action. Once you know *who*, *how*, and *what*, you need to be ready to take action: Do you want to maintain the evidence for possible future actions (for example, prosecution)? Do you want to get back to operations as soon as possible with little regard to evidence preservation? Do you want to tolerate the infection while you develop workarounds? These are decisions that you should have thought out ahead of time and practiced with both your incident team and your top-level management.

Let's look more closely at step four, action. To properly contain the incident, you'll need to know three things: *who*, *how*, and *what*.

1. *Who:* Who is behind the attack? Is this an accident? Is this an insider? Is this an act of terrorism? What do the threat feeds say about who's behind it? What is the motive? Understanding the *who* will help you develop methods of containment and treatment.
2. *How:* What is the attack vector? Malware, and if so, which kind? Is this the result of a virus? A Trojan? A worm? Did someone plug in an infected USB somewhere? Did someone click a link on an email? Was this a "drive-by shooting," such as malware dropped on a computer while someone was just browsing? Or was the breach perhaps the result of stolen credentials? It may be one or more of these things, or none of them. There could be some entirely other, more unusual

way that the attacker used to compromise your systems. Your team will need to identify the *how* in order to contain it and potentially identify ways to preserve forensic data.

3. *What was hit?* A single end point? Multiple ones? Servers? Applications? Networks? Your forensic people will need to do a detailed end-point analysis on the affected systems to collect evidence. This will include any kind of tracks that the attacker left behind, including a bit-by-bit copy of what is in the volatile memory (not just the permanent storage [e.g., hard disk, SSD, etc.]). They will need to establish the incident timeline: When did the attack start, how did it propagate, what did it leave behind, what are the effects? Part of this process involves highly technical work that may include isolating the malware on a system for observation, or reverse engineering the malware to understand what the code is doing. Once all this is understood, then all systems across the company will need to be forensically verified that they have not been infected as well.

It bears repeating that in the incident-containment phase, knowing what *not* to do is as important as knowing what *to* do. If your company does not have the resident expertise, a panicked executive, or IT person being flooded by alerts, may be tempted to pull the plug of the infected computer, try to use some I-got-it-from-the-Internet-malware-removal-tool, or—worse yet—log in as the administrator to investigate it or call your friend in the FBI.

This is why it is so critical to have a plan in place before the incident, and to practice, practice, practice! Knowing what to do and how to do it gets you half-way toward resolution.

## Treating Incidents

When it comes to treatment, I have bad news and bad news. First, the bad news.

Sometimes, you may have to live with the disease. You may need to live with it because of critical business considerations that prohibit you for isolating or rebuilding one or more systems. Or, you may need to keep the infected systems running so that the attackers don't realize that you are aware of them while shielding more valuable assets, or sending Delta Force over to kick in their doors. Similarly, there may be upstream or downstream dependencies that require you to get creative. For example, because of business requirements of nonstop use, you may need to restore the infected system onto brand new hardware and then reinsert it into production while taking the infected system out. That can prove about as easy as replacing an aircraft engine while it's in flight. It's doable but very, very windy.

Other times, you may be required to preserve the infected systems for evidence. That's all fine and good if you have one server that's infected; it's a whole other story if you have 50 of them sneezing and wheezing with a virus. Complicating things further is virtualization. These days, you can have multiple virtual computers running on one physical one. Despite ironclad assurances from virtualization vendors that there can never be cross-contamination across virtual machine boundaries, I remain a skeptic. I am a firm believer that if one person can build it, another can break it. So, I would not be surprised if a virus was created that could jump the virtualization boundary, despite whatever assurances you've been given. Remember, everyone lies.

Finally, after evidence has been preserved, requirements have been met, all the *t*'s crossed and all the *i*'s dotted, there is the fun part of coordinating one or more infected systems. Not only do you need the incident-response team on the same page, you need the whole organization to know that the following systems will go offline, for how long, what the impact may be, and so on and so forth. Depending on the number of systems, this can be an expensive, resource-intensive exercise. Plus, you'll make a whole new set of friends when you announce that all the passwords have been changed.

Which brings us to the bad news.

The only way to ensure that an infected system has been cured is to go to bare metal. This means that you need to completely and thoroughly wipe the infected system and rebuild it bottom-up from clean installation media. There is no sugarcoating this. If you need to be 99.99 percent sure that the infection is gone, the only way to do it is by burning the box and reinstalling everything new.

Why only 99.99 percent sure, even after a clean wipe? Because, word on the street has it that some agencies have developed malware that infects the actual hardware itself. Allegedly, this type of malware can infect the BIOS (basic input/output system) of a computer, or certain EPROM (erasable programmable read-only memory) chips, such that even after you wipe the computer, the malware can reinstall itself.

Of course, even wiping a single system is a time-consuming exercise. Not only do you need to have the clean installation media at hand, you also need to account for configuration settings, clean backup availability, data synchronization when the system gets reinserted into production, etc. Now, multiply this times the number of infected systems. This is where your disaster recovery planning will shine. Having clean, recent, whole-image backups per system will go a long way toward a rapid recovery.

## Incident Recovery

With the incident treated, you are ready to bring your systems back online. There are several questions that need answering here, bridging the incident treatment process and final incident recovery.

First, way before any incident, you must have considered the need for evidence preservation. If you are required to do forensic preservation, then you cannot wipe the infected equipment and rebuild. You'll need replacement gear. Moreover, the documentation needs and requirements for evidence preservation are extensive. Your team will need to be familiar with all the laws and requirements for evidence handling, chain-of-custody documentation, proper evidence gathering. Your best bet is to retain a forensic firm to help you. They will interface with your attorney and your incident-response team, and make sure that all the evidence is taken care of properly.

Second, your incident-recovery strategy hinges on your known values of MTD, your maximum tolerable downtime, the RPO, your recovery point objective, and the RTO, your recovery time objective. You have documented all of this before any incident, and they have governed your disaster recovery strategy. Here and now is where all this will be tested.

As with all things, recovery from an incident will fall on a spectrum. There will be companies whose MTD is practically zero and will therefore have hot failover sites, air gapped (i.e., non-Internet accessible) backup and archives, and multi-timeline mirrors (mirroring strategy and the necessary equipment that creates isolated versions of mission-critical systems over predefined timelines—for example a real-time mirror, a day-old mirror, a week-old mirror, a month-old mirror, and so on). Those companies will be using an army of resources to recover, because that's what it's worth to them, and frequently *is* what is required of them (think utilities, national security installations, water purification, air traffic control, etc.).

Then, there are the majority of companies that can afford an MTD of hours or days. Their strategy is more appropriate to that timeline, meaning that your team has some runway to be able to restore systems to production. That is not to say that there is a company out there that doesn't want the absolute minimum MTD. This is to say that the majority of companies are smart enough to not overpay for disaster recovery when they can tolerate a few days' worth of an outage. There may be a question about if those smarts are developed from proper risk management–centric thinking, or from "Are you crazy? I am not paying all this money for backup!" reactions. Either way, most IT departments have in place a budget-appropriate solution that has been implicitly accepted as appropriate.

Lastly, there are (hopefully) a minority of companies that have not thought through any of this. For them, incident recovery is … challenging. Some may never recover and go out of business (consider malware that destroys all data in the absence of a backup). Some will pay a dear price in both time and money and get only a partial recovery. Either way, if you are reading this book, and you're this far in and have realized that this paragraph describes your company, you have a lot of work to do, and you'd best hurry up!

In our case, I am confident that you have evaluated and vetted your disaster recovery strategies and solutions as appropriate to your risk appetite, cybersecurity exposure, and so on, so we'll accept that your environment falls squarely into the smart group of companies! While your team is restoring your production environment, you are making sure that they are following a pre-rehearsed checklist that affirms proper and normal operation of all systems, following the communications and notifications protocols, and all departments are working together in incident-response harmony. At the same time, you are making exhaustive notes on the incident that will help you in your post-incident review and action plan.

## Post-Incident Review

There will be *incidents* and there will be *INCIDENTS!* Both will require your careful review. People call post-incident review many different things (lessons learned, postmortem, etc.), but no matter what you choose to call it, the review process is essential to the evolution of your cybersecurity program and team skills. To begin with, you need an answer to a whole list of questions, starting with:

- *Who's responsible for this outrage?* You should be able to answer this with confidence. And yet the question is more complex than it seems. It's not about merely assigning a name to the attacker; it is about building a complete profile. Sometimes getting a name will be impossible. You will still be able to glean quite a bit from the tools used, origin, threat intelligence feeds, and plain old Internet searching. Try to build as good a profile as possible. Understanding your attackers, their motives, and their methods will help you prepare for the next attack.
- *Just the facts, ma'am!* After the *who*, you need to document the *how*, and you need to do it in excruciating detail. You need to know exactly what happened, when it happened, how it happened, what vulnerabilities were exploited, how it was discovered, which alerts were triggered, and which were not. You need all the facts about the incident, in as much

detail as possible. This will help you tune your defenses and identify holes in your control deployment.

- *Knowing now what you didn't know then, what do you need to change?* This is the introspective component of the exercise. You need to look inward and understand how your organization reacted to the incident. Look at everything and leave no stone unturned. How did the incident-response team act? Were procedures followed? Were internal communications effective? Was the response time adequate? Were the response actions timely and adequate? Did you meet MTD, RPO, and RTO targets? How did the executive team support the effort? How did the staff react? How was the IT-cybersecurity partnership performance? Once these questions are answered, you can collectively sit down and tune your incident-response plan such that next time you can perform better.
- *How do you stop this from happening again?* Having understood the organization's and team's performance, plus all about the incident itself, you need to plug the hole that allowed the incident to occur in the first place. This sounds a lot easier than it is. If the breach was due to a phishing incident, for example, your options may be limited to better email sandbox tuning and targeted cybersecurity awareness training. Neither of those will plug the hole completely. They may narrow it, but there is no guarantee that another member of the staff will not fall victim to such an attack. In which case, you're going back to layered defenses (sandboxing, role authorities, monitoring, training, etc.).

## Do It All Over Again!

As we discussed earlier, cybersecurity program development in general and incident-response planning specifically are living programs. They change over time, they change with your environment, the market, the technology, and they change because you change. You learn, you grow, you adapt.

The good news is that as you learn, grow, and adapt, you can apply your knowledge, experience, and adaptation to your cybersecurity and incident-response plans. You get a second chance! And, a third, and a fourth ....

Change is the only constant here, and it represents a wonderful opportunity in keeping your cybersecurity program constantly tuned. Embrace this, and take advantage of it. The alternative is catastrophic: An obsolete cybersecurity and incident-response program are just as bad as not having any.

# CHAPTER 12
## People

Remember our initial definition of *cybersecurity? Cybersecurity is the ongoing application of best practices intended to ensure and preserve confidentiality, integrity, and availability of digital information as well as the safety of people and environments.*

And, of course, the triad from our defense-in-depth discussion? *People, technology,* and *operations.*

Finally, which is one of the most effective controls in cybersecurity? *People!*

People, people, people! You may say I revel in stating the obvious, but all the work we've done so far is not about data, assets, or some document that defines a corporation. It is only about people. I've emphasized this in every chapter: Our work, your work, is people-centric.

People, it bears repeating, are at once your biggest asset and potential liability. As assets, they create value, they align with goals, and help protect the values they create. As liabilities, they can just as easily destroy these values through lack of awareness, carelessness, or ill will.

Your challenges in creating your cybersecurity program are twofold: First, you are creating a program for your people. Second, you must engage the same people to make the program a success.

That last one is trickier than it sounds!

## What's in It for Me?

Up until now we've been asking the question, "How much is it worth to you?" That's the right question to ask of the board of directors, shareholders, and so on in determining risk appetite and crafting the right cybersecurity strategy and program. Obviously, we never want to apply controls that are more expensive than the assets we protect, but between that floor and the ceiling set by risk appetite we have a lot of room and a lot of choices.

Now, we are asking people to engage with us and help us make our cybersecurity program a success. Why should they? Because we ask nicely? Because the company mandates it? Because of the "Only You Can Prevent Cybersecurity Incidents" poster in the break room?

I've emphasized how important senior management buy-in and support is for a cybersecurity program. We've discussed the significance of board engagement, and the role of company leadership in not only leading by example, but also conveying the message that cybersecurity is a shared responsibility. Now, though, we have to go from the abstract to the specific—from policy to people. That means confronting a new question: "What's in it for me?"

The literature on human motivation is extensive, and reviewing it in depth is clearly beyond our scope. But let's dip our toes in a little because you need to know a few basics in order to give your new cybersecurity program the best chance of success. This chapter will introduce some fundamentals about what makes people's attitudes shift, what kind of messaging works, and how to design a cybersecurity awareness program.

## Attitude Adjustment!

In their classic *Handbook on Social Psychology* (1986), McGuire, Lindzey, and Aronson defined *attitude* as beliefs and behaviors toward something. This something could be work, could be ideas, could be other people. Moreover, attitudes change with time, cultural influences, personal motivation, and knowledge acquisition.

A key factor in the ability to shift a person's attitude is a phenomenon called emotional resonance. Fear is a useful tool in provoking attitude change. When I used to teach computer science at the Stratford School in Rochester, New York, I used to tell my students that I considered "fear a valid educational tool!" I was, of course, joking, since I am one of those who prefer honey to vinegar any time of the day. Still, Professor Howard Leventhal at Rutgers University, in his 1970 paper "Findings and Theory in the Study of Fear Communications," makes two critical points that are particularly relevant to communicating a cybersecurity awareness message. The first is that "increases in fear generally increase persuasion, but there obviously are conditions where this is not so." The second one is that "when high fear messages fail to persuade, the failure frequently reflects the subject's felt incapacity to cope with danger."

There have been plenty of situations when I've tried to communicate a sense of urgency or danger to boards and executives, and those experiences fully confirm Dr. Leventhal's points. In general, following delivery of my message, there is a shift in the recognition that there is a problem to be solved, and in most cases, a follow-through action.

There is, however, a small percentage who inevitably reject the message altogether. They are the ones who will try every excuse in the book to ignore the new cyberreality ("We're too small," "Hasn't happened yet," "We'll look into it next year ... "). They are unable (or unwilling) to cope with the new dangers that our world now presents, and instead choose to hide their heads in the sand.

What I have found to be most effective in dealing with any stakeholder—be it the board of directors, the executive team, or the staff—is to stay on message. Be pragmatic about the threat as opposed to dramatic. Be equal parts diagnosis and equal parts prognosis. Be realistic, and always focus on the recipient, and their ability to process the information. Channel Peter Drucker:

*It is the recipient who communicates. The so-called communicator, the person who emits the communication, does not communicate. He utters. Unless there is someone who hears, there is no communication. There is only noise!*

Peter Drucker, *Management: Tasks, Responsibilities, and Practices*, New York: Harper & Row, 1973, p. 483.

## The Right Message, Delivered the Right Way

Back in 1951, Professor Carl I. Hovland and Walter Weiss of Yale University delivered a great paper, "The Influence of Source Credibility on Communication Effectiveness." It is in that paper that we learn that subjects, at the time of information exposure, discounted material from "untrustworthy sources." The problem is that with time, the same subjects tended to disassociate the content and the source, resulting in the acceptance of... Fake News! As a matter of fact, Hovland and Weiss discovered that "lies, in fact, seemed to be remembered better than truths."

As fascinating as this is, even more interesting is what happens with the retention of the message, depending on the source, over time. They discovered that although a message from a highly credible source had a higher percentage chance of being initially accepted, its acceptance dropped substantially over time (as short as four weeks). They also discovered that the reverse is equally true. A message from an untrustworthy source had an initially smaller chance of being accepted, but over the same amount of time, its chances increased, eventually exceeding that of the trustworthy source.

Why is all this important to our cybersecurity program's success? Because the messenger matters just as much as the message. And because you may have to dislodge false, entrenched beliefs from people whose cooperation is essential to the program's success.

For example, if your CFO is absolutely convinced that there is no way that your company is on any hacker's radar, you'll have a very hard time trying to get funding for the cybersecurity program. You will need to shift the CFO's attitude, and to do this you'll need to use language and tools that she, and she alone, can understand. This needs to be a very individualized communication, with a specifically tailored message, delivered by the right messenger.

Here's the vital point: Sometimes, the messenger cannot be you. If everyone in the company knows you're the one pushing for the adoption of a cybersecurity program, the staff may feel that you're coming to the table with a specific point of view, trying to shove a program down their throats. Your goal of adoption may be best served by using an ally as the messenger. Pick a well-liked manager, or the business team members who have helped you along the way, or even independent consultants as your authoritative messengers. Stay focused on message adoption, not the messenger.

For a message to be adopted, it must have certain qualities. Those include being:

- *Succinct.* If your message is more than a few sentences, it's too long. Edit it down to your specific point. One point per message. Don't ramble.
- *Specific.* The message needs to be as specific as possible and it should obey the communications principle of who will do what by when. (If you need more on that, look no further than the book by Tom Hanson and Birgit Zacher Hanson titled *Who Will Do What By When? How to Improve Performance, Accountability and Trust with Integrity*).
- *Meaningful.* Why does this message make sense to the recipients? How is it pertinent to their work life?
- *Authoritative.* What's the associated authority issuing the message? In other words, why should we listen to you?
- *Doable.* At the end of the day, your message must reflect a call to action that can be achieved. It cannot be aspirational or shoot for the stars. It has to be achievable by the message recipient in a reasonable amount of time and through reasonable effort.

By understanding your audience and understanding both the power *and* the limitations of your message, you can frame your internal communications accordingly. More importantly, you can use this information to tailor your cybersecurity-awareness training to the specific strengths, weaknesses, and culture of your company.

## Cybersecurity-Awareness Training

Just as no two cybersecurity programs are exactly alike, so it is with cybersecurity-awareness training programs. There are common elements, of course, and we'll examine them further on in this chapter. But you should never lose touch with the individuality of your company's culture and the specific needs of your people.

For any cybersecurity program to succeed, no matter its scope and delivery method, you must secure the vocal participation of your leadership team. They need to advocate for it, they need to participate in it, and they need to evangelize their middle managers on the importance of it.

There are several ways you can conduct cybersecurity-awareness training. Your choice will depend on the size of the organization, the level of existing awareness of the topic, and your risk and threat assessments. Speaking of assessments, an excellent way to establish a training baseline is by doing a skills assessment on cybersecurity. This could be as easy as a fun quiz, or even an interactive game that you can push out to everyone's computer. The results will be instrumental in designing the training.

## MY TOP CYBERSECURITY QUIZZES!

The following links represent my top general assessment cybersecurity quizzes. They are not as extensive or customized to any organization, but they certainly can help you get an overall sense of where your company's population cyberunderstanding is.

They are (alphabetically):

1. European Cyber Security Month (recurring, sponsored by ENISA and the European Commission) awareness campaign: https://cybersecuritymonth.eu/references/quiz-demonstration/ welcome-to-the-network-and-information-security-quiz/
2. FBI's "Cyber Surf Islands" games, especially made for students: https://sos.fbi.gov/?came_from=https%3A//sos.fbi.gov/ welcome-fbi-cyber-surf-island-fbi-sos-internet-challenge-text-only/
3. Federal Trade Commission's Phishing Scam "Avoid the Bait" quiz: https://www.consumer.ftc.gov/sites/www.consumer.ftc. gov/files/games/off-site/ogol/_phishing-scams.html
4. Khan Academy's Cybersecurity Quiz: https://www.khanacademy. org/partner-content/nova/cybersecurity/cyber/e/cybersecurity-101-quiz

5. Media Smarts: Canada's Centre for Digital and Media Literacy Quiz: http://mediasmarts.ca/sites/mediasmarts/files/games/cyber-security-quiz/index_en.html
6. Microsoft's "Test Your Cyber Security IQ": http://www.microsoft businesshub.com/internet-security-iq?CR_CC=200682284
7. Pew Research Center: Internet and Technology, Cybersecurity Quiz: http://www.pewinternet.org/quiz/cybersecurity-knowledge/
8. SANS Cyber Aces Courses and Quizzes: http://www.cyberaces.org/courses/quizzes

Once that's done, you need to decide which training strategy is appropriate to your audience. Is it going to be a trainer-led program or a learner-led one? In the first case, the trainer is in control. He or she presents the material, the learners participate to the degree that the trainer allows, and they may be subsequently tested. In the learner-led approach, the learner is in control, the training material is consumed asynchronously (people learn as they want and when they want), and the trainer's role becomes that of a facilitator and guide as the learners navigate the material at their own pace and share their experiences.

In some cases, the strategy is dictated by the size and geography of the company. For example, it will be very difficult to have an instructor-led workshop for a company with a few hundred employees distributed all over the country. Similarly, an intimate "lunch and learn" may be all your company needs to start on the cybersecurity awareness path.

Once you have identified the needs and arrived at a training strategy, the next step is to pick the best way to deliver the information. Your choices include:

- *Presentations*. Whenever I do a presentation, my second slide is a famous *New Yorker* cartoon by Alex Gregory. In it, the devil is interviewing a torturer, and says, "I am looking for someone well versed in the art of torture—do you know PowerPoint?" The point is well taken. You can certainly use presentations to deliver cybersecurity awareness training, but be certain to be as engaging and inclusive during the training as possible. Otherwise, you run the risk of the glazed, sleepy-eyed, disengaged audience. My recommendation is to use presentations for what they are good for: Deliver specific guidance to a specific targeted audience. Keep them short. Keep them to the point. And be sure to keep them interactive.

- *Lunch and learn.* This is a less formal presentation. If at all possible, avoid slides and the like. Set up the room in as round and inclusive a layout as possible (no podium, be part of the audience). Your goal is to have a discussion about a cybersecurity topic over lunch. Any material for your learners should be handed to them at the beginning, and let them peruse them at their pace. Keep the topic focused. For example, you don't want to have a "Cybersecurity Awareness Lunch and Learn." Be specific! You want to have "Phishing, and all the ways you can get hooked!" lunch and learn.
- *Group learning.* This is a great way to convey complex topics to either a small group, or sets of groups. For each group, you will need a skilled trainer in team-building and role-playing methodologies. The idea here is that you are taking a topic and really acting out everything there is to know about it. For example, if you're group learning about phishing, you may want to guide the group through an exercise in which members of the group alternate into the role of the hacker and try to fool the others to act on their instruction. What's the instruction? It can be anything, such as handing over a bunch of Legos! (Legos are a great interactive training prop! Don't leave your office without your Lego bucket!)
- *E-Learning.* If you have decided that your training strategy is a learner-led one, then e-learning will play a crucial role in success-fully delivering and testing your cybersecurity awareness program. To be sure, e-learning can, and should, complement *any* training methodology. It allows for constant assessments, reminder quizzes, and on-demand availability of information. It also reinforces all the other methods, since it can be a complementary resource to those who want to know more about the specific topic, or for those who for some reason or another couldn't attend the instructor-led training.

There are several excellent e-learning cybersecurity awareness programs. Consider, for example, the SANS Institute training offerings, Inspired Learning, Wombat Security, PhishMe, and Security Mentor to name only a very few. Please note that this is not an endorsement of any of specific program, and the preceding list is far from complete. I am mentioning them here to start you on a path to discovery for the right vendor for your specific company needs. Do your research and due diligence, and partner with the vendor that is right for you.

I cannot emphasize enough the importance of integrating your specific company culture and needs with cybersecurity awareness training. It also goes without saying that this is not a one-and-done type of activity. Depending on size and scope of your company, you will need to provide regular refreshers, training support, quizzes, reminders, and so on. Also remember that you need to integrate the training across the life cycle of all employees—from onboarding to offboarding.

Be sure to include in your training their at-home behavior. Your employees are exposed to cyberthreats both at work and at home. After all, if an employee uses the same laptop at home as in the office, then the cybersecurity risks don't stop at the office door.

The good news is that a successful cybersecurity awareness program can be one your most effective controls in your defense-in-depth strategy. Companies with an aware population have seen up over a 30 percent improvement in their ability to detect phishing scams, insider threats, even abnormal system activities.

My advice: Take cybersecurity awareness training very, very seriously. Just because it is a soft control (as opposed to all the high-tech hardware, software, and services ready), that doesn't mean it's any less effective. As a matter of fact, time and time again, security awareness consistently proves itself as one of the best controls against attacks. Invest in it accordingly.

## CASE STUDY: A CYBERSECURITY CLASS GONE AWRY: LESSONS FOR EVERY BUSINESS

### An Interview with Ms. F. Charlene Watson, Instructor and Cybersecurity Consultant

For Charlene Watson's first class teaching Computer Science at Florida A&M, she planned to follow the syllabus closely. She didn't have much choice. Hired as a guest instructor at the last minute to fill a vacancy, she had only a few days to prepare.

According to the plan outlined by the previous professor, the first class was to be spent in a review of basic networking principles.

"TCP/IP, Unix Stack, the whole thing," says Watson, who describes herself as a 25-year paramedic, turned martial artist, turned hacker, turned security specialist, turned teacher.

"Because you can't secure a network if you don't know network protocols."

Watson, whose teaching style is "very animated," came out of the chute with a bang. "I was going on and on about the TCP/IP stack, the OSI model, physical, data link, and network layers. And then I turn around and every single individual is looking at me with a blank stare. It occurred to me that they didn't have a clue."

She asked for a show of hands. "Anyone who knows what I mean when I say, 'TCP/IP stack?'"

One hand went up.

That student, through his background in the military, had been exposed to computer networks. The rest of the class—majoring in health informatics, business, and information sciences—had no background in IT. They were enrolled in Watson's course as one of prerequisites for an NSA certificate.

"Anyone with an NSA certificate is a highly desirable employee," says Watson. So that made sense. The problem was the course presumed the students had a certain a level of IT understanding. "A lot of them simply did not."

Immediately scrapping the entire curriculum, Watson remembered a class she herself had taken, called up her old professor, and got to work.

The TECO project, available on a general public license, is a course that takes students through the basics of networking. In fact, they have to build a network from scratch themselves.

According to TECO project documents:

The purpose of this exercise to help students understand how to design a network with only basic information available. When designing a network, the student may be given only a map and will have to make estimates from that little bit of information.

"I beefed it up and made it more security enabled," says Watson.

All her students were given building designs, architecture and security designs, IP addressing space, VLANS, and a set of expectations. "Each week, they had to ask me questions as if I were the client.

They had to call up Cisco and Dell and spec out everything from routers, layer 1 equipment, layer 2 equipment, layer 3 equipment, and edge equipment." She even made them draw the wiring using Visio.

From making wiring choices, to deciding why to use multimode fiber over single mode, to the security plan, to penetration testing, her students did it all. They went on field trips to small and large-scale data centers to see networks at enterprise scale.

Eventually, Watson enlisted her third-semester course students who'd been through her boot camp to manage the new first-semester students.

At first, she didn't receive rave reviews.

One student told Watson about his first reaction to her. "The first week, I told my wife, 'My Lord! This lady's crazy.' But my wife said to stay with it. I hated you every step of the way."

Then, that same student went to job interviews. When asked what experience he had, he put a binder down on the prospective employer's desk with all the network diagrams and landed himself a job.

"In the end, three or four of my students were picked up by the FBI, one by IBM, two by Cisco, and one by Microsoft."

Watson's experiences have critical lessons for hiring.

What businesses need to be aware of, says Watson, is that "data is the new currency." There is not a single job, she says, that doesn't involve data. "Even the cashier at Pizza Hut. They are touching and gathering customer and product data." Because of that, we need a digitally aware and digitally educated workforce, whether they are in an office, or in law enforcement, or health care.

As Watson's experience reveals, businesses must be careful about whom they hire and recall the binder-on-the-desk example from her former student. A solid, hands-on understanding of networks is a fundamental qualification for anyone being hired for a security position.

The way security professionals speak within the business, Watson says, is a second important criterion. "We taught students how to do it," Watson says. For example, the actual word *security* was off limits. "Executives have cybersecurity fatigue. They are tired of throwing money at the problem." She notes that the continued use of the word *security* implies to executives that they can create a company so cyber-secure it will never be hacked.

"But if it's IP-addressable, someone will get in."

Therefore, it was important for her students to learn to substitute the word *resilience*. "When you are breached, it's about recovering."

Effective communication wasn't about dumbing down the "geek-speak." According to Watson, it was about how to do the geek-speak in a way that would get senior leadership to listen.

Watson's experience also has implications for institutions of higher learning. They, after all, are on the hook for delivering newly trained security professionals into the corporate world. "It used to be a focus on research," Watson says. But now a set of new standards is required. Institutions that want to maintain their certification as a security center of excellence must require professors to have current certifications in their area. "Whatever the course is, they need an industry-standard certification."

This change, she predicts, will be good for business.

There are two possible solutions to the current shortage of security professionals, in Watson's view. The first is veterans, who, like her student, often have basic grounding in IT simply by virtue of having been in the military.

Inner-city youth is a second source, she says. "When you grow up in a tough environment and survive to 21 or 22, then you have mad skills. You can think outside the box to problem-solve. We have a ton of untapped talent K-12, inner city, low income. You give those kids a $35 raspberry pi kit [a very basic computer that teaches programming skills] and hire someone to go in and teach them how to use it."

# CHAPTER 13

# Living Cybersecure!

*Remember, no matter where you go, there you are.*
—*The Adventures of Buckaroo Banzai Across the 8th Dimension*

And, here you are! You made it! You plowed through chapter after chapter, stayed with me through some pretty tricky topics, learned a whole bunch of acronyms, reviewed cases studies, and now?

Now you know a lot more about your company than when you started! You know about its assets, its threat profile, and its risk appetite. You know where all the bodies are buried. You know what's worth protecting, and by how much. And you got to make a whole new set of friends in the process.

You are also in the proud ranks of the wise men and women! Wise people know what they don't know. The trick here is to recognize this and stay within their ranks. You need to take the knowledge that you gained, look at it critically, find ways to build on it, and always, always question it.

Cybersecurity is a science; a hard one at that. A science that's rapidly evolving. New discoveries, new approaches, new best practices are discovered, tested, and applied daily. Staying on top of this field is no easy task—some would argue it's impossible—but staying informed is something that you can, and should, do. As we've discussed, cybersecurity is a shared responsibility, and staying on top of it is one of the things that you must do.

When it comes to staying on top of things, how much is enough? Much depends on your role and day-to-day responsibilities. For a busy C-level executive, receiving pertinent alerts and a weekly summary may be enough. For a hands-on operations executive with cybersecurity oversight responsibilities, a daily briefing may be necessary. For a board member, alerts and a quarterly report from the CISO may be all that is needed. Frequency, quantity, and context will be determined by the size and needs of your specific organization. One thing is certain: You will need to stay informed and current. Forever!

What else do you need to know? Well that list is long. Very long!

What else do you need to know to support your newly created cybersecurity program? Now, that's more manageable, and I have some ideas!

In general, the things you need to be aware of tend to fall into one of the following categories:

- *Scientific developments*. These are straight-up developments in the field. Like I mentioned, there are thousands of cybersecurity professionals who are constantly pushing the envelope. Their dedication and breakthroughs are what makes this world a safer place, and books like this possible. Regarding where you can learn about their constant progress, my recommendation is to join one or more of the several worldwide organizations who support and advance the science and application of cybersecurity. For example, I have made frequent reference to CIS, ISACA, ISSA, (ISC)$^2$, ISO, and the SANS Institute. There are also government agencies like ENISA and NIST that also provide a wealth of information and best practices for a variety of industries and company sizes. A bit of research (and some well-spent membership dollars) will go a long way toward keeping you informed.

- *Regulatory developments*. These are typically legislative actions affecting cybersecurity implementation, and they can range from compulsory to strongly suggested. You certainly need to know about them—ideally, long before they're enacted—and plan accordingly. Moreover, you need to know about them everywhere in the world that you do business in. (See, for example, the European Union General Data Protection Regulation in Chapter 10.) You should expect regulatory actions at every level: city, state, and country. Whether your board, or whoever accepts risk in your company, chooses to comply is another matter. Yes, noncompliance is an option. Remember: If the cost of a control is higher than the asset it is meant to protect, then it doesn't make sense to implement it. Therefore, if implementing a regulation is going to cost the company so much money and time as to not be worthwhile when compared to the fine, then it may make sense to pay the fine. To be clear: I am not advocating that you take this position; but I would be remiss not to alert you to it!

How do you get to find out about all these possible exciting developments? Typically, your industry-specific publication keeps track and reports on legislative developments that may affect you. That said, there is no substitute for staying informed about what your government representatives are doing. Get involved and stay involved. Start with a reputable major daily newspaper, and graduate to picking up the phone and calling your representative with any questions you may have. After all, it's your business we're talking about here.

- *Information technology and computer science developments.* These developments are many, constant, and far-reaching. We're not talking business disruption here. We're talking life-changing discoveries and developments that will forever change the way we work, think, communicate, learn, influence, and behave. Aside from Moore's law that, in essence, predicted the doubling of computing power every couple of years, there have been breakthroughs in artificial intelligence, machine learning, pattern analysis (think big data), blockchain technologies, and the integration of computing and communications capabilities into everything from a toaster oven to a pacemaker. Why do you need to know about this? Because, as we've discussed, these things will dramatically influence your workplace, and since you're the one sensitized to the cybersecurity implications, you also get to be the one who needs to get in front of these developments and—at least—think about their potential impact to your program, if not your life. How can you stay informed on these changes? At a minimum, I would recommend subscribing to MIT's *Technology Review*, the *Harvard Business Review*, and at least one industry-specific publication. Are there any other publications that are reliable sources of this type information? Absolutely, and by all means, subscribe to them all! The important thing here is for you to stay continuously informed.

I will close this chapter with a look at what I consider to be *the* emerging technologies and trends that you need to be aware of for the next couple of years. I believe that each one will have a significant impact on how we understand cybersecurity needs, how we implement cybersecurity, and how we can safely interact with this increasingly cyberenabled world.

## General Data Protection Regulation (GDPR), Privacy, and Regulators

We discussed GDPR at some length in Chapter 10. It is worth your review, again. For that matter, it's best reviewed with a good friend, such as your legal department.

What we need to be sensitive about is that GDPR really is: a significant, international, far-reaching, cybersecurity regulation. I predict that it is just the beginning in what will be a long battle: various government regulations versus the inexorable advance of information technologies that push against a wall of real and perceived privacy rights.

There are many questions we need to ask: Why did the European Union even need to create such a strict data protection law? Does privacy need to be regulated? Better yet, what is privacy in the information age? That last one can take a whole book by itself, and it's one I plan to write, so for now, let's just stick with some basics:

The question of "Why, oh why, did the EU do such a thing?" is simple. According to their own statement:

> *The EU General Data Protection Regulation (GDPR) ... was designed to harmonize data privacy laws across Europe, to protect and empower all EU citizens' data privacy and to reshape the way organizations across the region approach data privacy.*

According to the American point of view, it is because they wanted to punish, or curtail and control the monopolistic behavior of the U.S. technology giants and their cavalier attitude toward privacy, marketing, and advertising. There were, and are, many in the EU who feel that by their practices and sheer size alone, the U.S. tech firms squeeze out the European competition. The most recent example of this kind of thinking is the €2.42 billion (about $2.7 billion) fine imposed by the EU on Google in an antitrust case over search.

All that aside, and going back to privacy, we're faced with no clear-cut, worldwide accepted definition of the word *privacy*. As a matter of fact, in several languages *privacy* doesn't even exist as a stand-alone concept: In Greek, for example, it is loosely, and poorly, translated as *secrecy*.

Then, there is the matter of the right to privacy. How you can discuss a right to something you can hardly define is mindboggling, but that hasn't stopped many a legislator from attempting it. The right to privacy, as locally defined by various countries, has therefore been introduced in a variety of documents from constitutions to bills. In the United States, for example, there is no constitutional guarantee to privacy. There is an *implication* of it in several parts of the Bill of Rights, but how far that privacy actually extends is open to debate. The Italians, on the other hand, are very serious about the matter and there is a right to privacy spelled out in their constitution.

Somehow, among all the definitions, codifications, and laws, we have to conduct business, exchange information, enforce laws, and treat each other's concept of privacy with a modicum of respect. Toward that end there have been many ongoing attempts to somehow frame the concept of privacy as a human right. This, of course, is far from trivial, with cultural, ethical, legal, and commercial interests fiercely competing for recognition of their definition of this elusive privacy.

Why do you care about all this, and how does this affect your cybersecurity program? You care because legislators of countries where you do business are not waiting on consensus definitions of terms. They write laws, and you're expected to comply, which brings us right back to the GDPR.

"But," you'll exclaim, "I don't do business with the EU." Be that as it may, even if you don't do business with them now, you may do business with an EU partner, vendor, or client tomorrow. If and when that happens, you will need to comply.

And even if you argue that this will never, ever, ever happen, I regret to inform you that this still doesn't let you off the hook. Many states plan to adopt a GDPR-like regulation to protect and serve their citizens. And, that's before the federal government makes its say in the matter.

Bottom line: You need to perform annual data privacy impact assessments. Make it part of your annual cybersecurity program review, and make sure that you carefully document the privacy impact of the data that you store about everything: employees, clients, vendors, partners, competitors, friends, and enemies! Think in terms of a continuous auditing of both your data and your practices. That is the world you should be prepared to live and do business in.

What else should you expect in the regulatory front in the next few years?

For one, expect to see many states following the recent example of New York, which mandated by state law that all financial and insurance firms must retain a CISO and show evidence of a robust cybersecurity program. You should further expect that these types of laws will extend past financial services firms to law firms, health care, and education.

There are many drivers for such legislation. Financial concerns are a big one, as is the notion of wanting constituents to be protected. (No one wants to answer the question: "What do you mean little Bobby's medical history is being sold on the dark web?")

Consider, for example, the continuously increasing risk that insurance companies are underwriting with their cybersecurity policies. Granted, that's their business and they know it well, so most of these policies are extraordinarily restrictive and prescriptive as to what's covered and how. Still, their exposure continues to grow. How long before a major breach produces a claim against an insurer that proves to be too much? Then what? Can an insurer exclude acts of cyberwar or cyberterrorism from their policies, and using which definitions?

All these issues, and many not covered here (e.g., national security interests, crime and fraud prevention, identity theft, etc.), will prove to be strong drivers toward increasing regulatory intrusion. In some countries, regulation will come more slowly than others, but you need to plan for these regulations now. Know where your business interests are, what your exposure is, and the type of data you're handling. You may need to turn on a dime and either produce a plan or mitigate your risk with business controls. The one thing you cannot do is ignore what's coming.

# Artificial Intelligence and Machine Learning

*Open the pod bay doors, Hal.*

*—2001: A Space Odyssey*

I suspect we all know what happens next, and although we haven't realized Stanley Kubrick's vision just yet, we seem to be rushing head-on toward it. For that matter, the list of scientists, technologists, futurists, and visionaries warning us on the dangers of rogue artificial intelligence (AI) grows daily.

Specifically, as of this writing, there are more than 8,000 signatories to an open letter posted at the Future of Life Institute, titled "Research Priorities for Robust and Beneficial Artificial Intelligence." The list reads like the "Who's Who" in science, technology, and arts, including luminaries like Stephen Hawking, Elon Musk, Michael Vassar, and Nick Bostrom.

So, why all the warnings and paranoia surrounding AI? And, what's the difference between AI and machine learning? Back to our definitions:

Let's start with machine learning. Machine learning refers to a type of computer program that can, essentially, write and modify itself based on the data that it is working on. These types of programs are great in dealing with very complicated and large data sets. Examples include pattern recognition, machine vision, and cybersecurity applications. Why cybersecurity? Because a learning system can use its algorithms to detect network intrusions before any other control flags them. For example, it may use its capacity in pattern recognition and statistical analysis to first learn what is "normal network traffic" and make judgments on what may be abnormal traffic as a result of a breach.

Machine learning systems are used extensively in the fields of data mining and data analytics. In those contexts, these systems can produce very sophisticated results that would be impossible using traditional computational methods. Consequently, these types of systems can single-handedly create value that was previously out of reach. Think in terms of analyzing behavior patterns of billions of Facebook users. What can that tell an advertiser? It turns out, quite a bit!

Why is this important to cybersecurity? Mainly for two reasons: First, there is a lot of hope that machine-learning systems will prove to be the "silver bullet" of intrusion detection. Already, there are versions of such systems in various stages of deployment, and results are encouraging. Second, the system itself, if in use by your firm, becomes a mission-critical value generator, requiring a disproportionate level of cybersecurity attention. By their nature, these systems process terabytes upon terabytes of data, some of it in real time.

Therefore, designing a defense-in-depth strategy around one of them can be a challenge.

Even if your firm is not using a machine-learning system yet, you need to be aware of them and stay informed. It is only a matter of time before these types of systems become widely used both as controls and as assets.

As you can imagine, machine learning systems and artificial intelligence systems are closely related. An AI researcher and a machine-learning researcher have a lot to talk about! Still, the differences are both subtle and profound, and well worth exploring.

First, I hope we can all agree that the term *artificial* is easy to understand. It is something that we humans make or create. Sometimes we make it so that it resembles the *real thing*, other times not.

Intelligence, though, is another matter. What, exactly, is intelligence? That is a very controversial question. To date, there is no definitive consensus on a definition. In 1994, Professor Linda Gottfredson of the University of Delaware drafted the now-famous "Mainstream Science on Intelligence" statement. She sent this to no fewer than the top 131 researchers in the field and got 52 of them to sign it. The statement was published by the *Wall Street Journal* in December 1994, and it included the following definition:

> *Intelligence is a very general mental capability that, among other things, involves the ability to reason, plan, solve problems, think abstractly, comprehend complex ideas, learn quickly, and learn from experience.*

There's a lot more one could say about intelligence but this definition works well for our purposes. If we marry Dr. Gottfredson's definition of *intelligence* with *artificial*, we get what AI researchers call strong AI. That is a computer that can basically exhibit the intelligence characteristics of a human. We are not there yet, but it may be coming—hence, all the warnings from scientists. If we are able to build a computer that exhibits strong AI, it will, in very short order, evolve into what Nick Bostrom refers to as "artificial superintelligence." The concern, of course, is that an artificial superintelligent computer may develop the same relationship with us that we have with a cockroach.

Where are we now? We are in what AI researchers call weak AI. This is specialized artificial intelligence. We have computers that can perform specific tasks very well, like beating the reigning Jeopardy champion at his own game, but the same systems would struggle with recommending the right evening outfit for a date.

Now, this may seem to trivialize the power of weak AI, and that would be a mistake. These systems are trailblazing and they produce incredible advances in science, medicine, even the arts. IBM's Watson is one of the prime examples of a very successful weak AI system that is having tremendous impact across industries and disciplines. And, keep in mind that, day by day, these weak AI systems are getting stronger and stronger.

This is why you need to care. These types of systems have direct implications on cybersecurity. They can be used as weapons themselves, they can be used as controls, and, since they are extremely valuable assets, they need to be protected for the value they represent. Consider, for example, that one of Watson's projects involves reviewing hundreds of thousands of medical papers and recommending potential life-saving treatments. Were it to be compromised, lives could be lost.

Even weak artificial intelligence systems have already affected the workplace. Today, they are machine-learning-on-steroids—the computer savant in the corner that is asked the incredibly complex question and has the right answer. Tomorrow, they could potentially be replacing hundreds or thousands of highly skilled jobs. I will leave the debate about social impact to others, but from a cybersecurity perspective alone, having a system that is responsible for such a big percentage of value generation changes the way we think about the role of assets, people, environments, and controls.

And that is your problem. You need to think carefully about the industry you are in, the kind of work your business engages in, and the ways your firm generates value. You then need to map this against an AI's capabilities, and project out the possible ways that an AI system may be integrated into your workplace. What happens then? What's at risk? How does value generation change? Where will the threats come from? How do you mitigate them, given this new target?

## Blockchain

By now, I am fairly confident that you've heard of the term *blockchain*, and certain that you have heard of Bitcoin. Blockchain is the underlying technology that makes cryptocurrencies like Bitcoin possible. But that's like saying, "The Internet is the underlying technology that makes music streaming possible." Yes, the Internet does that, but it does a lot more, and the same goes for blockchain.

Just as the Internet revolutionized our world, so will blockchain. Many have made similar, if not stronger, pronouncements, and—trust me on this—even the most grandiose are understated. Blockchain is truly a revolutionary technology.

So, what is it? It depends on how technical you want to be. At the simplest level, blockchain is a technology of distributed ledgers that are available to anyone, practically instantaneously, encrypted, with anonymized and indelible entries.

Why is this such a big deal? Because, for the first time in the history of humanity, we have a robust, redundant technology that can combine transparency and assurance of transactions. The minute that Sally pays Bob using blockchain technologies, everyone on their blockchain can know that the transaction occurred, for how much, and so on. There can be, of course, private blockchain systems (e.g., blockchain systems linking Federal Reserve Banks, or financial institutions, or title agencies, law firms, and so on) or public blockchain systems like the one Bitcoin uses. Either way, using blockchain technologies, Sally is assured that Bob got paid, Bob can never dispute it, and Jim can't steal the money. Moreover: There is no need for a third party to verify that all this is true. Blockchain, by its distributed and secure nature, assures it.

Blockchain technologies can be used for any transaction. It doesn't have to be about currency, stocks, or some trading instrument (e.g., derivatives). It can be about art. It can be about property. It can be about sacks of potatoes. If there is a transaction between two parties, no matter what that may be, it can be coded into a blockchain system and tracked. As you can imagine, there are many industries that blockchain could outright eliminate: clearinghouses, payment processors, brokerages, escrow services—any intermediary that exists solely to ensure a smooth transaction between two parties, and thereby collect a fee, is likely to go out of business.

The estimates vary on how fast and how widespread this transformation will be. One that stuck in my head was that by 2025 we may be looking at a 40 percent loss of finance-related jobs. Jobs that were involved somehow in the verifying and clearing of transactions, all eliminated because of blockchain technologies. Whether this number and date are true is anyone's guess. What's indisputable is that the technology is here, and that practically every govern-ment and financial institution in the world has active blockchain programs in development.

What does this all mean to you and to your cybersecurity program? Well, it depends. First, ask how will your business be affected by such a technology? Second, do you plan to be involved with blockchain systems? If so, there are many serious technical considerations you'll need to work through, far outside the scope of this book. Suffice it to say that a blockchain rollout, private or otherwise, carries significant cybersecurity implications.

In short, you cannot go at this alone. If you plan to play with blockchain, then you'll need to retain experts to help you throughout the life cycle of the project. And, fasten your seatbelt . . . .

## Quantum Computing

"God doesn't play dice," said Einstein. Actually, he didn't exactly say that. What he did say was "Quantum theory yields much, but it hardly brings us close to the Old One's secrets. I, in any case, am convinced He does not play dice with the universe." He wrote this in a letter to Max Born, a founding father of the branch of physics called quantum mechanics.

Quantum mechanics, or quantum physics, is the study of nature at the smallest scale possible. Think atomic, and subatomic studies. Scientists like Max Planck (considered the father of quantum mechanics), Niels Bohr (with his hydrogen atom model), Werner Heisenberg (and his uncertainty principle), Erwin Schrödinger (and his infamous cat), and, of course, Max Born, who was the receiver of Einstein's letter, described a world of chance, uncertainty, entanglement, and very bizarre behaviors, that to date continue to puzzle and confound our understanding of the universe.

The problem, if you want to call it that, is that this strange world described by even stranger mathematics is true! It has been repeatedly and independently verified by experiments. Go figure! We have, for example, indisputable proof of a concept called "action at a distance." NIST proved it as recently as 2015 in a paper to *Physical Review Letters*.

Enter quantum computing. Those are systems that instead of using the now-familiar digital states—bits of "1" and "0," "true" or "false," and the like—they use quantum states, of which there can be many. These quantum bits, or qubits, can occupy multiple states and can do so at the same time. Crazy, I know, but trust me. The math works.

The implications of such a computer exceed the wildest science fiction descriptions. A quantum computer will be powerful enough to simulate the most complex phenomena. Imagine a hurricane simulation in which you can tell exactly what each water droplet is doing at any one time. Imagine the ability to simulate the growth of cancer cells, or photosynthesis, or solving the most complex mathematical problems we've encountered. Also, think of the ability to break any size encryption in no time at all. And, think of that power in the hands of a … hacker? Or perhaps a nation-state with unchecked ambitions?

As of this writing, there is a quantum computing race going on. Google and IBM are two of the trailblazers in the field, but there are many, many more. Some are known (universities, privately funded researchers, and the like), and some are unknown. For example, we don't know if there is a quantum computing research lab in North Korea or elsewhere.

As to the cybersecurity implications of this technology, I leave you to your imagination!

Are there other developments that will affect your cybersecurity program in the next couple of years? You bet! There isn't a single technology company that is not working on bigger, better, smarter systems to protect and defend, including bleeding-edge technologies being tested all over the world.

There is no crystal ball that we can use to predict the impact of these technologies, only the knowledge that change is coming, and the impact of these changes will be profound. The thing you need to do is to commit yourself to staying engaged and continuously informed. That is the only way that you can protect yourself and your company. And the only way you can contribute to helping everyone live in a cybersecure world.

Which is how I want to close this book: By imagining a cybersecure world, without being particularly sappy. Just optimistic!

I would like to think that world governments can create treaty frameworks that protect our countries, our businesses, and our privacy. I would hope that our research institutions and international organizations and agencies work toward this goal through advocacy and education.

I would like to think that our business leaders, boards of directors, and executives will take on the challenge of cybersecurity and address it head-on. I would hope that lessons learned, professional voices, education, and awareness contribute to their decision to allocate the right resources in a timely way. I want to see business decisions include privacy and security considerations as well as profit. And I want to make sure that we, as professionals, all work proactively and stay engaged in making sure that the value we create every day is protected.

Finally, I would like to think that we, as individuals, will own up to our responsibility—be it civic, professional, or personal—and act responsibly toward each other, using technology with respect and with the wisdom it is due.

# BIBLIOGRAPHY

O ver the years that it took to prepare this book, I have consulted with, attended, read, and visited thousands of primary sources, be it in the form of books, seminars, workshops, classes, conferences, vendors, and cybersecurity professionals of every specialty that you can imagine (and some that you cannot!). It is clearly impossible to list all the material that I consulted and that influenced my thinking, and I therefore apologize for any omissions from the following bibliography.

For even more up-to-date resources, you might also consult the website for this book, www.cybersecurity-for-business.com.

*The Alien Vault Incident Response Toolkit: Putting the OODA Loop to Work in the Real World.* San Mateo, CA: Alien Vault, 2017.

*Americans and Cybersecurity.* Washington, DC: Pew Research Center, 2017.

Atluri, Indrajit. "Managing the Risk of IoT: Regulations, Frameworks, Security, Risk, and Analytics." *ISACA Journal* 3 (2017). https://www.isaca.org/Journal/archives/2017/Volume-3/Pages/managing-the-risk-of-iot.aspx.

Bandos, Tim. *Incident Responder's Field Guide.* Waltham, MA: Digital Guardian, 2016.

Barlow, Mike. *Governing the IoT—Balancing Risk and Regulation.* Sebastopol, CA: O'Reilly Media, 2016.

Bodeau, Deborah, and Richard Graubart. *Characterizing Effects on the Cyber Adversary: A Vocabulary for Analysis and Assessment.* Bedford, MA: MITRE, 2013.

Bonime-Blanc, Andrea. *Emerging Practices in Cyber Risk Governance.* New York, NY: The Conference Board, 2015.

Borg, Scott, and John Bumgarner. *THE US-CCU CYBER-SECURITY MATRIX.* Draft Version 2. Washington, DC: United States Cyber Consequences Unit, 2016.

Bostrom, Nick. *Superintelligence: Paths, Dangers, Strategies.* Oxford, UK: Oxford University Press, 2014.

Bosworth, Seymour, M. E. Kabay, and Eric Whyne, eds. *Computer Security Handbook.* 6th ed. Hoboken, NJ: John Wiley & Sons, 2014.

Brenner, Susan W., and Leo L. Clark. "Civilians in Cyberwarfare: Casualties." *SMU Science and Technology Law Review* 13 (2010). http://works.bepress.com/susan_brenner/3.

Cameron, Kim, and Robert Quinn. *Diagnosing and Changing Organizational Culture—Based on the Competing Values Framework.* San Francisco, CA: Jossey-Bass, 2006.

Cappelli, Dawn. *The CERT Top 10 List of Winning the Battle Against Insider Threats.* Pittsburgh, PA: CERT Insider Threat Center, Software Engineering Institute, Carnegie Mellon University, 2012.

Carnegie, Dale. *How to Win Friends and Influence People*. New York, NY: Simon & Schuster, 1936, 1964. Revised 1981.

*CGEIT Review Manual*. 7th ed. Rolling Meadows, IL, ISACA, 2015.

Cichonski, Paul, Tom Millar, Tim Grance, and Karen Scarfone. *Computer Security Incident Handling Guide*. Gaithersburg, MD: National Institute of Standards and Technology, 2012.

*Cisco 2014 Annual Security Report*. San Jose, CA: Cisco Systems, 2014.

*Cisco 2015 Annual Security Report*. San Jose, CA: Cisco Systems, 2015.

*Cisco 2016 Annual Security Report*. San Jose, CA: Cisco Systems, 2016.

*Cisco 2017 Annual Security Report*. San Jose, CA: Cisco Systems, 2017.

*CISM Review Manual 2015*. Rolling Meadows, IL: ISACA, 2014.

*CISO Board Briefing 2017*. Rolling Meadows, IL: ISACA, 2017.

Clinton, Larry. *Cyber-Risk Oversight—Director's Handbook Series*. Washington, DC: National Association of Corporate Directors, 2017.

*Closing Security Gaps to Protect Corporate Data: A Study of U.S. and European Organizations*. Traverse City, MI: Ponemon Institute, 2016.

"Cloud and IoT Threats Predictions." *McAfee Labs 2017 Threat Predictions*. Santa Clara, CA: McAfee, 2016.

*COBIT—A Business Framework for the Governance and Management of Enterprise IT*. Rolling Meadows, IL: ISACA, 2012.

Cole, Eric. *Insider Threats and the Need for Fast and Directed Response—A SANS Survey*. Bethesda, MD: SANS Institute, 2016.

Council Decision. "Security Rules for Protecting EU Classified Information" (2013/488/EU). *Official Journal of the European Union*, September 23, 2013.

*The Current State of Cybercrime 2014—An Inside Look at the Changing Threat Landscape*. Hopkinton, MA: EMC Corporation, 2014.

*Cyber 7—Seven Messages to the Edge of Cyber-Space*. Heraklion, Crete: European Union Agency for Network and Information Security (ENISA), 2015.

*Cyber Security Planning Guide*. Washington, DC: Federal Communications Commission, 2012.

*Cybercrime: Defending Your Enterprise How to Protect Your Organization from Emerging Cyberthreats*. Rolling Meadows, IL: ISACA, 2017.

*The Cyberresilient Enterprise: What the Board of Directors Needs to Ask*. Rolling Meadows, IL: ISACA, 2015.

*Cybersecurity Fundamentals Study Guide*. Rolling Meadows, IL: ISACA, 2014.

*Cybersecurity Questions for CEOs*. Washington, DC: Department of Homeland Security, 2013.

*Defense in Depth—A Practical Strategy for Achieving Information Assurance in Today's Highly Networked Environments*. Fort Meade, MD: National Security Agency, 2010.

Dekker, M. A. C., and Dimitra Liveri. *Cloud Security Guide for SMEs*. Heraklion, Crete: European Union Agency for Network and Information Security (ENISA), 2015.

Drucker, Peter F. *Classic Drucker: Essential Wisdom of Peter Drucker from the Pages of Harvard Business Review*. Boston, MA: Harvard Business Review Press, 2006.

Drucker, Peter F. *The Essential Drucker*. New York, NY: HarperCollins, 2001.

*ENISA Threat Landscape: Top 15 Cyber Threats 2015*. Heraklion, Crete: European Union Agency for Network and Information Security (ENISA), 2016.

*ENISA Threat Landscape 2015*. Heraklion, Crete: European Union Agency for Network and Information Security (ENISA), 2016.

*ENISA Work Programme 2017 (Draft)*. Heraklion, Crete: European Union Agency for Network and Information Security (ENISA), 2016.

European Commission Press Release Database. "Informal Justice Council in Vilnius." European Commission Memo, July 19, 2013. Updated September 28, 2017. http://europa.eu/rapid/press-release_MEMO-13-710_en.htm.

*EU-US Privacy Shield Framework—Key New Requirements for Participating Companies*. Washington, DC: U.S. Department of Commerce, 2016.

*Evolution of Incident Response*. Boulder, CO: Enterprise Management Associates, 2017.

Flynn, Lori, Carly Huth, Randy Trzeciak, and Palma Buttles. *Best Practices Against Insider Threats in All Nations*. Pittsburgh, PA: CERT Division, Software Engineering Institute, Carnegie Mellon University, 2013.

*Framework for Improving Critical Infrastructure Cybersecurity—Draft Version 1.1*. Gaithersburg, MD: National Institute of Standards and Technology, 2017.

Gottfredson, Linda S. "Mainstream Science on Intelligence." *Wall Street Journal*, December 13, 1994.

Grance, Tim, Joan Hash, Marc Stevens, Kristofer O'Neal, and Nadya Bartol. *Guide to Information Technology Security Services*. Gaithersburg, MD: National Institute of Standards and Technology, 2003.

Grance, Tim, Tamara Nolan, Kristin Burke, Rich Dudley, Gregory White, and Travis Good. *Guide to Test, Training, and Exercise Programs for IT Plans and Capabilities*. Gaithersburg, MD: National Institute of Standards and Technology, 2006.

Greenough, John. "34 Billion Devices Connected to the Internet by 2020." *Business Insider*, January 26, 2016. http://www.businessinsider.com/34-billion-devices-will-be-connected-to-the-internet-by-2020-2016-1.

Gresham, Rob. *Are You at Risk? 2016 Data Protection Benchmark Study*. Rolling Meadows, IL: ISACA, 2016.

*Guide for Applying the Risk Management Framework to Federal Information Systems: A Security Life Cycle Approach*. Gaithersburg, MD: National Institute of Standards and Technology, 2010.

*Guide for Conducting Risk Assessments*. Gaithersburg, MD: National Institute of Standards and Technology, 2012.

*Guide to Sound Practices for Cyber Security, Version 2.0*. London, UK: The Alternative Investment Management Association, 2017.

Hanson, Tom, and Birgit Zacher Hanson. *Who Will Do What by When? How to Improve Performance, Accountability, and Trust with Integrity*. Longwood, CA: Power Publications, 2005.

Herzog, Peter. *The Open Source Cybersecurity Playbook*. Cardedeu, Spain: ISECOM and BARKLY, 2016.

Hovland, Carl I., and Walter Weiss. "The Influence of Source Credibility on Communication Effectiveness." *Public Opinion Quarterly* 15, no. 4 (January 1, 1951): 635–650.

*IBM Security Services Cyber Security Intelligence Index.* Somers, NY: IBM Corporation, 2013.

*Implementing Cybersecurity Guidance for Small and Medium-Sized Enterprises.* Rolling Meadows, IL: ISACA, 2015.

*Implementing the NIST Cybersecurity Framework.* Rolling Meadows, IL: ISACA, 2014.

*The Importance of Cyber Threat Intelligence to a Strong Security Posture.* Traverse City, MI: Ponemon Institute, 2015.

Industrial Control Systems Cyber Emergency Response Team. *Recommended Practice: Improving Industrial Control System Cybersecurity with Defense-in-Depth Strategies.* Washington, DC: Department of Homeland Security, Office of Cybersecurity and Communications, 2016.

*Information technology—Security techniques—Information security incident management—Part 2: Guidelines to plan and prepare for incident response (ISO/IEC 27035-2).* Geneva, Switzerland: ISO (International Organization for Standardization) and IEC (the International Electrotechnical Commission), 2016.

*Information technology—Security techniques—Information security management systems—Overview and vocabulary.* Geneva, Switzerland: ISO (International Organization for Standardization) and IEC (the International Electrotechnical Commission), 2016.

*Insider's Guide to Incident Response—Expert Tips.* San Mateo, CA: Alien Vault, 2017.

Intel Security. *Blue Skies Ahead? The State of Cloud Adoption.* Santa Clara, CA: McAfee, 2016.

ISACA. *Board Briefing on IT Governance.* 2nd ed. Rolling Meadows, IL: IT Governance Institute, 2003.

*IS Audit/Assurance Program—Data Privacy.* Rolling Meadows, IL: ISACA, 2017.

*The IT Archipelago—The Decentralisation of Enterprise Technology.* London, UK: The Economist Intelligence Unit Ltd., 2016.

Janis, Irving L., and Bert T. King. *The Influence of Role Playing on Opinion Change.* New Haven, CT: Yale University, 1952.

Jones, Jeffrey M. "In U.S., Telecommuting for Work Climbs to 37%." *Gallup News,* August 19, 2015. news.gallup.com/poll/184649/telecommuting-work-climbs .aspx.

Kaplan, Robert S., and David P. Norton. *The Balanced Scorecard: Translating Strategy into Action.* Boston, MA: Harvard Business School Press, 1996.

Kissel, Richard, ed. *Glossary of Key Information Security Terms.* Gaithersburg, IL: National Institute of Standards and Technology, 2013.

Klahr, Rebecca, Jayesh Navin Shah, Paul Sheriffs, Tom Rossington, Gemma Pestell, Mark Button, and Victoria Wang. *Cyber Security Breaches Survey 2017.* London, UK: Crown, 2017.

Kohen, Isaac. "5 Layers of Defense that Prevent Insider Threats." *Cybersecurity Nexus,* June 12, 2017. https://www.isaca.org/cyber/cyber-security-articles/Pages/5-layers-of-defense-that-prevent-insider-threats.aspx.

Kral, Patrick. *The Incident Handlers Handbook.* Bethesda, MD: SANS Institute, 2016.

Lacey, David. *A Practical Guide to the Payment Card Industry Data Security Standard (PCI DSS).* Rolling Meadows, IL: ISACA, 2015.

Leventhal, Howard. "Findings and Theory in the Study of Fear Communications." *Advances in Experimental Social Psychology* 5 (1970): 119–186.

*Managing cyber risks in an interconnected world—Key findings from the Global State of Information Security Survey 2015.* London, UK: PwC, September 30, 2014.

*Marking Classified National Security Information, Revision 2.* Washington, DC: The Information Security Oversight Office, 2014.

Mark Mateski, Cassandra M. Trevino, Cynthia K. Veitch, John Michalski, Mark J. Harris, Scott Maruoka, and Jason Frye. *Cyber Threat Metrics.* SANDIA Report SAND 2012-2427. Albuquerque, NM: Sandia National Laboratories, 2012.

*McAfee Labs 2017 Threat Predictions.* Santa Clara, CA, McAfee, 2016.

*McAfee Labs Threats Report.* Santa Clara, CA, McAfee, 2016.

McFarlan, Warren F., and Richard L. Nolan. "Why IT Does Matter." *Harvard Business School—Working Knowledge,* August 25, 2003. http://hbswk.hbs.edu/item/why-it-does-matter.

McMillan, Rob. *Gartner Security and Risk Management Summit Security 2020—The Future of Cybersecurity.* Stamford, CT: Gartner, 2016.

Moar, James. *Cybercrime and the Internet of Threats 2017.* Basingstoke, UK: Juniper Research Ltd., 2017.

Moen, Ronald D., and Clifford L. Norman. *Circling Back—Clearing up Myths about the Deming Cycle and Seeing How It Keeps Evolving.* Milwaukee, WI: Quality Progress, 2010.

Mortakis, Georgios. *Cyber Security and Information Assurance Controls Prevention and Reaction.* Coral Gables, FL: Enterprise Risk Management, 2013.

Moschovitis, Chris, Erica Pearson, Hilary W. Poole, Tami Schuler, Theresa Senft, and Mary Sisson. *The Internet: A Historical Encyclopedia—Chronology.* Santa Barbara, CA: ABC-CLIO, 2005.

Murray, Anna P. *The Complete Software Project Manager—Mastering Technology from Planning to Launch and Beyond.* Hoboken, NJ: John Wiley & Sons, 2016.

NACD Advisory Council on Risk Oversight. *Cybersecurity Oversight and Breach Response.* Washington, DC: National Association of Corporate Directors, 2015.

National Vulnerability Database. "NVD Dashboard." Gaithersburg, MD: National Institute of Standards and Technology, September 28, 2017. https://nvd.nist.gov/general/nvd-dashboard.

Needle, David. *Business in Context: An Introduction to Business and Its Environment.* Mason, OH: South-Western Educational Publishing, 2010.

Northcutt, Stephen. *Security Controls.* SANS Technology Institute—Security Laboratory. September 1, 2009. https://www.sans.edu/cyber-research/security-laboratory/article/security-controls.

*Operational levels of Cyber Intelligence.* Arlington, VA: Intelligence and National Security Alliance, 2013.

*Overview of Digital Forensics.* Rolling Meadows, IL: ISACA, 2015.

*Overview of the General Data Protection Regulation (GDPR).* Brussels: Information Commissioner's Office, 2016.

Patel, Hemant. "IoT Needs Better Security." *ISACA Journal* 3 (2017). https://www.isaca.org/Journal/archives/2017/Volume-3/Pages/iot-needs-better-security.aspx.

Paulsen, Celia, and Patricia Toth. "Small Business Information Security: The Fundamentals." *NISTIR7621 Revision 1*. Gaithersburg, MD: National Institute of Standards and Technology, 2016.

*People and Technology in the Workplace*. Washington, DC: National Academies Press, 1991.

Petty, Richard E., and John T. Cacioppo. *The Elaboration Likelihood Model of Persuasion*. Cambridge, MA: Academic Press, 1986.

Proctor, Paul E., and Katell Thielemann. "To the Point: Implementing the Cybersecurity Framework and the Risk Management Framework." Gartner Security and Risk Management Summit, Stamford, CT, June 15, 2016.

Read, Opie Percival. *Mark Twain and I*. Chicago, IL: Reilly and Lee, 1940.

*Responding to Targeted Cyberattacks*. Rolling Meadows, IL: ISACA, 2013.

*Review of Cyber Hygiene Practices*. Heraklion, Crete: European Union Agency for Network and Information Security (ENISA), 2016.

*The Risk IT Framework*. Rolling Meadows, IL: ISACA, 2009.

Rogers, Everett M. *Diffusion of Innovations*. New York, NY: The Free Press, 1983.

Ross, Ron. Stu Katzke, Arnold Johnson, Marianne Swanson, and Gary Stoneburner. *Managing Risk from Information Systems—An Organizational Perspective*. Gaithersburg, MD: National Institute of Standards and Technology, 2008.

Schafer, Robert B., and John L. Tait. *A Guide for Understanding Attitudes and Attitude Change*. Ames, IA: North Central Regional Extension Publication 138, Reprinted August 1986.

Shackeford, Dave. *The SANS State of Cyber Threat Intelligence Survey: CTI Important and Maturing*. Bethesda, MD: SANS Institute, 2016.

Shalm, Lynden K. et al. "Strong Loophole-Free Test of Local Realism." *Physical Review Letters* 115, no. 250402 (December 16, 2015).

Smallwood, Robert F. *Information Governance—Concepts, Strategies, and Best Practices*. Hoboken, NJ: John Wiley & Sons, 2014.

Snedaker, Susan, and Chris Rima. *Business Continuity and Disaster Recovery Planning for IT Professionals*. Waltham, MA: Elsevier, 2014.

Snyder, Joel. *Six Strategies for Defense-in-Depth*. Tucson, AZ: Opus One, 2007.

*Standards for Security Categorization of Federal Information and Information Systems* (FIPS PUB 199). Gaithersburg, MD: Computer Security Division, Information Technology Laboratory, National Institute of Standards and Technology, February 2004.

*State of Cyber Security 2017*. Rolling Meadows, IL: ISACA, 2017.

*State of Cybersecurity—Implications for 2015—An ISACA and RSA Conference Survey*. Rolling Meadows, IL: ISACA, 2015.

*State of Cybersecurity—Implications for 2016—An ISACA and RSA Conference Survey*. Rolling Meadows, IL: ISACA, 2016.

*Talent.oecd—Learn. Perform. Succeed—Competency Framework*. Paris, France: Organisation for Economic Co-operation and Development (OECD), 2014.

*The 2016 Cyber Resilient Organization Executive Summary*. Traverse City, MI: Ponemon Institute, 2016.

*Transforming Cybersecurity*. Rolling Meadows, IL: ISACA, 2013.

Trites, Gerald. *Information Integrity*. New York, NY: American Institute of CPAs and Canadian Institute of Chartered Accountants, 2013.

*2015 Data Breach Investigations Report*. New York, NY: Verizon, 2015.

*2016 Cost of Data Breach Study: United States*. Traverse City, MI: Ponemon Institute, 2016.

*2016 Data Breach Digest. Scenarios from the Field*. New York, NY: Verizon, 2016.

*2016 Data Breach Investigations Report*. New York, NY: Verizon, 2016.

*2016 Internet Security Threat Report*. Mountain View, CA: Symantec Corporation, 2017.

*2016 U.S. Government Cybersecurity Report*. New York, NY: Security Scorecard, 2016.

*2017 Data Breach Investigations Report*. New York, NY: Verizon, 2017.

*2017 Internet Security Threat Report*. Mountain View, CA: Symantec Corporation, 2017.

*The U.S. Army Operating Concept—Win in a Complex World* (TRADOC Pamphlet 525-3-1). Washington, DC: United States Army, 2014.

*U.S. Cybercrime: Rising Risks, Reduced Readiness*. Dover, DE: PricewaterhouseCoopers, 2014.

Wang, Sichao. "Are Enterprises Really Ready to Move into the Cloud?" Cloud Security Alliance Education White Papers and Educational Material White Papers, February 2012. https://cloudsecurityalliance.org/wp-content/uploads/2012/02/Areenterprisesreallyreadytomoveintothecloud.pdf.

*Website Security Statistics Report 2015*. Santa Clara, CA: WhiteHat Security, 2015.

Weiss, Walter, and Carl Hovland. "The Influence of Source Credibility on Communication Effectiveness." *Journal of Abnormal and Social Psychology* 46 (1951). Reprinted in *Public Opinion Quarterly*, Winter 1951–1952.

West-Brown, Moira J., Don Stikvoort, Klaus-Peter Kossakowski, Georgia Killcrece, Robin Ruefle, and Mark Zajicek. *Handbook for Computer Security Incident Response Teams (CSIRTs)*. 2nd ed. Pittsburgh, PA: Carnegie Mellon Software Engineering Institute, 2003.

Wheatman, Jeffrey. "State of Security Governance, 2016." Gartner Security and Risk Management Summit, Stamford, CT, 2016.

*WhiteHat Security Web Applications Security Statistics Report 2016*. Santa Clara, CA: WhiteHat Security, 2016.

Whitteker, Wes. *Leading Effective Cybersecurity with the Critical Security Controls*. Bethesda, MD: SANS Institute, 2016.

Wolak, Russel, Stavros Kalafatis, and Patricia Harris. "An Investigation into Four Characteristics of Services." *Journal of Empirical Generalisations in Marketing Science* 3 (1998).

Wrighton, Tyler. *Advanced Persistent Threat Hacking—The Art and Science of Hacking Any Organization*. New York, NY: McGraw-Hill Education, 2015.

# Clear and Present Danger

*In early 2017, I wrote an editorial titled "Clear and Present Danger" for the website "From CEO to CEO." It presented my thinking on cybersecurity at the nation-state level.*

On December 13, 2016, the *New York Times* published a feature article titled "The Perfect Weapon: How Russian Cyberpower Invaded the U.S." In it Eric Lipton, David Sanger, and Scott Shane do an excellent job in framing in detail the recent state-sponsored cyberattack against U.S. interests. But the story doesn't end there.

Russia is not alone in excelling at cyberwarfare. Many nation-states see this as the new "arms race." They believe, rightly so, that this is a race they can win. North Korea, Iran, and China have demonstrated their capabilities time and again. So have the United States and Israel. There is little doubt that practically every country is actively participating in the development, management, and deployment of cyberwarfare infrastructure. They all are, and they are building massive defensive and offensive cyberwarfare capabilities. Moreover, they are "in it to win it," and they think they can.

What has made Russia's cyberattack particularly egregious is not that it is the first, but that it is a blatant, in-your-face show of power, ridiculing the last superpower standing. What makes it particularly deadly is that it is coupled with Russia's deep scholarship in propaganda. I have read recent interviews from officials downplaying and demeaning Russian propaganda as "par for the course," and "things we've seen before from the Russians." If so, then we have not learned, and that has cost us dearly. We have been badly defeated and ridiculed by what we all thought was a vanquished enemy of a cold war gone dead. In my view, news of the enemy's demise is premature, and the cold war is very far from over.

On April 4, 1949, with the memories of the Second World War brutally fresh, an alliance was entered into by the United States, Canada, and several European countries. The North Atlantic Treaty Organization (NATO) was formed. Article 1 of the treaty reads: "The Parties undertake, as set forth in the Charter of the United Nations, to settle any international dispute in which they may be involved by peaceful means in such a manner that international peace and security and justice are not endangered, and to refrain in their international relations from the threat or use of force in any manner inconsistent with the purposes of the United Nations."

Many more treaties followed, and the world's doomsday clock reflected the threat: 7 minutes to midnight in 1947; 3 minutes in 1949, after the first USSR nuclear test; 17 minutes—the lowest value—in 1991. Now, it is back to 3 minutes to midnight.

The lowest value, 17 minutes to midnight, was reached when the world thought the cold war to be over, and the United States and Russia were engaged in nuclear arms reduction. Since 2015 it is back to 3 minutes as "Unchecked climate change, global nuclear weapons modernizations, and outsized nuclear weapons arsenals pose extraordinary and undeniable threats to the continued existence of humanity," and world leaders fail to act.

Sadly, this is not their only failure. As catastrophically serious as both climate change and nuclear arsenals are, and about that there should be no doubt, a third blight has surfaced: cyberwar. Most think that hacking or cyberwarfare is a threat, to be sure, but not on the same level as nuclear weapons. Yes, millions of dollars may be lost, political careers may be ruined, and service interruptions may be inconvenient, but a cyberwar is thought to be confined to the virtual world, not the real one. They are deadly wrong.

Acts of cyberwarfare may have already claimed lives in Ukraine, when Russian hackers attacked that country's power grid, leaving almost a quarter million residents without power. Lives may have been lost when the centrifuges in Iran's nuclear enrichment facility were destroyed by Stuxnet, a suspected U.S./Israeli cyberweapon. And, of course, there are many victims of cyberbullying who have taken their own lives, demonstrating the power of reputational damage, an easily attainable effect of hacking any individual's life story.

Experts warn of the certainty of real human casualties from cyberwarfare. Consider what would happen if the electrical grid was hacked and the country, or regions, went dark for weeks on end. Ted Koppel did so in his book, *Lights Out*, and the implications are devastating. Consider the ramifications of hacking medical records and facilities, water purification plants, traffic control, or telecommunications. I am sure that you can come up with your own nightmare scenario that leaves thousands, if not hundreds of thousands, of dead or injured, and our country in chaos.

I also have no doubt that there are brilliant minds working around the clock in our security services that continuously analyze and respond to these threats, as well as advise our leaders. But I know from experience that their advice frequently falls on deaf ears. Just as executives don't want to hear about risk, be it cyber, technology, or otherwise, neither, I suspect, do government "executives." Certainly, recent rhetoric on the value of intelligence briefings demonstrates this, just as did the inaction and hesitation of the Obama White House in responding to the Russian attack against our political process.

We need a concentrated effort on this new front for the survival of humanity. We need our leaders to be educated and alert to the danger this poses. We need our people to be sensitized to the danger of cyberattacks; think "duck and cover" for the cyber-age. We need our allies to reinvigorate their frameworks for resolving conflicts peacefully to include cyberwarfare. A cyberattack against one country should be considered an attack against us all, with a commensurate and immediate response. And we need our international organizations to recognize the danger of cyberactor proliferation and take immediate and decisive action.

It's a start, when nothing less will do. My Cyber Clock is set to 1 minute to midnight, and the seconds are ticking.

*Originally published on January 17, 2017, in "From CEO to CEO" (http://www.ceo-to-ceo.com/trends/clear-and-present-danger/).*

# INDEX

Printed and bound by CPI Group (UK) Ltd, Croydon, CR0 4YY

27/10/2024

14580316-0001